VAGINA-MITE WAS NO MORE

JOURNALS 2009 - 2010

CHRISTINE FONTANA

Published by VirginiaDiddit in 2025
Melbourne, Victoria, 3000
www.virginiadiddit.com

Copyright © Christine Fontana 2025
The moral right of Christine Fontana to be identified as the author of this work has been asserted.

All rights reserved. Apart from any fair dealing for the purposes of study, research, criticism, review or as otherwise permitted under the Australian Copyright Act, no part of this publication may be reproduced, stored in a retrieval system, or transmitted, in any form or by any means, electronic, mechanical, photocopying, recording or otherwise, without the prior written permission of the copyright owner/publisher.

National Library of Australia Cataloguing-in-Publication entry available for this title at www.nla.gov.au

Title: Vagina-Mite Was No More, by Christine Fontana
ISBN: 978-1-923221-07-9 (Paperback)
ISBN: 978-1-923221-06-2 (Ebook)

Cover design and typsettting: Christine Fontana

CONTENTS

1. Introduction i
2. January 2009 1
3. February 2009 8
4. March 2009 17
5. April 2009 24
6. May 2009 36
7. June 2009 46
8. July 2009 66
9. August 2009 83
10. September 2009 96
11. October 2009 111
12. November 2009 120
13. December 2009 134
14. January 2010 153
15. February 2010 170
16. March 2010 180
17. April 2010 188
18. May 2010 198
19. June 2010 206
20. July 2010 211
21. August 2010 216
22. September 2010 222
23. October 2010 229
24. November 2010 235
25. December 2010 245
26. Acknowledgements 257

To the offspring, same same xx

Introduction

New Abode

Not long before the end of 2008, I went into hiding of sorts by closing my first blog and starting again at a new online location. This introduction begins with my first entry:

> *I feel like I've just carried in a million boxes and a shitload of heavy furniture. Single-handedly. Thought I should bring my files over from Old Blog before settling into a new home here. Can't just offload your old self because you suddenly [temporarily] hate your lovely friends and feel the need to run away.*
>
> *So now I've killed the illusion of having just popped into existence, and New Blog is burdened with the past. Which means that nothing's really changed except the privacy, and maybe my voice. So new, so honest, such manners now...*

Invisibility – nailed it. Finally. As an attempt at wholesale extroversion, *Vagina-Mite* lasted longer than expected. But by the time 2009 arrived, the winning of the battle to preserve some degree of invisibility against the perpetual struggle to overcome this inclination was a circumstantial necessity.

I wouldn't call it a victory, though. The retreat into hiding was prompted by two things. The first was the gradual removal of support for the arts blog site by its host; the second was the interference of a close friend. The latter drove home the imbalance created when sharing personal writing with readers generally, where they have access to your inner thoughts without giving you access to theirs. When your readers are friends this can be problematic, depending on the nature of the friendship. If you're susceptible to being ashamed of the product of your mind, it's natural to want to disappear from view.

Speaking of Which...

I'll repeat a summary that appears in the introduction to Volume Two here, which explains that the introduction to *Vagina-Mite* – the first volume in this series – applies to all volumes, and contains:

> ...*a necessary reflection on the nature and impact of personal writing; the delicate handling of people's privacy while satisfying the compulsion to record life with candour; subjectivity as the default setting in the reader/writer relationship when it comes to memoir formats; and the outrunning of the [thievin', violatin'] AI machine. It also explains the performative nature of writing about private life on a public platform, and affectations adopted in the construction of a strong alter-ego (which increase in frequency according to the degree of stress younger-me was experiencing, and which older-me has diligently cleaned up).*

Unsurprisingly

True anonymity is a lonely thing, and at my new blog location I was writing into the void for real. I was still lively and still in the World Proper, but as my new profile described, I was *'friend to many but close to nobody'* at the time. This volume traces the beginnings of a long period of emotional isolation that was to follow, brought on by a complicated domestic situation and subsequent diminishing confidence.

This domestic extravaganza is as usual characterised by the relationship between art/writing and life, which is sometimes as gentle as nurturing the germ of a particular novel, or the painting of particular works, and sometimes as cataclysmic as the direct impact your writing has on somebody you love. Here the life-writing dilemma mentioned above – that tension between feeling compelled to write and the desire to protect people's privacy – grows into something immediate, specific and very personal.

The volume is characterised also by that ongoing contradiction, where I give in to the instinct to disappear, while holding [desperately] onto the need/right/drive to speak.

Repeat, Repeat

Distilled and clean, a hashtag paints a thousand words. I've added a couple of things but the hashtags lazily thrown together in Volume Two still apply, including the intrinsic struggle of being an artist itself. I can't for the life of me think of a better way to conclude:

> *Hashtag art and motherhood and all of the complications that go with it. Hashtag Australian writer. Hashtag domestic life, the aftermath of a marriage, the raising of an angry teenager. Hashtag the joys of motherhood, hashtag the struggle. Hashtag I'm an idiot, hashtag I am not. Hashtag art and economics, hashtag what was I thinking. Hashtag why didn't I just get a normal job. Hashtag I tried, hashtag I failed. Hashtag I succeeded, hashtag I had no idea what I was doing. Hashtag Tourette's, that simmering, bastard thing. Hashtag love, hashtag sex, hashtag too-much-information. Hashtag the end of sex as we know it. Hashtag queer relationships, hashtag hetero, hashtag unconventional family structures. Hashtag Mother wrote a book, hashtag she shouldn't have done that. Hashtag now what [?]. Hashtag how we mess up our kids. Hashtag school refusal and its poor cousins: cleaning-bedroom refusal and doing-dishes refusal. Hashtag undiagnosed neurodivergence. Hashtag overcoming introversion, hashtag succumbing to introversion. Hashtag – ultimately – life.*

Vagina-Mite Was No More
Journals 2009 – 2010

January 2009

Friday, 2nd January, 2009.

Conquerage

Time for a sit down and a think. What about, painting? *Again?* Needless to say, I've been busy painting, but that doesn't need thinking about. The painting's been going great guns. I may even be skipping the second-layer angst this time.

No, today we need to congratulate ourselves for having faced The Kitchen Bin Problem. More specifically, the unidentifiable smell coming from the kitchen bin cupboard. Until today I dealt with the problem by closing the door of the kitchen bin cupboard and hanging a plastic bag on the door handle. New Bin. Ingenious, I know.

If I sound light-hearted it's because the smell is *gone*. I scrubbed that bin cupboard all over and not once did I find the cause of the smell, but it somehow vanished. Whose idea it was to invent bin cupboards, I don't know, but instead of smelling like a cupboard that holds a bin, my bin cupboard now smells like a Nordic forest. I think that has to be the recipe for a good year ahead.

Saturday, 3rd January, 2009.

A Curious Case of Not Really Curious

I went to see *The Curious Case of Benjamin Button* yesterday, despite being put off by the incredibly dorky title. I'm not exactly saying ho or hum about it, but I guess my reaction is at best lukewarm. As I sat through it – neither bored nor particularly interested – I kept wondering what appealed to both actors and producers when they read the script. All very forrest-gumpish. Bit of a wanna-be epic, all "this happened" and then "that happened" and then "et cetera".

I mean, really. It emphasised the tragedy of life being limited no matter which way you look at it (yah, poignancy), but the story lacked depth. It was running almost entirely on charm and period setting (i.e. a film maker's playground). There were characters who were developed but never taken anywhere. Details that amounted to nothing. All of the superfluous *Don'ts* you're supposed to leave out of a story, because they're a distraction.

What bothered me most was that I didn't give a flying fuck about any of the characters. We were even *told* to care about some of them, but there was no demonstration of how important they should be. (Writing rule: show, don't tell.) I only cared when he left, because there were still twenty good years of adulthood left in him, and twenty years should be plenty for raising a child to adulthood. So why leave? That didn't make sense, and it was the crux of the story. Therefore its guts fell out around its ankles. Not the kind of caring they were after = big *fail*.

Something I do care about: a bird in a cage at work. I was in a different wing yesterday (no pun intended), and that's where I found it – one of those green and red ones. Is that a love bird? Well the poor thing was alone. I can't stand seeing birds in cages. I tried apologising to it and gave it some of the cake before I served afternoon tea to the residents, but what can ya do? The worst thing about birds in cages is that you can't set them free. There's no such thing as a good intention, because if you do the right thing the bird will die.

It's no win, and therefore the saddest thing.

Friday, 9th January, 2009.

The Day the Earth Yawned and Took a Nap
Actually it wasn't that bad. I took Son to see *The Day the Earth Stood Still*, and he hated it because of the female lead actress. I, on the other hand, could watch it again and again because of the lead actress's scarf. That scarf should win an Oscar for Best Supporting Garment. It was

in almost every scene, so I was outrageously content. Just the most perfect colour combination ever. I need it. I must have it.

Obviously I'm [again] discovering within myself a shallow side, and I'm liking what I find. I suppose I should mention that I rather enjoy a good fantasy about obliterating the human race for once and for all, so the storyline was okay. If you overlook the inherent flaws in the alien reasoning (i.e. they could have just taken away our access to electricity etc. and sent us back to basics to teach us a lesson). And the cheesiness of alien rationale being as cold as an iceberg, wot melts when witness to the human capacity for emotional extremes.

Awwww, and *awwwwww*.

But forget all that. Scarf. Scarf scarf. *Beautiful*.

Wednesday, 14th January, 2009.

Hard Day's Night

Gosh, Wednesday already. Not the Wednesday I'd planned, exactly, but here I am because every day there's something that needs to be thunk out loud and never the time to think it. This is a disciplinary sitting, to offload before bed.

Because I worked *hard* today. First by saving lizards. Quite a few. Every time I went to the loo I'd find one running around on the bathroom floor. GrandKitten doesn't normally bring her toys downstairs, or at least I thought, but now I'm beginning to wonder just how many little tail-less lizards are running around inside our house. I tried to return them all to the same patch of garden, so that they could gather as tail-amputees and reminisce about their time as Prisoners of War.

Secondly, I finished what I was supposed to finish yesterday, as in the under-drawing for a three-panel drawing. It took ALL DAY, that being a day that was supposed to be put aside for painting. So I'm feeling down because paid work is getting in the way of my at-home work. And my feet hurt.

Also, my broken glasses broke more, so I've tied them up with embroidery thread. This enhances the crooked way they sit on my face in a decorative kind of way (wispy thread ends), but does make me feel even more poverty stricken than before. Then there's the smoky exhaust from my dying car. And the lists of kids' school books to be gotten. I don't know why all of this chose today to get to me.

Anyway, doesn't matter – tomorrow I'll get to the fun part of the drawing (the top layers), and because I've been doing these drawings in my head for so long I'm pumped. I need to make the transition from thought to reality before I feel good. Today's feeling is a bit of *blah*, a bit of *nothing seems possible*.

But look at that – brain a little bit emptier, so now I can sleep. And beg myself to get up early. I'm not a night person, and I hate wasting the best hours of the day by sleeping late. I need to realign my body clock. If I can just get up early every day, things will be fine.

Thursday, 22nd January, 2009.

A Sucker Born Every Minute

And I'm one of them! I love being one of them! There are probably few things less interesting than what I'm about to write about, and yet I'm absurdly excited, so in my bid to brain-dump as necessary it just has to be dealt with.

It's my new car. Somehow I've misconstrued this buying of a new car as a serious step towards being Normal. Possibly very adult-y? Because *other people* do it. They do it *all the time*. If anything I'm latent, and this fact is helping me get over the guilt of spending money like a normal [adult] person. Maybe it's a symptom of almost turning forty? Who knows? Who cares?

I know I should've shopped around a bit more (i.e. at all), but I'm really bad at making decisions, so the less I have to choose from, the better. Also that would have involved shopping, a process best avoided (time! care factor zero!). So I test-drove two cars. Second day of hunting; I found the car I liked, I bought it. I find this kind of decisiveness thrilling. Uncharacteristic, and thrilling. I shouldn't have even made those pleas for advice from certain men, who seemed determined that I beat the price down.

This because I had two types of car to choose from, and when First Advice Man started telling me about all of these others, my head swam before teetering on the edge of a complete meltdown. No. Don't listen to other people – they will confuse. It's much easier to be a dupe-able consumer. The world needs people like me, to pay full price and keep the economy going.

And if I'd walked away from the offer, as these men advised, I might have missed out on the car I wanted. I can't imagine me beating anybody down. That salesman had me correctly pegged as a caverinerer. I wanted the car. It's an ex-demo with a long warranty. I don't have to care about cars once I have this one. I don't have to *worry*. I can just paint pretty stories and write fascinating pictures.

Tomorrow, when I drive my new car, I'll be so invisible to the world, just a nondescript every day kind of person, that I can do whatever I want. No more conspicuously loud engine, no more conspicuous exhaust pipe plumage. *I am not here*, and *I am not-here with style*. I love being normal – I should conform more often.

Saturday, 24th January, 2009.

Sub-Standard

I'm not sure how the standard came about, or why my car doesn't measure up, but apparently its so intolerable as a vehicle that First-Born has refused to learn to drive in it.

I was so excited when I picked it up that I took it to First-Born as soon as I could. I had L-plates ready. Thought they'd be so happy to learn in a smooth-driving car that doesn't deafen every pedestrian it passes with its roaring exhaust.

Something about how dare I buy a car without getting their approval first. But more likely its a classic case of transference, the car just an ugly extension of the ugly owner. No one in their right mind would buy me if they found me parked inside a car yard. Good to know. Guess I wont be teaching them to drive after all.

Monday, 26th January, 2009.

Mind Over Matter

Matter being paint. Of course. What else is there? There's liverwurst, granted. I was making sammiches for the Germans at work tonight and they do love their liverwurst. What I discovered is that if you mash it into a spread it's a delight to smear over the rye bread (feels very average on wholemeal), and all I could think was *wouldn't it be nice to paint with liverwurst?* I'd never eat it, but I appreciate the sheer joy of the stuff.

I was just telling my friends that I've been letting my paintings control *me*, instead of the other way around. It's all about the upper hand, isn't it? *I'm* boss of the world, and those paintings will do as they're damn well told. None of this angst they're putting me through.

So far so good. Fine Art Illustrator Friend came over last night, and according to her the paintings aren't crap. I have to trust her because she's as blunt as a mallet. There's gotta be a better simile than that out there for her – I've got to stop writing when I'm tired. (When am I not tired?)

Long story short = today painted with confidence instead of fear, though slightly scared, or maybe scared shitless but in a confident way = going so well but then had to go to work and it drives me crazy having to interrupt my real work to go and earn money.

Am tired = the end = goodnight.

Saturday, 31st January, 2009.

I Got to Put My Feet Up

It's not that I want to write about movies again, but it's nice to say something as easy as "I saw a movie" and put in my two bob's worth about things that have nothing to do with my mental innards.

So for starters, have you ever noticed that Wil Smith's face looks like it's been stuck together from odd parts, kind of like Mr Potato Head? And have you ever seen Mr Potato Head pash?

I only went to see that movie because somebody told me it had a letterpress in it. I braved both bad reviews and an un-air-conditioned cinema. And the letterpress had a such a pissy little role, a fraction more than a cameo, but it was nice to watch people kiss (I don't get out much).

I suppose you can call it arty that the first proper kiss followed a very emotional letterpress moment, although it wasn't a particularly sensual-looking kiss, probably a 7 out of 10 in Real scale, and 9 out of 10 in Voyeuristically Satisfying scale (because of the very emotional letterpress moment) (I REALLY DON'T GET OUT MUCH).

Whatever. Not even going to bother mentioning the title. Not as bad as the reviews say, but nothing earth shattering either. Was "okay".

―――

By The Way

I should say more about the heat wave, because it's exciting and as I can't help repeating, *I really love the heat*. When it's this hot in Melbourne, suddenly everybody's talking about the weather. You can't wait to see the news and watch footage of people being hot in public. And you really love finding out how high the temperature soared. The higher the number, the more it feels like Melbourne's winning some kind of competition. *Score! [!!]*.

―――

February 2009

Monday, 2nd February, 2009.

School's In
No offence to my offspring, but jigger off already. I'd forgotten how utterly blissful it is to be home alone. And now I'm outdoing myself with the sitting and thinking business. Have I not sat down like this all summer? Maybe if I change the locks before they get home, it can be like this forever. I can wear ear plugs to block out the sound of thumping and screaming coming from the front door.

I also haven't swum since the holidays began, so the first thing I did was go to the pool this morning, assuming that all of the world's children were in school, so the pool would be silky and flat. And it would have been, if every other lap swimmer on the planet hadn't had the same brilliant idea. Doesn't matter; they were okay swimmers, so apart from accidentally groping some guy on the arse as I came in from a lap of backstroke (I'm so glad he was facing away from me), nobody was in anybody's way.

You can imagine the peace that started to infiltrate my body. It was important after that to rush home and dance naked on the table top, but the tabletop was dirty so I did housework instead. I know! Housework! And you wonder why I'm single. But you can understand, really, when I say that doing dishes and mopping floors was so much more relaxing today, because I knew that for at least half a day nobody would come home and mess up ~~the~~ *my* [!!] house.

I'd wander intermittently into the studio, look at paintings, then wander out again and clean some more. It's possible I had a cat nap. It's possible I sat at the [clean] kitchen table with a mug of hot chocolate to watch the rain fall and enjoy the rip-cracking thunder. Doing *nothing*.

All of this in one day. I don't think I can stand the excitement. And only a few minutes left before I go to pick Son up from school.

I wonder what the year's going to be like. With house clean = we can start afresh. Even though it may be difficult. So far the brilliant new routine has fallen flat, because First-Born's most common spoken phrases [to me] are *'shut up'* and *'get fucked'*. Makes me very sad, but I'm not gonna think about it.

Just, I like this feeling, with silence all around, cats sleeping at my feet, and optimism that the new routine will wipe out First-Born's anger. If I can just get them to cooperate. Fingers crossed.

Still Monday.

No Fucking Food

You said it, sister. And you'd be right about that if you couldn't count salad, fruit, bread, soup, and about a million et-ceteras as "food". ALL OF WHICH ARE ABUNDANT IN OUR FRIDGE.

Ah, First-Born and the sabotage of my new menu system. I printed out calendar pages to write our menu onto in advance, so that as life gets shitfully busy this year we can still keep on top of the food. This makes me a superb provider of necessities for my children. It's the soup, I tell you – the secret to good living.

I'm scared of First-Born messing the system up, because I'm going to need a bit of smoothness to survive. I'll be working at the nursing home, teaching two classes, and attending Elite Art School/ uni full-time. On top of this I have manuscripts to work on. Frankly, the food needs to cook itself.

In my imagination I see my children chopping vegetables before I get home each night. Then I take some prepared food from the fridge and we all prep the meals together. Awww. Look at us.

I wanted us to practise during January, but First-Born told me artfully to *get stuffed*. They haven't eaten a single thing I've prepared over the past two weeks. Whereas I think I'm a hero for preparing anything at all during that heatwave. If I was alone I'd be eating nothing but cherries and watermelon. (And chocolate, that's a given.)

So am I worried, well of course. After the vandalism of my bedroom wall incident, I left art school last year so that I could be home more, and for a while that was okay. But they still hate me. I find it unsettling that I'm not receiving any love from my child. First-Born can't stand me. I don't have to do anything to achieve this level of hatred from them, just existing is enough. Last night they got angry that I hadn't cooked a big meal, *'There's no fucking food'* again, and ordered me to go shopping and cook for them. I don't know, it's all very stupid. I of course said no, seeing as I'd planned salad sandwiches for dinner. They said no to my offer but ate the sandwiches that Son made.

First-Born wants to feel looked-after, I know this. And I'm failing to make them feel looked-after. But, see looking-after-my-children information above. What is it that I'm missing? Self-sacrifice? Submissiveness? A different personality? What'll it take to please them?

I never describe this very well, I get far too emotional as I write about it. I don't know what I'm supposed to do. What if they make the year impossible? Must not anticipate. Must see how it goes. Keep a low profile. Maybe wear a bullet proof vest.

Still Monday, 2nd February, 2009.

Secret Agent

Here I get to blow my own trumpet, but not really because I don't want to quote all of the outrageously generous comments on the manuscript appraisal report. It arrived how many weeks ago now? I don't know, but I emptied the letterbox at the top of the driveway on my way out, and said letterbox contained my returned manuscript, which sat on the passenger seat of the car (my desk) for a good ten minutes before I couldn't stand it anymore and had to pull over to read.

Long story short: the manuscript has been declared "finished", "complete", "no need to make any changes" and *get ye to a publisher* sort of thing, with some very flattering et ceteras. The best part is that I didn't know a certain somebody was an agent, and he left a note saying *'Let's talk'* on the report pages. Talk we did, and he asked me to please read over the notes and send him the manuscript. That's gotta make a girl feel lucky.

That he's secretive about his role as an agent has made me suspect he wears Italian suits and sunglasses and drives a shiny black car with heavily tinted windows. Probably smokes cigars.

I don't know why I'm not frothing at the bit to get the suggested revision done. Possibly because it's hard to let go of an unfinished painting. But I've signed both canvases now, and during today's studio checks couldn't find anything to work on. I'd feel better about calling them finished if one of them wasn't bothering me. The self one = I never use proper references and so do stupid things to my anatomy. So dumb. But the other one's had rave reviews from friends so far. Another friend will be coming to see them this week; he's my high executioner, so I'm waiting for his opinion with baited breath. In the end it might be necessary to scrap one and keep the other. Who knows?

The subject of the rave-review painting, a lovely friend who so kindly modelled for me nude, is waiting for me to send her images, but I'm just taking my time. Still operating under the belief that nothing good will ever really happen, very disconnected from any sense of merit and not in the mood for praise.

Same with the manuscript, everything so calm, no sense getting excited until the ball really starts rolling. Because what if he hates it? Nobody's hated it yet, so that's a stupid thing to think. (Actually one person has, an agent I sent an early [unappraised] draft to [before I knew appraisals were a thing].) But I'll get my sense of *finished* with the paintings, and my housework has been done, so maybe tomorrow I'll start reading over the manuscript and writing him a cover letter.

Isn't this the moment I've been waiting for? After years and years of work? A potential agent waiting in the wings. How nice is that – to have at least one reader ahead of me, and that reader a potential doorway to other readers. So I should be getting off my arse. Any minute now.

Sunday, 8th February, 2009.

The John Doe of Bushfires

You see why I need to be spanked and sent to my room. I *still* love the smell of bushfire. It's just so *pretty*. So when I ducked my head outside the balcony door yesterday for about the hundredth time to feel the lovely heat press against my face, as is my want, and this time I smelt smoke, my first reaction was to inhale deeply and sigh.

My second reaction was to remember that I live less than a hundred metres from a forest, on a forty-six degree day, with the air being stirred up by a hot northerly. I grabbed Son and we hit the computer, straight to the CFA site. But the major fire events weren't major yet. The list was humongous, but only really Bunyip was big. The rest were trickfully small.

The night sky's a beautiful kind of eerie after a bushfire, the moon all orange-like, with phantasms about. Hence my heartless pleasure in Very Bad Things.

It wasn't until I was at work today that I found out about Kinglake. And that people had DIED, meaning that my smoky bushfire perfume was probably laced with intolerable tragedy, and that should learn me. And then this evening, when a friend visited, I found out that Marysville had been razed to the ground. Marysville! I almost lived in Marysville!! When he left I tried to find the news, but it wasn't until late-late that I caught a couple of proper bulletins and saw it all.

I'll spare you my sentiment because there'll be sentiment aplenty over the airwaves for some time to come. KRudd PM, for example, who's undoubtedly very sincere but even now, in the midst of chaos, comes across as a salesman. This time of emotional goods and empathy. (But really, he can hug a man to comfort him in a way that John Howard never could. You have to admit. I'd buy a car from him. I would.)

All praise to Channel Ten for not interrupting their news broadcast with advertisements. For presenting the facts without getting overly down and dirty with the huggy prime minister. At least not as much as Channel Nine did. Which brings me to the comparison, because Channel Nine played ads and the ads were so tacky I was shocked. You just don't *do* that. You don't go from *Devastating Broadcast of Widespread Tragedy* to *Superficial Consumer Glut*. And, really, couldn't they have stopped the consumer clock from ticking out of respect for their own, said being Brian Naylor? Those advertisements were offensive, nothing short of.

But on another note, our burning state event needs a name. Death and destruction needs a worthy title. We saw it with Ash Wednesday, we saw it with Black Friday. Why has nobody named our awful day yet? Is it that this time we can't find words to encapsulate what's happened? A tight phrase to make it easier to define what we can't get our heads around? A reference to sum things up and convey magnitude? I don't think I've ever known us to be so lacking in labels. It's not tacky to have a label for this kind of thing – the label helps us respect the enormity of the experience, and allows us to communicate a whole gamut of emotion with its mere mention.

I'm waiting for the title the way you wait for a baby to be named. The words are going to become part of our national memory and community identity. This is no small thing.

Thursday, 12th February, 2009.

Horror and Shock

Have I taught them nothing? My students are lovely people, and every week I look forward to kicking back at the head of the class and listening to them tell stories. But if any student of mine – *ever* – starts a paragraph with '*I gazed deeply into his eyes*' again, I'll expel them from my class and not let them back until they've washed their brains out with soap. If I haven't already spontaneously slashed my wrists in one swift and reflexive move, before my mouth even stops gaping.

What could I do but bite my tongue? A sentence like that's beyond help. I couldn't be the one to break it to her. Even though it's my *job* to break it to her. And if I could do it (I can't! I can't!) I certainly wouldn't be able to do it gently. Maybe I should've given her a subtle hint? Something like vomiting onto her lap.

That bit of fiction I have out there may beat readers over the head with its lack of tact, but I've never before been more grateful to be a writer of things gritty. I'm so sorry, Anonymous Student, but that was a revolting display of "niceness". I know this makes me a Very Bad Person, but oh puh-*leeze*.

Friday, 13th February, 2009.

Inadequacy

It takes a lot to confuse me [?], but today I'm confused. I've been considering the nature of the synopsis, because I have to rewrite one. This should be easy, because we have dictionaries to help us with them. Synopsis, in a nutshell, equals outline-of-story, and the function of this outline is to inform an editor of what the book contains.

My most recent manuscript appraiser has a nicer way of looking at a synopsis. She's the big kid and I'm the little kid and I want to grow up to be just like her, but I almost can't get my head around it. She suggests that my synopsis is an explanation of what the book's about, but it would be better if it had a narrative quality and was more like a small version of the book itself.

It's so nice in theory. I love that she suggested I include *'the more breathless energy of the book itself'*, which is outrageously flattering. But maybe I'm pooped? Maybe my brain needs an asthma pump, and to collapse after the marathon?

I'm failing, and need to try again. I think I can, I think I can.. (ah shit, I *don't* think I can – that's the problem).

Saturday, 21st February, 2009.

Forty is the New Nothing

Can't I just skip forty and go straight to forty-one? It's really interfering with my invisibility. The problem isn't that I'm growing older, seeing as I like growing older, because it allows me to feel very wise and be condescending to Young People. I wouldn't go backwards even if I could. The problem is that people want me to *celebrate*, and I'm really not in a celebratey mood.

Forty's like this philosophical juncture where you're tricked into considering the quality of your life.

I think First-Born had already mentioned planning a fortieth for me before Xmas, in between growling and calling me a c_ _ _. (Note my new evasiveness, as though I'm suddenly shy about writing the word *cunt*. Is this what growing older does to you? Am I suddenly *mature*?).

Then at the Xmas table the rest of my family started getting in on the act. At the time I thought *okay, I'll do it for them*. This because I'm extremely generous. They all have parties because parties are normal. Parties are what normal people want. *I will be normal.*

Mostly I wanted to do it for First-Born, giving them a chance to do something nice for me, filling our house with people and music and wine just like we used to, which would make them think nice things for and about all of us, putting life into perspective by punctuating it with celebration. Theoretically, our relationship would suddenly improve because of this. And I was touched that they thought I was worth the trouble, given the way they've been lately.

But as December moved into January things didn't change. The C word was still the most prominent label applied to me. First-Born was doing crushing little rejection things on a daily basis. I made it known to everyone that I do NOT want a party. In fact, a party would upset me, because it'd be a farce. I don't want the attention. I don't want to be celebrated. There's nothing to celebrate. I'm content to be content and nothing more. I'm at Art School and finally belong somewhere. It's nice. And it's all I need.

At home First-Born's maturing a little because they're also at a new school, and they have a new outlook. But last night they mentioned the party/get-together/whatever. There's very little time left to plan it. Or alternatively, very little time left to somehow make people forget my birthday altogether. But we talked, and it was literally the first actual conversation we've had in well over a month, possibly two or three. As in, they didn't raise their voice at me once.

Long story short, when I said I don't want to celebrate until we get our family life back, First-Born said we've never had a family life. When I told them I'm a good mother, they said I'm not a good mother. There was a lot more to it than that, but all of it contextualised by my idea of happiness. I'm not happy. I mean I'm happy in countenance, but I'm not happy with our life and am powerless to change it. When First-Born says these things I see just how far away from improvement we are, and how embedded in bad feelings our life together is. I just have to wait it out, and while I'm waiting I don't want to pretend to be happy for a party when that's just not the kind of happy I feel.

So you see, a party is asking people into your life, and I can't do that. They have no idea how little love First-Born has for me at the moment, and how heart-breaking it is. In the softest, most private way. Things I don't tell them about. A party's just going to highlight how sad I feel deep down. I don't want to have to look that in the eye.

My Birthday, 2009.

Pat on the Back

For a few weeks I was hoping that the synopsis fairy would sneak in at night and re-write my synopsis for me while I slept, but by Tuesday I was beginning to suspect that there's no such thing as a synopsis fairy [!!]. So I did the damn thing myself.

This needed announcing. Anyway I'm forty now, and have decided to ditch the misery and drink wine instead. Bottoms up.

March 2009

Sunday, 1st March, 2009.

Fifty-Bound

I've probably mentioned before that teenagers smell, but I think it needs reiterating. THEY STINK. I was walking behind Smelly Hair Guy when I picked First-Born's friends up from the station yesterday, and nearly gagged at the idea of his long and obviously unwashed hair being anywhere inside my new and shiny car.

We're talking at least three-day unwashed hair, here. Why don't teenagers know about the unwashed hair smell? If humans weren't so capable of producing other offensive smells, I'd say it's the most offensive smell ever generated by the human body. I should've gotten First-Born to shave it off while he slept and thrown it over the balcony. Some befitting fantasy about griffins spiriting it away to some blistered landscape where they use it to build nests in which to store their human corpse rations.

Apart from this, First-Born's new friends from Serious New School are okay. Except that they keep me up all night and then wake me up early, and Performy Guy feels the need to perform in my face every time I walk into a room, with card tricks and balloon animals. I guess that's okay really, because when I met him he handed me a balloon dog he'd just made and I discovered I quite like blue balloon dogs. Also he makes me laugh. I think he'll go far in showbizness, except that some of his tricks are magiciany and magician tricks are a pet hate of mine. So I both like and am thoroughly bored by his theatrics.

Anyway nice people, yeah yeah, but they can fuck off now. They can fuck off twelve hours ago. Closer to old age now, I'm equal parts cantankerousness, intolerance, and miserly aspiration, hence the alarm bells ringing in my head when I heard kitchen cupboards banging at 7 am. I was worried they'd raid my newly replenished chocolate stash.

Why am I writing about teenagers? That's just wasteful. I can't believe I have to go to work today. Work is for commoners. I don't know why I thought it was so noble to be doing my bit to help the world go 'round when there are books to write and pictures to paint. I'd like to take the good-citizen's halo from my head and shove it up somebody's nostril, because two jobs plus full-time study equals no time for anything else. I'm so fucking tired I can't even be bothered remembering what I was going to say next.

p.s. I secretly love that First-Born brings their people home. I like knowing who their friends are, and that they're happy.

Amused [Again] by Xtians

When she rang to say *happy birthday* from sunny old interstate I asked an elder relative about her Hard Times, which are a result of an unfortunate business investment with a fellow church member. Churchy Relative could lose their house, for example. And during that pleasant conversation she said that she'll *'just have to put more trust in [gawd's] ways, but that's really hard to do right now'*.

'Or trust less in human beings,' I cleverly suggested, respectfully amused that she thinks gawd's up there controlling the funds and orchestrating her very bad luck. In the old days if gawd wanted to smite you or test your faith, he'd send in a plague or make you sacrifice your offspring. I think Churchy Relative's getting off pretty lightly.

Monday, 9th March, 2009.

The Long Piece of Rope, De-Mystified

Instead of giving in to her usual suspension of disbelief this evening by chasing the rope-end as I twirled it around her, GrandKitten kept lifting her eyes to watch my hand. As though the rope wasn't really a long snake that needed to be caught. As though it was *a cheap human trick*.

What will I do if she suddenly flicks her tail and walks away, saying *'What a load of bullshit!'*? If only they'd stay young forever.

Chris Fontana

Tuesday, 17th March, 2009.

Later Gater

I've somehow become the kind of person who doesn't open their mail. There's a pile of unopened letters on my bedroom floor to prove it. They're there because they fell off the drawers where I keep my overflowing in-tray, also containing unopened letters.

I remember all of those years of listening for the postie, when the sound of letters dropping into the letterbox was exciting. What's happened to me that I'd rather burn the damn things? Too much paper being wasted, that's probably it. Plus who can be bothered. *Really.*

Friday, 20th March, 2009.

Between Me and Sleep

I don't know whose idea it was to strip the bed today so that the linen could flap happily in all of that autumn sunshine. I've spent a good hour pondering the possibility of the bed making itself before I go in there. It could be that I'm avoiding a little bit of effort, what with my muscles feeling so flu-ey. It could be that I'm just full of good intentions that are far too difficult to realise. It could be that I'm just too tired. So tired lately that I've been thinking I should get a clinical diagnosis, but am not sure if there's such thing as a diagnosis for pure and unadulterated buggeredry. Plus I'm pretty sure the doctor would just examine my pooped little body and say '*I'm sorry to be the one to have to break this to you, but, YOU'RE FORTY, so get used to it*'.

I'm desperate to get myself to bed, but it really is a lot of effort to make the bed from scratch. Maybe I could just sleep on the couch?

Saturday, 21st March, 2009.

Slow Motion

It's like I live inside an old kung fu film, but without the lip-synching. It's not that I can't get things done, I just need about a million years per task and then I'm okay with it. I realised this both yesterday and today, when I let things run on slow time. These are the first two days of not having to rush between one place and another. This because I not only stayed home from art school, but also I said yes when some person I know rang and offered to remove two of my paintings from an exhibition they were hanging in. Which was pretty brave of me because it means risking damage, but time is time and well you know, even paintings have to leave the nest and make their own way in the world eventually.

It's taken me two days to do what I'd planned to get done in one morning. But the sun's shining, and I'm sitting here having a think – haven't I needed that? The Australian in me is wanting to say *fucken oath*. So yeah, *fucken oath*.

I'm also wagging work tomorrow, due to exhaustion and sort-of flu and me weary old bones et cetera. That means if I'm lucky I can get last week's things done by the end of this weekend. Well some of them. Like the seven canvases I meant to stretch today and started but didn't finish.

I'm so slow-motion that if I was playing tennis, I'd throw the ball up to serve, and before I'd swung my body to follow through with the hit you could have gone out for a cup of tea and not missed anything.

Does anybody even drink tea anymore? This is why I could never be cool – if I could do cool I'd have known that other people really drink beer. Is this a temporary metaphor problem, or a tennis problem? I'M TOO TIRED TO THINK STRAIGHT.

Saturday, 21st March, 2009.

Week-Old Thoughts

Probably stale by now, but better late than never. Secret Agent finally called and then called again. We spoke and yea there was rejoicing, except that I don't quite manage rejoicing much these days. So yea there were many calm feelings of pleasantry across the land. We touched intellects, and it was *good*. He's lovely to talk shop with. And although it'd be in my best interest to stop resorting to metaphors it really is blind-datish, this agency business, and scary as all fuck.

Anyway it looks like I have a literary agent. The sweet nothings have been whispered, so now we're at the hand-holding stage. I'm not getting too excited, just in case. I don't expect good to happen to me. Ever. Although, all of this being-sensible is making me feel like I'm wearing somebody else's clothes. I can't wait for my impetuousness to return so I can go back to doing reckless and stupid things. I'd at least like to feel excited about something. Anything.

I guess I am? But only in small doses. I suspect I need to shed some people to manage this. Develop a fuck-the-world attitude. Didn't I used to fuck the world? I'm sure I did.

There's something to ponder. But first, I'll just hold onto the nice Secret Agent experience. Being a week behind my own brain means that I haven't even done the work I was supposed to do to get the manuscript submitted, so that's tomorrow's job. Only I'd better not do that one in slow motion. Write first, fuck the world later. Even *that's* sensible. What's gotten into me?

Sunday, 22nd March, 2009.

When In Doubt, Make a Scarecrow

I was supposed to be making deeply profound art, but I made a scarecrow instead. I had no idea how much *fun* it is to make a scarecrow. Making scarecrows is the secret to everlasting happiness. And this explains why I was so tired for the rest of the day that I fell asleep at least three times whilst working on my manuscript; because I was a veritable god who'd fashioned a creature out of nothing (which has gotta knock the stuffing out of you). NOT because the manuscript is boring.

Despite this joy, I experienced two sadnesses today. The first was because in the past my kids would have helped me make the scarecrow. If only I hadn't come to scarecrow-making so late in life. I miss them being young and enthusiastic. Their kind of dumb wonder at everything. It's no fun feeling dumb wonderment on my own.

The second sadness is that I made a roast dinner. It smelled beautiful and was beautiful. I haven't made a roast dinner in about a century, so it reminded me of the life we had before. And I realised that a roast dinner is really an in-love meal. I want to be in love again.

I think it's Secret Agent's fault. He's an astute reader, and for a week now some of his comments have been floating around in my head. Because the novel's so personal, when his feedback got personal it was like psychoanalysis. As in, other readers have been intelligent and given me detailed feedback, but they haven't done what he did by thinking out loud about the narrator's thoughts. When he was talking about what he'd read in the narrative, he was telling me about my life, and he got things so right I was taken aback. How did he *do* that? It's like he read with x-ray glasses or something. And now that I'm reading through the manuscript it's all coming back to me. What I had, what I'm missing now. Where the emptiness is.

But I have a scarecrow to fill the void, and if I start talking to it there's a chance I won't feel lonely anymore. First I have to turn it into sophisticated "art", seeing as it's part of an obscure project for art school. Twist of a phrase here and there and I should be able to manage it. I have enough integrity. I'm not an installation person like some of the other people at school, so I know it's gonna turn out on the stupid side. Do I care? No. All in a day's work.

Tuesday, 31st March, 2009.

Sonya Hartnett's New One

Butterfly. There were sentences that describe teenage boys as being '*medieval with sweat*' and made spectacular declarations, such as '*a mother and a father have no right to feelings… a parent should be a person the way a door is a door*', and explained things like '*Plum had been accepted as part of the deal, like Spam in a raffle-won hamper*', and so instead of returning it to the shop the way I planned to if I didn't like it, I had to keep it. Which makes me feel like a Good Consumer and not somebody who treats a bookshop like a pay-as-you-go-but-only-temporarily library. Of sorts. (Which I only did because I bought it from AMERICAN CHAIN Borders, so it's practically my duty to return it. At this I will fail.)

And there's the worry. I always think I'm going to re-read a Sonya Hartnett, but actually I never do. It's like I get my fill and I stay full. Really I don't mind the brown tracksuit pants flavour of the title. And even though I sometimes flinched at the number of similes and wondered if she wouldn't be better off building them up as metaphors, I'm stunned by the devastating and beautiful torture of the story. She's a wonderful writer.

I do need to squeeze a but in there somewhere, because she ends the novel on a character I can't stand. I get it, I'm supposed to feel that way about her – but it left me with a lingering taste of something awful, and when I pick up the book (I now don't have to be careful not to smudge it with chocolate or Vegemite) and open it to drink a little bit in here and there, I see this revolting character and the awful taste returns.

It's not that I'm having fiscal regrets. I think I'm worried I won't be able to enjoy the potential re-reading because of that ending. I want it all again, brand spanking new and painful.

April 2009

Saturday, 4th April, 2009.

Pilgrimage

With camera, picnic blanket, some cheese and biscuits and a bottle of wine, a friend from Art School and I went to visit some bushfire sites today. Which makes death and destruction sound like a picnic (what gave it away? the picnic blanket?), but I promise we were very respectful.

It's confronting while the news is drip-feeding the stories through, but we drove out to Healesville and Yarra Glen and then on to Kinglake, and I realised it's not until you're in the thick of the charred landscape that you really get a sense of the magnitude of the thing. Which is an offensive thing to say, because while the fires burned I was in a safe elsewhere, so the only magnitude I can rightfully touch is a distant one.

I won't even try to convey what it's like to be there. Sad, obviously. And beautiful, despite the stink of spent rage (and really, the smell of burnt landscape is overwhelming). Kinglake is so small. While we were driving through I saw a street sign that hinted at wide vistas, so that's where we went, and that's where we found a whole area full of destroyed houses (not a single one left standing). From there, the most extraordinary view of an expansively burnt Everywhere. Leaves you speechless inside.

Although I hate that there are so, so many cars on the road, I'm going to encourage everyone I know to go there. It's almost like a responsibility to witness how violent nature can be, to see for yourself what can happen.

I lived out past the Yarra Valley once upon a time, and feel guilty that the peace of the place was sinking into my bones the minute we reached the other side of Lilydale, despite the destruction. I still hope I can find somewhere peaceful one day, because I miss it.

And when I do I should build my house out of corrugated iron and steel roofing – that stuff is everywhere. Bent to buggery but looking like it could survive anything. As in, the rubble that makes up a burnt house is a tiny pile of dust and a shitload of mangled roof. Build a house out of steel and there's no way the big bad wolf would be able to huff and puff the place down.

Wednesday, 8th April, 2009.

Escape From Alcatraz

Ever since I discovered it on the weekend, I've been hatching a plan to bust a cockatoo out of its cage at work. (Hatching, get it? Birds? Eggs?)

As with the caged love bird – *with no other bird there to be in love with* – seeing the cockatoo filled me with despair. But the cockatoo's more robust. I mean it's big, innit. Surely if you set a big bird free it doesn't die? There are so many cockatoos around here, it's sure to find a family. Problem is, I hardly ever get rostered onto that wing, and I was planning on giving up the Sunday shift that took me there. Should I keep that shift on the off chance of finding a way to free the bird?

I tried to work out how the cage was secured but couldn't. Bugger the bird-trapping elderlies and their need for tea n' coffee. The cage doesn't even have enough room for wingspan. When I tried to give it cake it hissed at me, because it's *not happy Jan*.

The other problem is the security cameras. I don't think they're out in the courtyard, but they might be nearby. Then again, security cameras are there to protect residents, not to stop escaping cockies.

I don't know. There has to be a way. I can't stand birds in cages. Or fish in tanks. All I have to do is open a door and leave it ajar. You wouldn't think it'd be so hard.

Sunday, 12th April, 2009.

Spit n' Polish

If my house was a creature I'd have ripped its head off with my teeth. I've been doing some aggressive cleaning, but have to admit defeat.

I've discovered that Ex-Husband has stashed junk in every nook and cranny – and *ohmigawd*, the *garage*. That man never throws anything out. But he's in Peru… and I'm here…

I wish I had a trailer. But here I am back at Square Zero. To make this house a home I have to make it somewhere we love. And we do love it, don't we? No. Yes. Sort of. But not the way I would *if*. Such a big if. Home isn't home until you share it, I think, and the kids don't seem enamoured by being here, so there's a sadness about this place, even though it can be happy. And beautiful. We're just existing here.

I think that'll change if I plant carrots.

But anyway I can't just hang around hoping to find love. First thing I have to do is a cathartic clean out of the past, which requires throwing away some of Ex-H's things. I have to think about how lucky I am to have space. We visited a studio a couple of weeks ago (at Art Skool) and it got me thinking about how expensive it is to rent a studio. I wondered why people don't set up their studios at home, and why they don't live further out from the city to make this possible, because it's cheaper. Really I can set myself up properly here IF I JUST RESIGN MYSELF TO IT, even though I don't have somebody to love and having somebody to love is probably the most important thing about studio building.

But I like working from home, with all of the peace n' quiet, and being able to start early and work late, often uninterrupted. Life at home has always been family, a bit of painting, a bit of writing, walking and swimming, and I have friends, so what's the problem?

Carrots – I don't have home grown carrots. Right.

Tuesday, 14th April, 2009.

Feijoa Heist '09

This time it wasn't dark when I left my parents' house, so I had to drive around the corner and wait for a whole sunset to happen. Which allowed me to stake the joint for longer, but was ultimately boring. I'd not brought a book with me – I usually have a book in my bag, but how was I to know I'd need to squeeze in some pre-burglary reading?

I forget about the feijoas every year, until I remember them, and experience a glorious surprise at what the season is about to offer me. Still, forgetting them equals a failure to plan the day properly. When I saw them on the tree in the afternoon I nearly died, and made sure I drove very slowly to visit Old Uncle in his nursing home, so that we could get back as late as possible. That was easy because I was playing Enya on the CD for Mum, and we had the sun in our eyes all the way back from Warragul. A BASTARD DRIVE.

If you're going to burgle in broad street light, around dinner time isn't the best time to do it. The sun had gone down, but after I parked my car, turned the interior light off and crept across the road, I had to run into my parents' driveway to hide behind Dad's car because wherever it is that people go to on an Easter Monday, they all come home at around 6:45 pm. This wasn't going to be easy.

I watched Mum and Dad through their windows for a bit, thinking again about how they're such good people, and how they'd be horrified if they knew what I was doing. That afternoon, while Mum and I were looking at the fruit, she suggested I ask the man next door if I can take some. Does she not know that if I ask the man for his fruit, I'd be alerting him to the fact that the fruit's worth eating, thus making him want it all for himself? And what if he told his friends about it? What if he gave some to his family? No – feijoas are the best kept secret in the world, and need to stay that way. If people start protecting their trees with shot guns I'll be in trouble.

So anyway, I had my canvas bag emptied of contents and was wearing dark clothing. I braved the leaves crunching underfoot to get in under that tree in the darkest place possible. The dog started barking but I didn't care, and when the man inside the house came to the back door to deal with the dog I just kept shoving that fruit into my bag. I was hidden by the fence and a few leaves, and as he scooped dog food into a bowl I just kept thinking *'That's right, Mister – the dog's barking because it's hungry, not because there's somebody stealing your feijoas out front'*.

When those blasted cars kept driving past I'd freeze in my hunched-over position and make like a rock. I even pulled a muscle; don't ever let it be said that being a rock isn't hard work.

At home, my two little feijoa trees are still in their pots, and have started to wither and die. I have to decide where to plant them and get into the garden. Not near the adult feijoa tree on the bottom tier of our property, which flowers but doesn't bear fruit. Planting's another thing to think about, though, isn't it. My fear of the garden, and the endless work it requires. Maybe some other time.

Wednesday, 15th April, 2009.

Weak Tea, No Flavour

I'll try not speak ill of the dead, but I'm going to be honest. Which isn't as bad as it seems because you're allowed to dislike somebody's book whether they're alive or not. It's just the recentness of her death that makes it insensitive. *Sorry*. But really, why did she bother?

I mean, there's dark, and then there's *dark,* and I don't know what draws people to *dark* when dark will do just fine. In fact normal dark is instructive, takes us somewhere it might be good for us to go. Like cabbage. The other dark (*dark*) is just Brussels sprouts.

No offence Dorothy Porter. But before I get to *El Dorado*, I also recently read *The Road,* Cormack McCarthy, and faaark, what a head spin. That was good dark – an unpleasant thing to imagine, but speculatively realistic. Drags you through the mud of ethical questioning. What would you do, n' all that. Not something that needs to be analysed, just experienced.

El Dorado, though. The only thing I thought was strong was the tug of the storyline, and the Dorothy Porter way of telling so much through well-crafted and efficient snippets. But the snippets themselves this time didn't move me. I had no empathy for the murdered children, and was appalled that empathy was expected from the start. The characters were unattractive in every sense of the word. I didn't care about any of them. The storyline itself, despite the pull of it, seemed so pointless.

Like *The Monkey's Mask* (which I LOVED), it's very *seventies cop*. Has that homicide tv feel about it. If you could smell the characters I think they'd stink of old ashtray. And that's what I've come away with – the whole thing was like an imagined evil scenario that had no bearing in the real world, much like a typical police drama, American style. So much of it unlikely to the point of being stupid (sorry sorry).

Before I read that I read *Akhenaten*, which I'll go out and buy because the writing's stunning, and well worth re-reading. Again with the darkness, but it at least makes some sense here. To me. Because she took each fragment of the story and made art out of it.

I didn't get that from *El Dorado*, and the kind of darkness it wallows in makes me think that she goes for the *extreme* where the *moderate* might be more effective. As though this one revealed – because it's at the tail end of so many – a loss of touch with the value of real-life drama. The bigness of the small.

I don't know. Anybody can do death and murder. It's almost cheap cultural currency. Keeps us in touch with our primal potential, I guess. So to go there, you need to do it with more something or other. More what? I don't know. I just thought it lacked integrity. The love story that seemed to dominate was kind of irrelevant, and I got the feeling that the whole thing was some tawdry background excuse for a tale of who-gives-a-shit lust. (Sorry sorry sorry!!)

I should probably shut my mouth, but my aversion to this book is too strong. I admire her writing in so many other contexts, so I can't even say it's not my cup of tea, because it is. She's not my type of person, I know that. I witnessed her being very unfriendly once and it stuck with me. I only ever admire her from a safe distance.

I guess it's one thing to go into darkness, but to dwell there is another. To dwell on sensationalist darkness, where there's no light. I had a friend who was like that. It's not that I want life to be all fluffy slippers and sunshine. I just think there are stronger ways of finding the edge, of taking other people there with you. In a very evasive, jumbled way, I think I've said enough.

Friday, 17th April, 2009.

Brain Clutter

I know that work is leisure to me, but in the old days I was a bit more desperate about making time for whatever project I was working on, as though I had to be in a hurry to do everything. It's possible I was right to be that way, but my self-sacrificial days are over. Meaning that I still grope for time, but clearly I'm in denial about it. And that's why instead of painting yesterday morning I was able to watch a movie.

Don't ever let me do that again. I hired *Nights in Rodanthe* because My Lovely Mother told me she liked it and I thought it'd be nice to sit around watching people be in love. I don't think I've ever seen such bad on-screen kissing. They didn't so much suck face as slap heads together, and that made a crappy love story rather up-chuckful. I couldn't care about them, and I hate not caring. Caring's just about my favourite thing.

Is this not-caring about characters thing happening to me lately because the characters in books and movies are sometimes badly written, or am I becoming heartless? Maybe a bit of both.

———

Playing Hard to Get

Evil Ex-Friend is back. I've said that already, but she's back a lot now, so I need to give her a think.

I don't know if we'll ever talk about the past, but it looks like the friendship will go somewhere. And she's coming back to Melbourne. With her lovely baby. Which means we won't just be phone friends the way we have been since I heard from her last year – there'll be visiting involved. The way it used to be. The phone friendship has been the warm up for the renewal of our vows. Gradual but real.

I'm still surprised that she's walked back into my life. And humbled herself to do so. You know how you mourn something as though it's gone forever? What she did devastated me. I was once upon a time a very forgiving type. Or not so much forgiving as very forgetful, because as soon as somebody I love is nice to me I forget all of the horrible things they've done before. Because *love*. Ya know? I love love.

I've tried playing hard to get, aware that I need to protect myself. But I'm discovering that it doesn't work as a friendship strategy, because by playing hard to get (not calling too often, making myself not too available) I've missed out on seeing her. I was so suspicious it took me a while to realise she was being genuine.

I spoke to her again a couple of days ago and realise that she's in the same position I'm in. This is going to sound irksome until I contextualise it, but I'm shy about the way she talks about my "mind" as though it's a phenomenal thing. Flattery will get you everywhere, yes? On the one hand that kind of thinking serves to isolate us from other people. At first I thought she was doing this because she can be snobby when it comes to braininess, and leans towards the academic world a lot more than I do. I have no time for loftiness – in fact, it shits me. (She went to an elite high school – she's bound to be intellectually snobby.)

On the other hand, she's right. It's hard to find peers, especially peers who you can also relate to as friends. Even now, when I'm surrounded by people who love what I love (art), I'm still isolated. And she's isolated – both of us with plenty of friends, but only a handful that we can call peers. It's a crux. And that's why this type of friendship is a drug. The sheer thrill of talking to each other.

So will we be close again? We talk as though we're close already. The way we were before, no ceremony needed. I like that. But I'm still aware of needing to be careful. She's one of the reasons I can't feel safe with people. I love them but feel like everything's temporary, that I'm not welcome anywhere forever. I hope that changes. I spend my life looking for somewhere to belong, that's all I want. This has everything to do with knowing who your friends are.

So I'll need to sit down and write about another problematic friend soon, because he also requires a think. People are *such* hard work.

Saturday, 18th April, 2009.

Definitely A Writer He Ain't

I've done the loathsome duty of writing another summary of my manuscript, to head the publisher submissions that'll be sent off this week.

But now I have to re-write the about-the-author section, which I corrected for Secret Agent during my last e-mail, but which I can't help noticing he didn't change properly. My inner editor is *screaming*.

Because I can correct it again now and slip it in unnoticed, but he might not use this actual document. He might cut and paste the about-the-book and then send the original version in with its VERY BAD SENTENCE STRUCTURE, and I'll DIE ON THE SPOT.

What do editor/publishers think when they receive a manuscript with bad grammar in the intro section? Do they forgive it in mere agents, or do they think of it as unacceptably sloppy?

I don't know enough about this and it makes me nervous. Maybe I'm a control freak? I can't stand editorial sloppiness. In e-mails from friends I think it's cute and only sometimes correct them [!], but this is professional. *Shit.*

Tuesday, 21st April, 2009.

Cough. Cough Cough.

Finally I've managed to get myself up at zero o'clock every morning, the joyful reward for that being an earlier-than-early walk around the hills. But now the world's burning all over again. The controlled burns have stripped the air of moisture and filled it up with smoke, so no walk for me today. I was only just recovering from the bushfire season. If this is the way the world's gonna be from now on, we'd better find a way to not-die from respiratory disease. Air is *important.*

It's back to Art School today. Actually it was meant to be back to Art School yesterday, but I stayed home to paint and to be quiet. In doing so I managed quite a few perfect things. Painted all morning, and then the window. It's been so long since I've been able to relax I'd forgotten all about the window. May I never live in a place that isn't north facing – the autumn sun through that lounge room window makes for perfect reading, so I bunkered down on the carpet with *Rant* (Chuck Palahniuk) and had me some bliss.

I also managed time for laps at the pool, then came home to conquer a Big Fear.

Let's not mistake Big Fear with Rational Fear. The garden's a beast and quite overwhelming. On a hillside you can't do anything alone or unobserved. The neighbours – if they find you fascinating –

can watch you whipper-snip the lawn, for example, if you happen to have left it for so long that the lawnmower bucks and whinnies before running away at the sight of it. No privacy, and as a person who hates to be watched, I can't stand the idea of it.

That idea gets more overwhelming the longer I leave it. On the other hand, I hate being in a place I don't experience, especially because it's really beautiful out there. Aside from potential people watching. Once I'm down there I don't care anymore – I get in and then wonder why I don't do this more often. I think I have an inner gardener that's screaming to get out.

Son is wonderfully good. He helps without complaining. Well maybe a bit of complaining, but no aggression. He could stamp his feet and say *no way*, but he doesn't. I tell him I want company and that's good enough reason for him to help me. He needs a halo. And now I have big plans to get myself out into the garden a lot.

I think I can tame this garden. Become friends with the monster. It's all about interacting, living life, being part of the world you're in.

Friday, 24th April, 2009.

We Have Lift-Off

...so now I can do as Secret Agent advises me to do: settle in, kick back and relax. Maybe watch some grass grow. I'm pleased the manuscript has been sent off to a juicy list of publishers, able to exist without me holding its hand for a while. But having been kicked in the guts by life enough to feel no optimism, I have no expectations. I don't not-have expectations either – just, I'm not impatient and will go about my business without worrying about what happens.

But if the universe would consider throwing a little kindness my way, I'd appreciate it. Per favore. Ta.

Monday, 27th April, 2009.

Weevils is Evils

But they did take care of that surplus food I had stockpiled for some flippant purpose, such as feeding my hungry family. And throwing spoiled oats over the balcony at night is like watching moonlit snow. Cornflakes over the balcony – not so much like snow. Like leaves, maybe. Very pretty. And I suddenly have a good excuse to reminisce about times past, when weevils were a fact of life. Probably half a century before I was born, which is giving me an olden-days experience better than the ones you have to pay for when you go to olden-days recreation venues. And they did prompt me to spring-clean my [admittedly not even dirty] pantry, which is now oh-so-shiny.

It's also empty. I do love a bit of empty. When I overlook the tragic waste of so much thrown-away food (not even pretend waste – there were weevils in unopened packets of things!!), I think Old Mother Hubbard was onto a good thing. If Old Mother Hubbard wanted to write a novel, for instance, she probably could. With empty cupboards I feel so unburdened. I realise this is feeding into my throwing-things-away frenzy, and with hard rubbish collection coming up I could probably go nuts over it.

Nice buggies. Cutesy-wutesy. Maybe not so evil after all.

Wednesday, 29th April, 2009.

The End, Nigh?

I'm so tough I eat carcinogens for breakfast. Not literally, but I do rub them into my skin. Allegedly.

A while ago Ex-H told me about a carcinogenic ingredient found in the basic brand of moisturiser I use, and I had to panic. I'm addicted to moisturiser, and being a loyal sort I don't like to change brands. I've used this [allegedly] killer moisturiser since forever. I use their soap and I have pump-tubs of the stuff in my bathroom, swimming bag, studio at home, studio at school, upstairs bathroom, bedroom. I take a portable one with me to drawing groups. And whenever I go anywhere that might be moisturiser-challenged.

I need it, mind. Dry hands are intolerable.

So when he told me this I thought a) bugger, I'm going to die; and b) bugger, I'll have to wait until I run out to replace them with a non-carcinogenic brand. Because I'd stocked up recently, this would be well into the Distant Future, thus ensuring that by then I'd be even closer to Death. (Hell forbid I waste the product by not using it.)

Well, the Distant Future is here. I'm running out, but I'm too scared to do the research, in case I find out that what he said is true. And what about the other brands? How do we ever know? Are we all just lab rats? Lab rats with incredibly supple skin?

I use so much [allegedly] killer-moisturiser that if the rumour's true then there's no way I couldn't have cancer. My only saving grace is that if it *has* given me cancer then I've used so much that my cancers have undoubtedly developed their own cancers, and the new cancers have undoubtedly killed the original off, leaving me cancer free.

I like this theory. But it doesn't help me chose my next moisturiser brand.

May 2009

Wednesday, 6th May, 2009.

Back in the Real World
Sydney, city of bad hair. What's the point of using a hair straightener to work your way up to looking normal enough to blend invisibly into a crowd, if the humidity's going to frizz you up into something hideously conspicuous? I like my invisibility, however, I am intrepid, and I love Sydney. My niece's new apartment's on a lower floor in King's Cross than the last one, so I can hear even more sirens, even louder, even more often, and it's still an evil thrill. It's like somebody's always dying in Sydney, and dying with great aplomb.

And oh yes, the art. The usual gallery hopping. So many thoughts thunk but I don't have time to think them again. Sydney is art is Sydney. Sensual overload. Joy.

Mum almost burnt my house down while I was away, there's an excitement I should mention. She tried to heat coffee in our coffee plunger by placing it on a gas burner. (*Dear Mum, the coffee plunger is PLASTIC. Love, Me.*) I didn't even know we had a coffee plunger, but I suppose I should be pleased to have a new, replacement coffee plunger that I'll never use.

Another excitement = ferry ride. In all the years I've been going to Sydney to see exhibitions, I haven't managed to squeeze in one ferry ride. When was my last ferry ride? Ten years ago? So I took the Manly ferry to – GUESS WHERE – to *Manly*. Alive, so alive. The only experience in the world that can make cold wind feel pleasant.

I had a difficult day today. Some days just are, even when they flow smoothly. Because of feelings I don't have time to filter through. Things sad and things beautiful. Some things pointless but interesting anyway. How does a person write on days like these? Where would I even *start*?

Chris Fontana

Sunday, 17th May, 2009.

nnnnnnnnnnnnnnnnnnnnnnnnnnnnnnnnnnnnQ1

That title is the cat's contribution. And just as well she's contributing because I'm completely brain dead. So brain dead I'm letting a cat sleep across half of my keyboard, and I have so many things to think out loud I can't grab onto a single one of them. Partly because of stimulus overload, but also because Ex-Husband has returned from Peru and is now staying with us for an extra week before going back to Perth. How's a person supposed to think when there's an ex husband in the house? A person can't, is the answer. He's a presence loitering around the periphery and interfering with my wiring.

Ex-Wife visited today. The place crawling with exes again. Only it was like a visit from Santa Claus, because she came bearing gifts. A lot of serious gifts – the kind that make you wonder if you're really a good mother because why didn't you buy those things for your children?

Also, Evil Ex-Friend's coming to stay with us at the end of next week. That's three exes in a row, and it's making me wonder who are my present people? Do I have any non-exes? Wherefore are my people?

I'll tell you where. I was invited to a thing at a friend's studio in St Kilda today, but couldn't go because of my many ex commitments. And what with offspring needing to be picked up. So now I'm thinking about how I never go out anymore. I mean I do, but not to socialise. Always pinned down by something. And that's bad, because how will I find out who my new people are if I don't go out and get to know them properly? I'll be trapped in ex-land forever.

Evil Ex-Friend's an interesting one. We still click. I still feel like I should be saying *'out with the past'*, and something like *screw you*, but there's a lot I'd like to share with her, and it seems equal now. Is it equal? I wonder.

Sunday, 17th May, 2009.

Too Freaky for Naked

Reading my first David Sedaris novel has been a complete mind fuck. I couldn't do it. And that's bad, because David Sedaris is a name any self-respecting reader/writer needs to drop these days. *Sedaris*. You see the ring it has – stinks of culture and literary uptodatedness.

But *Naked* was a bad choice for me to start with and it's made me feel like a freak. (Ach; I just realised I wrote '*but naked*', as in butt naked. Unintentional, sorry.) I started it on the train and felt immediately dark, because it's about a Tourette's Syndrome sufferer and my tics are serious enough for me to relate to what he's written. Even though the '*it was telling me to do this*' kind of commentary's a bit clunky, and exaggerated (as though the compulsion's being directed by voices), the essence of the physical preoccupation is realistic. So as I was reading it I could feel my own compulsions kick in, in the same way they kick in if I'm watching somebody else twitch. (That happened over lunch once – it was hilarious.)

I had a similar reaction when a documentary about a Tourette's sufferer was given to me by Ex-Husband; I started watching it one night and couldn't handle being in the man's headspace because it was too close to home. It felt painful to be in somebody else's experience. And depressing. And so sad. And it made mine more determined to torture me, so that I had to turn it off and distract myself as best I could to survive the prolonged moment.

These things bring to the front of my mind things I spend every day trying to contain in the back, an in-your-face reminder of the awful inability to feel freedom inside your own body. The Tourette's body is like a prison. And mine isn't even anywhere near that bad, is only very serious when I'm very stressed or very tired. But it's always there and I don't want my attention drawn to it, thanksverymuch.

So do I try another Sedaris? Or do I associate him with torture forever from now on? I don't know if he's very clever or just a prick.

Saturday, 23rd May, 2009.

Things That Go Bump in the Night/Shakin' That Ass

Well I *was* shakin' my arse. Until First-Born pushed through the crowd of teenagers who were dancing around me, screaming *BAD MOTHER!! BAD MOTHER!!*, then ripped the stereo cable out of my iPod and put it back into their own, as though ABBA isn't good enough for their party.

I've tried about four times and First-Born's been on me like lightning. If I just wait until they've had a little more to drink and then persist, ABBA will kill that dance floor. In the meantime *I See You Baby* aint so bad.

Except things really are going *bump*, so often that I have to keep running upstairs to see which part of the house is breaking. Nobody's coming down here because I put the child gate on at the top of the stairs, with a sign saying '*No Scumbag Teenagers Beyond This Point*'.

Who'da thought they could all read? Except, they don't seem to be getting the point of the *Romans Go Home* sign I stuck up on the wall beside it.

Not to worry, they're good kids. I'm enjoying this party even though I haven't fortified my nerves with a glass or three of wine. I think that's because the smell of alcohol is so strong it's reaching me down here, and I'm getting tipsy just on the vapour. This is killing my plans to hide down in my bedroom with *The Age A2* section, to think bookish things and reflect upon my morning-slash-afternoon with Evil Ex-Friend, who I might just have to rename.

What I love is that Ex-Wife has dropped Other Son here for the night, and he hasn't stayed here for so long. Other Son's Younger Brother is a scream, I wish he could've stayed too. How a four-year-old wasn't scared of the devil music belting out into the house I don't know.

Oh well. *Party party*.

Q: Is it too soon to try ABBA Again?

A: It's never too soon for ABBA. *Oi*.

Still Saturday, 23rd May, 2009.

Brick Pillow

I'm typing this in the dark so that I can enjoy my fluro glow-in-the-dark wristband. That's just the kind of thing a hip party goer would do. I know all about hip party goers, because apart from being one [allegedly], I've been subjected to the ongoing me-me-me aren't-I-fucking-wonderful spiel of a hip party goer wannabe *all freaken night*. It never ceases to shit me that the most boring teenagers are the ones who put so much energy into demonstrating how interesting they are. He even did the I'm-such-a-crazy-guy speech, though he used words like "unusual" and "weird" to disguise the socially suicidal quality of his braggery.

Doesn't matter because I got my revenge, and while the teenagers run around saying *'First-Born's mum is so ace'*, I'm secretly a real bitch who derives perverse enjoyment from making them suffer.

Me-Me-Me Guy made the mistake of being overly drunk at this so-far vomit-free party, of failing to accept his ride home, and being all show-offy about sleeping on the garden as though somebody [me] was going to eventually say *'Nah don't, ya big silly, you come back inside'*.

That was his worst mistake, because after wandering back inside three annoying times, I eventually locked the door on him. When I later heard soft music coming through a window I went outside and found him passed out on the brick path in front of the rose garden. I'm leaving him there all night. I'll act surprised in the morning and ask *'Gosh, why did you sleep out there?'*. He'll think I'm full of the milk of human kindness. He'll think I don't think he's a complete twat who deserves to develop varicose veins overnight. Hangover? I hope so.

Yeh, well. I'm pretty happy even though it's about a million o'clock, because I've already tidied up and done the first mop of the floor. I estimate that this time I'll only have to mop once more in the morning. That makes this party a domestic success. And that's why I'm being generous, by sitting here for five minutes before chasing those talkallnight teenagers to bed.

It's so nice that the annoying ones are on the outside of the house. And I've already done the kettle, so Hottie #9 is tucked into my bed, a-waitin', and in a few minutes I'll be lying in the dark looking at my glow-in-the-dark wristband as I drift off to sleep. Thinking happy thoughts, even. Because I have wonderful kids, and tomorrow I get my life back.

Chris Fontana

Monday, 25th May, 2009.

A Woman's Monthly

Being behind in anything that isn't slapping me in the face, making the world fall down or containing somewhere a description of the consistency of oil paint, I only just this minute (yes! you saw it happen!) caught myself up on the hoo-hah about Sally Warhaft and *The Monthly*. What a lot of he-said she-said. Can intellectuals do that? I mean, our dignified public opinionaters aren't this human, surely? It's practically entertaining.

I was reading Robert Manne's schoolyard side of the story and had such conflicting thoughts as *gosh, how reasonable* and *fuck, that's a bit patronising, innit?*. Then I got to the end and came across this comment by nsproule on the Crikey website:

> *Well thank goodness that Manne was able to tell his side of the story and paint Warhaft as both an overwhelmed woman (as women with responsibility are prone to be) in addition to being hysterical and unreasonable. Isn't it lucky that there were two reasonable and benevolent patriarch's at hand to save her and then screw her publicly afterward.**

Pisser. My feminist radar's in the crowd waving a banner as Feminist Affront wins the race, because look at his language. He suggests that Sally W. was, from the start, dependent on their support – not as an equal team member responsible for making the determining decisions for the publication, but as a woman who was being done a huge favour by being allowed to continue in this high-pressure role, despite her gender handicap. Exactly what nsproule said, only nsproule said it better.

Who's ever going to know the truth? Maybe she did a few unprofessional things, or maybe she didn't. Maybe they're all acting with integrity based on their own perspectives and nobody need be slandered. But reading this article, I wonder if it might be a case of the men being baffled by something that might have been more obvious to them with a little self-knowledge? Because if Robert Manne was capable of examining his own words here (possibly whilst dissecting them on plate as he prepares to eat them), he might see that any "irrational" behaviour on SW's part might have been a legitimate reactionary response to years of frustration at working with people who don't realise how [albeit subtly] condescending they are.

Ya just have to *feel sorry* for men. But I do like being able to read his article and witness his first lesson in adolescent girl-speak. Welcome to the world of bitch-fighting. And here's where we remind ourselves that bitch-fighting has an evolutionary function, which is to teach people to examine, articulate and resolve relationship issues. Once you've learnt this, you can outgrow this kind of discussion and skip straight to the rationality bit.

Yey adulthood! (You would hope.) When things get irreconcilable, don't even bother. Trumping the situation is impossible, so the best thing you can do is maintain your dignity and move on. A lot of cavemen don't realise that it takes a lot more skill than wielding a knotty club.

Tuesday, 26th May, 2009.

Minding My Own Beeswax

Having a naturally big mouth and not much inhibition when it comes to things private, it's taken me years to extend the respectful discretion I reserve for other people to my children's business. Because they're mine, you know? And when does a child stop being your business and start being their own anyway? It's one of motherhood's big dilemmas, because to not exercise your big mouthery for the sake of getting things off your own chest (in order to respect their privacy) can often mean suppressing things that you really need to talk about.

So here I am, not talking. For months on end not talking, even though a lot of what I'd like to say involves things being better. First-Born's lost some of their aggression towards me and we've been having quite a few nice family conversations around the place. Just the three of us.

So I'm erasing almost everything I've just written, except for two little phenomena. One of these is First-Born's nocturnal wiring (i.e. not sleeping, sometimes not at all). Like last night, despite my announcement a few nights ago that this house requires Night Time every night, and that means all technological things turned off by 10:30 pm. They've gone to school today without sleep.

The second is First-Born's fixation on Sweden. It's not that they believe Sweden's this great place where things are better (they offer a huge litany on this score) that worries me. It's that they *must have* Sweden. They want me to give them Sweden for their birthday. I don't know how to purchase, ship or wrap something like a whole country, so they're having to content themself with the dream.

This dream has evolved into plans to do a student exchange, and First-Born's asked me if they can do it if they work hard for the rest of the year. (This because I've been giving them serious advice about earning – and therefore being more satisfied when attaining – the things you want.)

Last night they said that it's tragic to be seventeen and have achieved "nothing". What, exactly, should a seventeen-year-old have achieved? They think everybody in the world (excluding the people of Sweden) is revolting and has shallow values. Unfortunately they don't believe me when I reassure them that they've yet to meet the Much Bigger World that exists outside of school.

First-Born needs to care about something but I can't find something smaller than Sweden for them to care about. It's awful not being able to make your child happy. I want them to be young again – when they were young I could make everything alright. I love my kids. Parenthood can be so sad.

Saturday, 30th May, 2009.

Big Fat Fibber

Okay, let's get this straight: when I'm not telling lies, I'm an extremely honest person. More than honest – I'm probably foot-in-mouth kind of honest. I'm especially honest about the lies I tell, and here I go with that, because telling lies is my lifeline. Lies are good, don't let anybody tell you otherwise.

The thing is, if you write or paint (take your pick), nobody but nobody's going to understand when you tell them that you can't go out to their whatever social occasions (of which they seem to have a million a week), or bum around doing nothing for hours on end, because you need to finish a chapter/painting/drawing. No matter how professional a part of your life you make these things, the things you do are [to them] just your *little hobby*. They will never [NEVER] understand why you might give these things top priority.

Because of this and *only* because of this, I've lied all my adult life to protect the time I spend on these things. I've used them all: headaches (migraines are a priceless excuse, I don't know how many people think I die regularly from killer migraines); sick relatives, dead relatives, motherly commitments, and the important washing of hair.

I don't feel guilty, because experience has taught me time and time again that if you tell the truth you both offend and annoy people. They hate you for it, which may be their way of showing how much they love you but still, fuck them. I love these people and I even love their company, but I lie to protect their feelings, and I lie to protect my time. At times ruthlessly. It's dog eat dog.

I'm writing this now because I'm pissed off. I accidentally told the truth. The truth is my enemy. But I told the truth because I thought that by now people might understand. Especially My Lovely Mother [!!]. I told her that I can't have my nieces stay over after my sister's fiftieth because I HAVE WORK TO DO. How much? A LOT. How urgent is it? VERY. And yet, somehow I not only have them here now (having been talked into bringing them home after the dinner last night), but I'm also having them here tonight (after the surprise party).

Not only did I get to bed late last night = no early morning start for me, but I've also lost two hours since getting up, and can see another hour spiralling down the toilet, because it's taking them forever to get themselves out of the house (I told them they have to go out for the day). I COULD CRY.

So I'm upset with My Lovely Mother, but it's such a pointless upsetness. I accepted years ago that getting upset achieves nothing, because you can never show them or express it to them. They don't get it. Worse: they don't care. The concept of both official and self-imposed deadlines means nothing to them. The only thing you can do is strengthen your resolve to get even more ruthless when protecting your time.

So this is my resolve: fuck them all. No more mr-nice-guy, and no more truth. I like being social, and I love my people, but but and more but. It's every woman for 'imself. Declared.

———

p.s. I do love my nieces very much; I'd just prefer to love them at a different, more convenient time.

p.p.s. I'm TORN between love for them and needing to get work done. A position I don't want to be put into, where I have to make a choice. I CAN'T make that choice. They all KNOW this. That's why my nieces are HERE. Hence, FUCK!

———

nsproule comment = posted on Crikey = *Monday,* 34^h *May, 2009, at 9:45 pm.*

June 2009

Saturday, 6th June, 2009.

Intermission

Last night I found myself trapped inside the house with dvds and a pizza. When I expressed my alarm at this the kids cracked up laughing. I asked First-Born could I borrow one of their flannelette shirts and by the way do they have any beer?

I don't drink beer, and I don't like pizza [much]. And I didn't realise that some of the dvds were overnighters. Did this mean we'd have to spend the next 24 hours watching movies? You can see why I panicked. But it works. You know. Joining the human race.

I marvel at being in the land of the living like this, because reading Zoe Heller's *Notes on a Scandal* made me want to die. It's both that good and that bad. Good because of her scathing wit. Astounding, even. Bad because it's distressing to be in that headspace for very long. I knew this already because I loved the movie, but had already decided I'd never watch it again. Inadvisable. Don't do it.

I even hesitated when Reformed Hippy Friend told me about the book. But I'm desperate for powerful writing, see. So I bought it. Assessment is over (at Art Skool) and having a Guaranteed Good Read was my unwinding-gift to myself. I lay on the pillowy couch in the sunny lounge room for two afternoons in a row, and I read. I absorbed total peace, I fell asleep, I read some more. Then I finished and wanted to die.

I love that Zoe Heller is brilliant, I just wish she was brilliant about something other than loneliness and the emptiness of everything. Desperation and need. All of it wrist-slashingly insightful and *profound*.

So I went for a walk and thought about how I could go about a non-surgical lobotomy, as an alternative to suicide. I thought about how I grew up loving football and cricket, and wondered how I could go back to that even though I HATE watching sport. I remember myself as an eleven year-old watching players tackle themselves into a clinch, and calling out *'Aw, give 'im a big kiss, ya poofter!'* (an affectionate slur, not the hateful kind). I want to be like that again. I want to like beer so that I can hang out with sports fans in the edifical church of Aussie Culture and never turn into a lonely Barbara (a la` *Notes on a Scandal*).

When I started the walk I was disappointed because I wanted to take the kids to see the new *Terminator* movie, but Son wanted to wait until a friend could come. By the time I got back he'd changed his mind, but First-Born hadn't seen the first and third and didn't feel like being in public, so we hired the movies, and that meant a totally unexpected nice night in together. I love spending time with my kids – they're both hilarious.

That's why even though it touched a nerve I can never be a Barbara, and I don't have to do anything as drastic as turning to televised sport. Thank fuck for that.

(Afterthought: I was going to give the book away, but I just flicked through it to find something spunky to quote, and changed my mind, because she's just so amazing. Maybe if I make a rule that when I feel like reading it again, I only read small segments, and only when I'm feeling exceptionally happy? One passage at a time, that's the way to do 'er.)

Monday, 8th June, 2009.

The House of Always-Awake
I think I need to live in a cave. Back in a time when people went to sleep because it was dark and woke up because it was getting light. I can think like this today because I'm doing such primal things as roasting meat. I usually cook the roast with love; today I've been cooking with defeat instead, but I figure it'll taste just as nice. Let's not start thinking of the thing as imbued with emotion and such like. Me caveman, me eat meat and sleep = me have good life. All very simple.

What I'm doing here is looking for the bright side of defeat. I've been aligning my patterns with the kids in some stupid attempt to get them to live properly, and now I have to let that go. Because I can't get the house to slow down at night. They won't. I've begged and pleaded my case (my poor old body) (NEED SLEEP!!), but last night had to throw my hands up in the air and give up. I got to bed late [midnight], leaving them awake with the modem on. GrandKitten woke me at 2 am by jumping up onto my pillow, and I didn't get to sleep again until well after my morning alarm had gone off at 5 am.

Friends call and isn't that nice, except that I didn't get a chance to squeeze in the very important information that I was awake all night. Isn't it funny how we humans need to have somebody give a shit about our sleeplessness.

Anyway First-Born has attempted to care. They got up at 3:30 this afternoon and cleaned the couch they'd trashed with food days and days ago. This was an outward gesture, but it's too late. I don't care anymore. I have to sit down to a roast with my children soon, and then go to a movie, but actually I don't want their company today. [To them] I'm not their mother. There's no woe-is-me in this,. Facts is just facts and I'm some invisible person who happens to be necessary for the running of the universe, but is of otherwise no significance.

The most I can do is make sure I stop giving up bits and pieces of my life. So my resolve has to be to leave them to fend for themselves at night. Go to bed as early as early. Use ear plugs. Close my door. Fuck you, world. Then I can get up at 3 am if I want to. And I do want to. Then the world'll be my oyster. AND I'LL HAVE HAD SLEEP.

The sheer emptiness of so many things. In the end if there's nobody to tell it to, you can live an entire life like this. And it'll matter nowhere.

Wednesday, 10th June, 2009.

It's Not Crap

I need to declare that I loved *The Slap* (Christos Tsiolkas) before I suggest that reading that kind of masculinity is like having a stiff penis shoved down your throat. Gag on that, Babe. If it wasn't for sweetheart little Richie, I'd suspect Christos Tsiolkas has a very gangster rap star approach to manhood.

I really did love it. But I have to laugh; I read it like I was Mother Superior and it was my job to monitor the author in his role as Moral Paragon. Because there are things I didn't like. I cringed here and there at the emphasis on appearance and the Greek Adonisness of so many of the characters (male and female). Fashion rag-ish attention to detail in the descriptions of clothes. But on the other hand, he had us watching The Beautiful People, and the trap of mediocrity within which they lived their Beautiful People lives didn't fly entirely over my head. Artifice and suburban agony. Growing old. It's just, there were times when I couldn't tell whether he was critiquing, reinforcing, or just exposing a few shallow interiors.

I'm guessing he was *exposing* because the book itself isn't the least bit shallow.

I also didn't like the drugs. That's because I'm a mother and am in DENIAL. They're not everywhere, see. But in this novel they are; they're everywhere and they have a major social function. Having never been one of The Beautiful People and therefore having managed fine on good old fashioned [occasional] boozing, I found this element of the story sad. But then I stood back and thought, *well that's his reality*. This is because I'm level headed. And because my children will never do drugs like that. [!!]

Oh, and the music. I find the listing of music in fiction tedious in almost any context. Music's everywhere in life, and I love it, but it comes across [to me] as borderline ostentatious when you list too many specific songs or bands in a certain way. Because trying to get people to experience what you experience when you listen to a song isn't likely to work. It takes so, so much crafting to transfer the experience of one art form to another. As a writer you need to be wearing your editor's cap to anticipate the effect it has. It almost always ends up seeming as though you're advertising your taste. *Hey everybody, this is what's in my extremely cool CD collection,* kind of thing. I do realise that if I was a Beautiful People I'd just nod my occasionally drug-fucked head and say '*Yeah*' when I read about a song being played. Like, *yeahhhh*.

You see why Mother Superiors never get laid. How uptight is that reading? Very. So I'll only quietly mention that certain sections sometimes [rarely] looked as though they were going on for too long before they bounced back and demanded your respect all over again. The writing's good. The content – good. Better than good. If he wins awards I'll be pleased.

I'm glad I can say that, because I had people in my ear telling me I'd hate it. They said the writing style was bland (it's not) (in fact he does a good turn of phrase). They were writery types, and therefore what would they know. It's funny how some writers love to love things, and some love to criticise the things that other people love.

Love is a many splendid thing and I'm happy to be feeling it now. For this novel. Its breadth is wonderful and exciting. Sophisticated. It's put me off men all over again, but what the hey. He's probably just done me a favour.

Apart from visiting Old Uncle in the far away nursing home and going to work and going to work and going to work some more, I've done nothing but read for the past few days. It's not my fault; I was strapped to the bed and forced to read at gunpoint. Sometimes strapped to the couch. Sometimes even to the front seat of the car. *That's* how good this book was, and is.

Thursday, 12th June, 2009.

Chasers Make a Reasonable Point

There are some opinions that you expect to be stoned for uttering. As in rocks, not spliffs. And maybe *The Chaser's "Make a Reasonable Wish"* sketch was tasteless, and you have to work a bit harder to actually get the point of this one, but the cry of heartlessness from the heartful is just as sickening. This may be KRudd PM's fault? With his trendsetting habit of unforgiving, knee-jerk expressions of outrage. As though the moral spectrum is a black and white zone.

Actually, I think that working out the point of the sketch is like working out the Rubik's Cube, and anybody who manages to stare down the moralistic hullabaloo to get to that point is very clever. That would be me, yah. And I can tell you now that I'm not a young adult (young at heart, maybe?), or from Generation Me Me Me. I'm a parent, and I've worked with sick kids, and I'm full of the stuff of human kindness.

So cut the crap. Insensitivity is bad, yes. But I just read Shaun Carney's article (from yesterday's *Age*) and considered his accusation that we lack empathy. Of course we lack empathy, we're a nation of selfish motherfuckers. But I'm sick of childhood being treated as a fluffy white no-go zone, and my reaction hit a particular height when I read this:

> *A Gerard Ryan from Cambodia wrote that the indignation at the sketch reflected Australian society's "hubris and collective solipsism". Dismissing the gifts given to families with terminally ill children as "overseas jaunts" that should be better spent on children in Cambodia, he called for Australians to redirect their sympathy and their charity.*
>
> *In fact, what Ryan was saying was this: my reality is the only true reality, yours is false. For him, the only deserving children are the ones in his midst, not the ones in ours.*

Because, Shaun Carney, you're not getting the point. Gerard Ryan wasn't claiming that his needy children are more deserving than our needy children. He's pointing out the disproportionate nature of the things we offer our delicate little flowers. I.e. We're giving the sick kids trips to Disneyland (which aren't a necessity), when we could be giving the needy kids in Cambodia food and medicine (a necessity).

The Chaser people aren't evil. What they're pointing out is that we're giving these children an unrealistic compensation for their illness and possible death, when these children are lucky already, because they have access to health services and a truckload of people who give them love and as much comfort as possible. What about other people? There are children who aren't sick but lead crappy lives and get no compensation whatsoever. There are sick adults who get no final wish. Offering them this final wish is nice, gosh yes, but from a broader perspective on human suffering and what might be needed elsewhere in this world, granting that wish is an enormous extravagance.

You're telling the kids that as individuals they're special, in a world where none of us are special, not really. Fostering that Western Child viewpoint, that *You Are the Centre of the Universe*. As though we deserve stuff. As though family and the et ceteras of normal life aren't fulfilling enough. As though if we don't give our kids iPods and overseas holidays *oh no! we mustn't love them enough! calamity!!*.

So get over yourselves and look a bit harder. Granting wishes: good. Not acknowledging the extravagance as such: dumb. Thinking of it as a right and not a privilege: taking things for granted. At first I thought it made no difference whether *The Chaser* group had made that sketch or not; as in, the bare bones of it was a non-event that contributed little to our intellectual evolution. But now I've changed my mind. Thank you for the challenging think.

Tuesday, 16th June, 2009.

Fusty Boobs and The Small World

I almost didn't hit the town with my bitches on Saturday night. What was I – tired? Sad? Oh for fuck's sake. I was almost an idiot, is what. I haven't hit the town for a long, long time. If I'd stayed home this time it would have been an irrevocable step towards becoming one of those reclusive old women who talk to their cats. (Note to self: stop being reclusive and old and talking to cats.)

I was so sure I'd not be going I did loads of washing, and in those loads of washing were a gazillion bras. The washing was all wet. So I grabbed a bra that I'd bought years ago and never worn. It was still in a packet. (I bought a bra that came in a packet? Where did I get it from, a vending machine?) It was comfortable, really, and it wasn't until I was diving up the freeway that I noticed the overwhelming smell of drawer liner. How does drawer liner penetrate plastic packaging? Well I don't know, but I could smell it ALL NIGHT.

The first thing I did when I got to Friend Girl A's apartment was get everybody to smell my boobs, but all they could smell was perfume. Nasal philistines. Obviously my nose is attuned to such things. (Possibly a result of spending so much time with cats.) Which would explain the great perfume dilemma, which I should write about some time. But in any case, it bothered me. Lucky I *am* half reclusive, because if I'd wanted to fall into bed with anybody I don't know how I would've explained such an old lady halfway-to-death smell.

Anyway, I'm not that kinda girl and I only have eyes for my friends. I'm in absolute friend-love with them. We kind of hit this euphoric state at first sight and we stay that way all night. So by the time we left the restaurant and stumbled across an old friend of Friend Rampant's, we were in the throes of passion, and he and his boyfriend got swept up into the euphoria. Two venues later we ended up at The Peel (which is boutique-y now and full of young people) with the three best poofters in the world. I'm so in love with them I wanted to take them home and lock them in a cupboard, where I could keep them forever.

It being a small world, I kicked off some conversation with the now-mandatory question: '*Have you read* The Slap?'. No they hadn't, but one of them knew Christos Tsiolkas so I was able to pry a little. Only a very little, because I'm not as interested in him as I am in his book, and I never have been a celebrity arse kisser. So forget Christos, but remember this: I had forty-year-olds to talk books with!!! I don't know how I contained my excitement.

So that's it, that's how to live. We'll see them again. Friend Girl A's about to go to Vegas to be married by Elvis, and when she gets back we'll wrest her from her husband and re-live old times with our new poofs. We'll sit around a bar and remember the past as though we're telling war stories.

I didn't know it at the time, but I needed that night. Desperately. It really is how life's gotta be.

———

You know how you get ripped out of bed early by necessity and it's like being aborted, so when you approach the roundabout on the way to dropping Son at the bus stop you think *there'd better not be any cars there* and [matter of factly], *I'm not stopping,* because you're both too tired and too cold to stop even if you wanted to? Even though the law says you have to?

It's that kind of morning. It was that kind of night.

———

I'm on an island of happy in a sea of shit.

———

Wednesday, 17th June, 2009.

Adventure On the High Seas

With an interest in the jolly rogery of Sea Shepherd and their interventionist fight for whales, I was expecting to find some eye-opening content hidden inside the adventure when I watched *Whale Wars* (and it *is* an adventure – I was gripping the seat through nine episodes in a row). But I wasn't expecting outright disillusion. I still admire Paul Watson, but I'm going to continue admiring him from a distance, because what a brilliant load of tossers the SS crew [mostly] are. (This fact hasn't come across as clearly in any of the books I've read. Sometimes you need to see and hear a person speak to really read them.)

First of all, riveting stuff. YOU MUST WATCH IT. Yey them, keep up the good work etc. But I think even the fearless Paul Watson should realise that a protester of any sort is more useful ALIVE than DEAD. He and his fearless appointed leaders (who're usually being fearless on behalf of the diminutive crew they're sending out on breakneck missions) take the stupidest risks. The amount of times they're recorded saying something like *'If you're not willing to risk your life [for the whales] then you shouldn't be down here'* is sickening. Because there's reasonable risk taking, and then there's suicide. I wonder if they're after a martyr? Is that it? Because that's the only way a dead person's going to help draw attention to the whaling problem.

This whole dying-for-the-cause business belittles their role as intelligent strategists. I know that fifty minutes per episode isn't going to offer an extensive insight into the mission, but from what I gather the crew are treated as though they're expendable, and as though they're there for the party and not to be taken too seriously, because proactive greenies are a dime a dozen.

Still, I'm glad they're out there. It's just I won't be thinking about joining them at any stage (and I was; I wanted to get my sheltered little suburban arse out there), so I guess that's my homework done. The Fine Captain's decision to take the Steve Irwin through the ice instead of safely backtracking was monumentally stupid and that made my mind up for me. A decision at sea shouldn't be driven by desperation of that nature, even I could see that. The poor crew; how could they respect their captain after that? Enter the cold reality of their said expendability, which you could see cross their faces. It must have felt like a betrayal to them, as though they'd just discovered they were about to be traded into slavery.

Well anyway, the vigilante interventionist path is kick-arse n' all that, but there are so many avenues of protest and each of them are important. Off the field, ignorance is the bigger enemy. And that goes both ways. So I'll go back to finding other ways to get involved [writing], because clearly the only frontier I'll be entering is the Great Downloading one. That was my first*, and what a doozy. I'm 0.1% geek now. Adventure is Us.

Whale Wars isn't available in Australia, which is crazy, seeing as Australia holds the cards and its people need to be encouraged to take an interest. What goes on, powers that be? Whyfore can't we have this on our tvs?

Thursday, 18th June, 2009.

Prodigal Friend

Prodigal Friend is Evil Ex-Friend's new name. Because I saw a lot of her when she was in Melbourne, and would have seen more if I'd been able to accommodate all of the visits she requested. She remembers all of the good things, and I am, according to her memories, a saint [!!].

The truth is, I *am* a saint. When I love a friend, I love them good and proper, with no ulterior motive. Just love. I'm patient, I'm forgiving, and I'm there for the taking. You wanna be my friend? Of course I'll be your friend – I love being friends. Happy happy. But there are so few people who I can really, really get close to. Friendship, once it happens, is easy; but a friendship as good and as important as hers is so freaken hard to find.

She knows that, and so she's back. We still seem to have friend-love, only she's more vocal and appreciative about it. She still talks about my *'mind, your wonderful mind'*, and sat on my floor with her baby, shaking her head as she said *'You're just so amazing, and you're the only one who can't see it'*. These things she says make me cry. Not in front of her, but especially because of her. She stripped my confidence. The way I am now, so small and shrunken, is to some extent because of her.

The other truth is, my mind is messy and impractical and I don't have the personality to make it otherwise. I'm trapped in an endless loop. Not "amazing" at all; just capable enough to generate the illusion of amazing. She'll work it out eventually, then let's see where we're at.

He Who Shall Not Be Named

What even happened? This happened?:

>He started at Elite Art School a year before me;

>Halfway through the year I said to Reformed Hippy Friend *'I'm so surprised he's still such a good friend; I expected him to drift off once he'd met new people'*;

>I was very happy;

>He said things like *'I wish you were here'*, and *'Art school just isn't the same without you'*, and *'You'll love it here – hurry up and get here!'*;

>We got together to draw regularly;

>When he pulled away it was very abrupt;

>Suddenly I felt uncomfortable calling him;

I felt disposable but I kept my chin up and was there when he wanted me to be there;

I tried not to be passive but actually I could only be passive;

Then he became argumentative about intellectual things, as though I was disagreeing with him when actually I wasn't;

He espoused Elite Art School philosophies as though they were only accessible to the initiated;

They ARE only accessible to the initiated;

I didn't dispute that and looked forward to having my mind opened, but never lost sight of my own perspective;

He continued to be argumentative and was very impatient with my perspective;

Was he just pissed off with me for walking away from my PhD? Was that a point of disrespect?;

By the way, I walked away from my PhD.

Then, he got angry about my blog. I felt uncomfortable about him reading it because reading a personal journal is a privilege, and it had replaced our real interaction.

He often questioned me about it and this time he was angry because I'd mentioned him (in the context of laughing at myself, totally self-deprecating and light); entered into volatile e-mail dialogue about it that surprised me. Said that I'd made him look like a something or other '*MALE*', which he'd written in caps lock, and that's when the penny dropped.

He made the never-write-about-him request and said '*I don't like the way you represent yourself in that blog, Chris*', and it was like getting a kick in the gut.

I wonder how to not-write about Friend Who Doesn't Want Me to Write About Him, when he does such crazy things as getting upset about me saying optimistically that he could *think beyond capitalism* when he described the problem of his future gallery-running plans, which don't cut it as financially viable, because he thought I was calling him a greedy capitalist ,when really I meant it as a basic noun and was encouraging him to think outside the square, because we don't have to limit ourselves to things we see around us, and went to the trouble of explaining that capitalism is the foundation of our whole society and it's not actually a dirty or accusatory word, which led to him throwing his head back with an ugly sneer and accusing me of backtracking to cover my obviously intended insult, which led to me asking *'You don't trust me, do you?'*, which led to him answering with *'No I don't trust you'*, with much seriousness, which led to the surprised asking of *'But why? Why not?'*, to which he said *'Because you're a compulsive liar, that's why!'*.

And how do I not then write about the subsequent last moment of our very beautiful friendship, or however much was left of it, when I threw my hands up in the air in a gesture of *'There's nothing more to say'*, because finally I've learnt that there's no point in talking when the other person isn't listening, and I should walk away, because this all followed a gradual and painful decline in the ease of our interactions, and many such unnecessary intellectual disagreements which weren't so much disagreements as misunderstandings or misidentified agreements.

And how – when this matters so much, and after many months of obediently not-writing about this important friendship – do I not think out loud [and in print] about how Friend Who Doesn't Want Me to Write About Him checked up on me an hour later by popping his head into my studio to ask if I was okay, when I was actually not okay [?]. How do I not describe how I nodded my head and kept on painting, and in fact ruined my painting that day, and was lucky to be able to bring it back from the dead [?].

Friend Who Doesn't Want Me to Write About Him keeps talking to me, has repeatedly visited my studio and been happy at me for a while, less so now because I'm not very responsive, which solves the problem of me wanting to write about him but having to resist, because soon there'll be nothing to write about, because the friendship is over, and soon he'll be gone altogether.

I loved his friendship. I loved his maleness, even. And I hate that it leaves me in the same place, not valuing my own worth, aware of my disposability, wary of the way people love me. I have so many friends who are happy to see me when I walk into a room, but I've cut myself off from daily friends. I don't talk to many people about things that matter. I experience happiness in small bursts, but it's no longer my natural state. I have no optimism where once I had shitloads of the stuff. I don't trust people. I spend most of my time alone.

My mantra, all over: *love everybody, need nobody*. I hope it's not like this forever.

Maths
It can take a year and a half to find out if a friendship's really a friendship. By then you've invested everything in a person, so if it doesn't work out... well. You have to find new people and start all over again.

Friday, 19th June, 2009.

War Paint
The sun's shining and it's quiet and I've done a very granny thing. I photographed a bird. Not just any bird, mind, but the invisible bird with the nice melody who I've been listening to for years but never seen.

I know, I know, get a life. But if you saw life as it is here you might change your mind and tell me to always watch birds. Buy binoculars, even, so that I can see things far away. Although, I kind of need to look close up to see where I'm stepping, because somebody hasn't cleared the broken crockery off the floor.

Funny how if you don't clear yesterday off the floor it'll still be there today.

Son turned vigilante a few days ago and hid the modem. I was at work and First-Born came home from school to find it missing and went berserk, thinking I'd hidden it from them. They started to raid my bedroom, so Son ran upstairs to get it. He didn't tell First-Born he was the one who'd hidden it, so they continued to assume it was me. The only reason they didn't scream at me when I got home was because they'd taken Valium to calm themself down. (Fucking doctors.)

I understand why Son did it – he's sick of First-Born controlling the house. It's the first sign I've seen in a long time that it gets to him. Like me, he's disappointed that what was good has turned bad again. For a while we were all happy together. Then First-Born started hating me again, and it was a shock, and it stinks of forever. But hiding the modem was the wrong thing to do, because First-Born's very fragile, and he was feeding their anger towards me.

Anyway, eventful days and eventful nights. First-Born throwing crockery and me cussin' like a bogan. They didn't calm down enough to go to school today, but they'd obviously done some thinking because they did concede that I'm not actually the ogre they accuse me of being. Said *'Alright you are tolerant and you are civil... but you're not supportive'*. A small breakthrough.

Still Friday, 19th June, 2009.

The Incredible Lightness of Brain-Fluff

It's all good. When times get tough you just need junk food for the brain, so every week I look forward to watching *Medium*. I teach a class where we discuss Very Important Issues and ride a euphoric intellectual high, and then I practically speed home so that I can be back in time for Allison DuBois (Patricia Arquette). It's disgusting.

Yesterday was *Medium* day [night], but *Medium* wasn't junk enough, so I went to the local cinema in the afternoon to see *The Proposal*. I don't think they get more junker than that, and the only reason I could stomach it is because I think Sandra Bullock's ACE. The humour's appalling in places (slapstick without the slap), and that lead actor guy whose name I don't even know is a wooden Ken-doll of a man.

I can't stand that pretty-boy look; half baby, half iconic masculinity, and incapable of insightful facial expressions. Sandra Bullock naked, on the other hand – well.

Sometimes you just need to watch people fall in love, is all. Even if half of those two people are revolting.

Saturday, 20th June, 2009.

Three Times Before the Cock Crows

I was talking to Baby Brother on the phone this afternoon and thinking affectionately of his very bogan-ness and the rough-n'-toughness of our conversational subject matter, and then he asked me *'So what have you been up to?'*. All I could think to say was *'Oh you know, just art school'*. I think that's maybe the purpose of art school; a good cover for the many things that take place between the earlobes, all of it exciting on the inside but amounting to a big fat zero in terms of general conversation fodder.

Did I mention to him that I'd just returned from the city, where I'd attended a lecture-slash-seminar-slash-panel-presentation-slash-literary-event thingy, about poetry and political change? No I didn't. It's obviously my own personal jesus and I'm into denying it because *oh the shame, the shame.*

So, publications notwithstanding, I'm still a closet writer and will stay that way until I put myself out there again. How I can love poetry and still think of it as a dirty little secret I have no idea. Today was like a homecoming, though. I feel like I've just been plugged back into The Big PowerPoint of Life. I could spin a few metaphors right now.

Well of course all things seem possible after an event like that. The bubble will take weeks to burst. Don't ever let it be said that poets aren't exciting; I love the way they collect little burs of information and connect them together for us. There's always the risk of being subjected to much postulating about what poetry does and doesn't do, but only the last speaker got a little close to the borderline of definitive declarations on the subject. He saved himself, just, but I held my breath hoping that Sophie Cunningham (Chair) would tidy up his little slip afterwards, and she did, praise be to her. (His other points were okay.)

Yes I'm avoiding going into detail. I have a notebook full of many profound and beautiful statements that I'm not ready to process just now, being as tired as tired. And I don't do that here, really. This is my place to be excited but lazy about it. I work hard enough elsewhere. And all of that work's coming together – today was another perfect step forward. Just what the doctor ordered.

Sunday, 21st June, 2009.

The Perfect Lady Hump

Never did I think I'd learn so much about vaginas from a group of woolly woofters, but there ya go. After graphic conversations about a documentary on the rise of labiaplasty over beer [theirs] and wine [mine] last weekend, I finally managed to make time for *The Perfect Vagina*, which you can find on the SBS website.

I'd never thought of this as a bastion of self-consciousness for women, but apparently it is. And all because most women are ignorant about the appearance of other women's bits. There's no realistic benchmark of normality out there. Having grown up with oh so many self-consciousnesses, I'm so glad that that one had never occurred to me. I'm feeling quite lucky right now to be free of something so devastating.

Anyway it's strange that something so interesting can be so depressing. I felt very dark after watching it, perhaps because it's sad that it's even an issue. And of course I had to scrunch up my nose at the hippy get-togethers, where women address their bits as though they have personalities, and then sit around looking at each other's clackers. All very nice, yah, go sisterhood et cetera et cetera. But the fact that they were all defensive as they introduced their genitals to their audience in an '*It's like this because...*' way was just misery making.

I think vaginas are best understood by loved ones. They're fascinating things, I know, but when you're getting them out there and making women Pro Bits in such an open way, I think something's lost. There needs to be exposure, but how does that happen naturally? Making a song and dance about it is like begging to be loved by people who don't know you as a person, thereby making your vagina a disassociated entity that has to stand in a cold and analytical spotlight.

Visibility: good. Desperate plea for approval: bad. How do you add to the consideration of appearance the tactile qualities of what is actually a very lovely thing to touch? How do you teach that to somebody who isn't your lover, without getting creepy?

The artist guy who did the wall of vaginas was interesting, to a point. The visual impact of that project is both good and useful. It's just, those body casts of his are to sculpture what photography is to painting. Except, photography's an art form in its own right; a body cast is just a slapping on of plaster and voilà. Boring. I think that's what I found most depressing – that the championing voice of the vagina (a male artist) is a bit of a dud (sorry, artist).

Solutions? I don't know. Maybe women (mothers, friends, grandmothers) need to be more opportunistically naked. And there are books out there, maybe they need to be shown and discussed in schools. Exhibitionism as empowerment. Just, do it *nicely*, hey?

Still Sunday, 21ˢᵗ June, 2009.

As it Happens…

!!!! I just watched Friend Girl A get married by Elvis in Las Vegas. I don't know why I did such a thing without champagne, something about not getting up early enough to make that appropriate. Also I didn't organise a get-together for the occasion with Our Other Bitches because it'd be weird having her wedding without her. I kinda regret that now; who needs the bride when we have the internet?

What a kick. Elvis hogged the spotlight but they danced on his face and I can tell you she was all demure-like. She doesn't dance like *that* when we're at The Peel. Is it because she's married now? The only disappointment was that they didn't play *In The Ghetto*, despite the fact that we hinted it should be on the play list last week by singing it at her all night. Plus the ceremony was very quick.

Happy! Here I am discussing nihilism with one friend over e-mail, and watching another friend's tacky Vegas wedding on-line. That's living, that is. Guess which friend I'd rather hang out with. [!!]

Tuesday, 23rd June, 2009.

Guillotine

There must be a cleaner way to sever yourself from your children when you need to. What we really need is to cut contact, First-Born and I. Just avoid speaking. First-Born goes about their business, I go about mine. But they're not the most co-operative of people.

I think I was screaming out something along the lines of '*Just leave me alone!*' last night, when GrandKitten jumped onto the couch where I was sitting and bashed her body affectionately against the side of my head a few times. It was the beautifullest thing. Made both First-Born and I laugh.

Problem: if I ignore one child, how do I continue to provide normality for the other? And beyond normality, a happy home?

Am not liking this. Am not getting much done. Am wagging a training thing I was supposed to go to this morning. Am making honey joys and thinking that Cornflakes really are little flakes of sunshine. Am thinking it's funny that honey joys are both First-Born's and my addiction lately. Am thinking sometimes chocolate just isn't it and a bit. Am thinking First-Born's like my double and if they stopped hating me they could maybe stop hating themself.

Still Tuesday.

Sartorial Eww

I wonder why one of my friends is so attracted to murky colours. Why she dresses herself in those drab winter coats that look like oppressive old Englandness. Something on the green side of brown. And that on her pale skin, all unhealthy-like. Why would you do that. Why such contrasting colours and curtainish aesthetics. How can she not see how ugly it is? It hurts my eyes and I have trouble hugging it hello.

Heh. Maybe I'm judgemental after all. Just not the way First-Born thinks I am. And not towards them.

Still Tuesday, 23rd June, 2009.

Watching Grass Grow

I don't know how geeks who download compulsively get anything else done. Now that I can do it I can't leave the damn thing alone, and when it's going I feel compelled to watch it. That little blue download bar is the worst kind of mesmerising.

And why would I watch something I can't tap my foot to? The unpredictable rhythm of the percentage counter is enough to do my head in. Especially now, when I'm hoping to watch another episode of *Whale Wars* before going to work, and I know that time's running out.

Is that why geeks never see sunlight? I was hoping that writing this would trick it into going faster because I looked away, but there are still two more excruciatingly slow percent[s] to go. [!!!]

July 2009

Wednesday, 1st July, 2009.

Me Dad Does Dali

To be honest I wasn't actually interested in Dali and I wasn't really interested in Surrealism, having been subjected to said phenomena over and over again as a repeated element of undergrad curriculum over my hundred years as a student [and counting]. I'm over it. I was never not over it – just glad it was in the world but equally glad that the world had done with it.

But I *am* interested in spending time with Dear Old Dad, so when he suggested Dali at the NGV I said yes. And didn't I owe that to Salvador? He played an enormous role in my formative years as an artsy teenager because a Dali poster – given to us by our neighbour – hung on our toilet wall for years. So maybe I wasn't always over surrealism, because I loved that poster. *Loved* it. Even though it was gradually graffitied by my childhood tormentors (one brother and one sister) with hate messages to me [literally], and such poetic statements as '*Chris is a slut*'.

Ya gotta larf. You could sit around on a psychiatrist's couch for years just chewing the fat over why my parents didn't remove the defiled poster from the wall, but really – it was a great poster. It didn't get removed until the walls were painted. I wish I still had it. With a skewed sense of nostalgia, I even wish I had the hate messages – they became part of the art.

So today we did the Dali exhibition and gosh, what a doing. It was a bit like viewing art from the inside of a traffic jam. Is it just me, or is The Blockbuster Exhibition evolving into something other than it used to be? In I-think a good way, I feel as though I just had Dali rammed down my throat. Very education-like. Or maybe that's not good? The jury's out on that. I love that I was surprised by a lot of things. I love that Dad pointed out that Michael Jackson's image was/is hidden in quite few of the works [!!!] in what can only be described as a subliminal *Where's Wally* way. I love the emphasis on skill. I love the works with political content and don't love so much the ones that're self-indulgent. I love that Dad thought the Skull Sodomising a Grand Piano was hilarious. I love that I got to think things I hadn't really thunk before.

BUT – and it's a big one – I left without having felt like I'd sunk my teeth into Dali at all. There seemed to be lots of padding and not much painting. And yet there were a lot of paintings, and they were significant. But but but? They weren't brought together in a cohesive way, maybe? There was no sign of the toilet wall poster painting, for instance. No major melting clock (just a few melting clock spin offs). The illustrations demonstrated breadth of interest and bully for Dali that he was smitten with Benvenuto Cellini, but did there need to be so many of those when two or so would have sufficed? I'm saying, there were things that were weighted more heavily than they could have been, and I wondered why the exhibition was designed that way.

So, not enough paintings = it was more like a documentary than an exhibition. Paintings are what the public want, aren't they? When you promise Dali, isn't that what they come looking for? I'm not satisfied, really. I'm a very tough customer. And although I thought I'd buy the catalogue, I ended up not buying it because of what was missing.

Being a student means looking at/for the way artists bring ideas together into a unified body [of work], and the main word I'd use to describe Dali's work is referential. At least in this exhibition, the majority of the work is referencing some other cultural icon, be it an art work or a literary work.

I think that's the thing that disappointed me most; the occasional referential work is okay, but repeated reference is boring. Do you get to see into the artist's mind, or just into what the artist was interested in? As in, there's engaging in the culture that surrounds you, and there's being trapped by it. I don't know enough to say whether he was doing one or the other, or neither. Maybe the dialogue with culture was more useful than you can tell at first glance. But still. I just know it doesn't appeal to me. Much.

Well there you go – the exhibition is an experience with small flashes of love but then an all-over-the-place sense of it being incomplete. Despite the scale of the thing. And the beautiful mounting of some works. And those wonderful cushioned walls. I guess, as Dad said, I'm *'all Dali-ed out'*.

Saturday, 4th July, 2009.

Germ

Enter the pent-up excitement of being on the eve of writing. A bit like the expansion of the universe until it's gone so far that it ends up springing back to its beginnings, lacker-band style. The novel I keep saying I'm about to really start writing [really really start] is this time for real about to start being written.

What I love about this is the slow evolution. I attribute the slowness of all things to the distraction of first thesis and then Art School. Plus perhaps the reworking of Other Novel. And many many other things. (Life!! You must laugh at it!!) But through it all, the idea's been turning over and it wasn't a matter of *would I write it*, but *when would I write it?*.

First, I started re-reading the book that triggered the novel idea (*Harpoon*, Andrew Darby). And today I finally dug out my old Spirax notebooks, through which I breathe, to trace the idea back to its origins. What I found in those notebooks is so simplistic that I had to scoff at myself. It was narrative baby speak, and had me so relieved that I didn't start actually writing the thing earlier. It's like I've spent the past year and a half re-learning to walk and speak, and am only now fit to tell a story.

This demonstrates the reality that without good think-time, a story just can't happen. Or at least can't happen well.

I know that the middle ideas (which are in other notebooks) are better and ready to use, and I'm about to go and dig them out. But how scary is this novel: the nature of the research leaves me ill-equipped for it no matter what. What can I really ever know about whaling? I have to brave my ignorance and suspend my own disbelief. And decide upon whether or not to make the geography real or made-up, for the sake of overcoming ignorance. Will start with real and see how I go.

This time I'm writing with a plan, embracing my new incarnation as an Organised Person. My aim is to finish the plan by tonight. Actually it's the only way to cope with immersion in a story when I have so many real-life commitments ahead on every given day. With Plan in hand, I can rise before the birds, write, then walk, then travel to studio, work in studio, then come home to feed the chillens, then collapse and think about the next morning's chapter (which will have followed me through each day anyway), and then sleep and rise early again. Squeeze my employed work hours in there also. But it is do-able. Isn't it? I'll make it do-able.

Creative energy is frenetic and I'm working hard at planning the hard work ahead. I have one week of holidays left to make it so well and truly started that there's no way it can stop. What a thrill!!

Sunday, 5th July, 2009.

Desperation

I'm going to pretend I'm full of testosterone so that I can do a male job of describing my illness. Sick as a dog, up all night, cough and splutter. Body so inflated with white blood cells that limbs are buzzing and refuse to sink into mattress. A little bit of *Princess and the Pea* happening, with an invisible jabbing just below my shoulder.

It's the awake-all-night bit that matters here, because I was. And while lying in bed with floaty limbs, I wanted something desperately. Not a Cure for said illness, not a bowl of chicken soup, but MY LAPTOP.

I know I did it to make First-Born happy, and it seems to be working, and they love it as much as I do so I know it's in good hands (they even cleaned up their bedroom so that it'd be housed appropriately, somewhat like royalty). But it's hurting, I tell you, that I gave it away. Ex-Wife had finally given them the long-promised PC laptop, but First-Born's been fully trained in the art of hating PCs. They're a pro. So the PC's currently shoved under their bed, because I gave them my MacBook on the proviso that I'm allowed to keep the very new desktop All to Myself. (Big, beautiful Mac, how I do love thee and thy download capacity, kiss kiss et cetera.)

Now – *suffering*. To be without a laptop. I first felt it yesterday, when I sat up on the couch trawling through my rather exciting and very large pile of notebooks. I had to work with [get this!] a PEN and PAPER. So primitive!! There I was with a carnal desire to run my fingers ever so lightly over those beautiful MacBook keys. Alas. During the night it was worse – writing happening in my head and no desire at all to sit here at a desk, in the cold, in the wee small hours. No offense, DeskMac, but who writes at a desk? *Who?*

I've been looking up the prices of new MacBooks and they ain't pretty. I can't justify it after buying this one. So I looked at second-hand; *depressing*. Then I looked up over-bed tables, to make this computer mobile. But sometimes I work on the couch. Kills that solution.

Will I have to resort to using the PC laptop Ex-Wife gave to First-Born? Can I sink that low? And what if I can't? If the keys don't feel right... and then there's the horrible PC desktop screen, which I hate hate *hate*. I suppose I could try to trick myself, by turning the laptop on and keeping my eyes out of focus as I set up Word, then going to the loo and returning to the bed to an open program that I can pretend is on a Mac computer, and not having to feel irksome about it until I go to back up the files the PC way, which is 'orrible.

I hope First-Born appreciates that I've made the Ultimate Sacrifice here. Writing this novel's about to get traumatic.

Tuesday, 7th July, 2009.

How Big is My Truck

Oh grow up, politicians. And maybe stop spending public money on sloganistic pissing contests.... please?

Friday, 10th July, 2009.

No Such Thing as Busy

Today I made an art and as a result have not walked in the sun. I was also making this art yesterday, and didn't walk in the sun then either.

Nor the day before, being still sick as a dog and figuring that being able to walk requires the ability to breathe. That's three days without a walk, and only this big art to show for it. Not even a good art, just a nutting of things out. Why oh why.

Anyway it doesn't matter. Did I mention I bought that MacBook? It's sitting in my bedroom and is home sweet home. I couldn't help it, I need somewhere to think. No consumer regret. Not a sign of feeling guilty. Although, it's occurred to me that my life has been somewhat streamlined this year with shiny metallic new things. That'll be computers [multiple] and cameras [multiple] and cars [singular], which are all practical things.

Shopping like a chick's not my thing, so I'm slightly embarrassed. And yet, paradoxically, I don't give a fuck. I'm back at school this week, and anything that makes life easier and more productive is worth it.

Segue: not sure I want to be back at school. Have grown fond of real life and want more of it. I need slow time. I cleaned windows two days ago and yea, there was light. I had no idea they were dirty, because I look through them all the time. Could be I thought the world was smoggier than it is. But no, it's clear as a bell and it bowls me over every time I go upstairs. *So pretty.*

When First-Born emerged from their bedroom the next morning they exclaimed with wonder, and this morning woke me early so that they could borrow my camera to take photographs of the sun-risey view. (Could it be that their mood problems were just a symptom of dirty windows? Might they be happier from now on, because they can see the clean vistas and how the world is beautiful from our house?)

I didn't know I loved clean windows so much until I had them. I love that I used rainwater I'd collected in a bucket to do the job. I was very Mother Earth that day, and would like to be Mother Earth every day. All I need is a squeegee and time.

I get to the point eventually – time. I'm planning to pretend I'm not really at art school. When I go in there, I'll just happen to be going to my studio in the city. I have two days of classes per week and three studio days, so I might spend one of those studio days at home. Three day weekends = lots of time for painting AND being housewifey, inasmuch as a non-wife can be.

There'll definitely be no such thing as *Busy* by the time I'm done with it. It's all just a state of mind.

Saturday, 11th July, 2009.

Armistice

I know there's a world out there somewhere, possibly in another dimension, where all cats love each other and can reside in the same house without spraying. I hear tales of other people's cats getting along. Not so here, but today I braved a potential battle in an attempt to shove world peace down their furry little throats.

I've had to lock the Big Three out for what must be over a year now, because every time I feel sad enough to let them in I catch them spraying. The smell of cat spray is truly evil. And pervasive, and impossible to remove. If you could bottle it you'd have a Perfume of Evil Intent. I'm appalled that such extreme malice exists.

I know this because I turned my fireplace on (a medium-sized radiator that I keep for special, because I hate ducted heating) and within an instant the foulest smell you can imagine radiated out into the house. One of Three Big Cats had *sprayed on my fireplace*. My advice is, if you do happen to bottle a specimen of cat spray, whatever you do DON'T COOK IT. The stuff is bad enough fresh.

Because it's windy as all heck today, I opened the doors to let them in. I try this every now and then and it doesn't work, but I love them all, and want them to resume their rightful places on their respective thrones [our beds]. Without pissing or spraying on the way.

You can imagine GrandKitten's disgust when she realised that Her House had been wantonly invaded by Other Cats. One's asleep above First-Born's bed, one has escaped eviction by settling onto my bed, and the other eventually settled on the couch. I had to abandon ideas of doing anything else today and just read, because she wouldn't stay put unless I did. It is, after all, an honour to be a slave to a cat.

GrandKitten's definitely not happy, but there's enough love to go around. So far so good.

Chris Fontana

Sunday, 12th July, 2009.

Art versus Heroic Acts of Saving

I didn't write much yesterday because I had to a) feed the offspring by way of hunter-gathering with Large Trolley as opposed to usual Small Basket, and b) save Son's head. Son's head was an emergency, because of a particularly nasty brush with a pair of scissors wielded by First-Born the evening before. First-Born was cutting his hair, not his throat, but I knew if I sent him to school on Monday without an interventionist hairdresser visit he'd be social toast.

The hairdresser, who looked like a drug-fucked bikie who doesn't eat his vegies and stunk of cigarette smoke, laughed his rugged little head off. And then said *hmmm, ahh... umm.. hmmm.*

'*Can you save him, Doctor?*', I asked. He pondered for a long time before answering with '*Maybe if I do this... or maybe if I do that... wow, they really went to town on you, didn't they? Do they hate you or something?*' (Really, First-Born means well.)

Anyway he managed to save Son's head, which was miraculous. When I saw the finished job I looked around me for loaves and fish and wine made out of water, such was his power. Although, I don't understand why it's trendy now to leave that bit of hair hanging awkwardly in front of the ear. It's a foul bit of messy on a normal cut. Maybe if I snip it off while he's sleeping? I bought him some gel to swipe it back but imagine Son using product. No, I don't think so.

With that crisis averted, today is for writing. And a walk, but mostly for writing. I've wiped the slate clean of all other things, including going to work, because I don't want to risk passing this horrible illness on to the residents. Even though handling their slimy dishes is probably how I got sick in the first place. Luckily for them I think art's far more important than revenges of infectious nature.

Tuesday, 14th July, 2009.

How to Write a Novel Without Even Trying

I haven't been able to visit Old Uncle because of STILL being sick as a god-spelt-backwards, and not wanting to infect everyone in his nursing home. I don't know why being such a saint makes me feel so guilty, but it does. I worry about him being lonely. So I picked up the phone, and isn't technology wonderful; it can bridge both the geographical gap (his geriatric prison's over an hour away) and the gap that separates the sane from the demented.

I listened to his concerns about Grandma (who died when I was three) who seems to be avoiding him, which is odd because '*You know what she's like*'. (No, I don't, Uncle – she died when I was three). I enjoy this slightly-uncomfortable world he's created, and never know whether or not to correct him when he gets things so wrong. It seems cruel to interrupt a fantasy that preoccupies him so fully; wouldn't that throw his head into a spin? And isn't it a huge problem that the only way to make him feel better about Grandma [his mother] avoiding him is to make him feel worse by telling him that she can't be avoiding him because she's dead?

All of these dementia fantasies are elaborate and prolonged, i.e. every time I speak to him I get an updated instalment on the same scenario.

Another fantasy is that he's about to start writing "another" book. His first book, a memoir called *The Boy from Black Snake Creek*, was apparently not only a best seller but won numerous awards, one of which came with a $250,000 cheque that was stolen from him by the government, who seem to refuse to partake in fair dealing despite Old Uncle's obviously honorary literary status.

It's noteworthy that all of Old Uncle's fantasies have an edge of both his-own-legend and paranoia/conspiracy-theory about them, but that's not the point. The point is that it's disconcerting when he tells me – the only writer in the family – that he's writing award winning books, because I start to put my own experience of writing (which is a bit more real) next to his and wonder *what if...?*

The *what if* being that I could really be the one in the nursing home with a cracking good case of dementia, who just happens to be imagining she's a writer at work on some very absorbing manuscript and a few other writerly things, and that everybody else is just humouring me because I'm so old I'll be dead soon anyway and I'm not doing anybody any harm.

I think I should start pinching myself a few times a day to check that I'm real. And if I win any more literary awards I'm going to be very suspicious about whether or not I'm imagining them.

Another part of me thinks I don't need to write any more books or stories or poems. Ever. Why live this gut-breaking kind of life with so much effort going into the production of what at the moment seems like so little? I could just spend what's left of my conscious life on holiday and watching tv like a normal person, and then enjoy my dotage by getting dementia and believing I wrote all of those *award winning* books and stories and poems anyway, without having had to do *any* of the *work*. It won't be any less real to me if it's imagined as opposed to being really real. You see? All of this preoccupation and isolation and over-thinking – why do I bother?

Welcome to my New Plan.

p.s. The good thing about the phone is that it's just me on the other end, whereas when I visit with My Lovely Mother she always corrects him with a harsh dose of reality. I flinch when she does it because he gets so confused. (Can you blame him? Reality's hard work!)

Thursday, 16th July, 2009.

Hit n' Run

I did one! I'm a criminal!! But only because I didn't feel the hit bit. Kinda hit the brakes hard as a red light turned to green, and the car in front of me was doing I don't know what. Staying stationary I think? But doing so in a trickfully moving way. I hit the brakes and thought *phew, that was close.* Then I stopped for a moment to wonder why his car wasn't moving. I thought he was pointing sideways for me to go around him because his hazard lights were flashing, therefore his car must be broken, and off I went.

He drove up beside me at the next set of lights. I wound down my window and he said *'You hit my car! And then you drove off!'*.

What the fuck? Such affront and gobsmackery on his face. I thought he had to be wrong, but I followed him to the curb, noting that his bumper had a couple of small white scratches but no damage. That's NO DAMAGE. Then when I got out he said *'You smashed my car up!'*. I looked at the bumper and I looked at him and again, *what the fuck?* Exaggerating, much? I asked *are you sure I hit you?*. He said *yes* and I examined the car. I guess the pissy little scratches looked fresh but really, get a touch up pen.

I know a few feminists who'd sock me one for saying this, but that's like touching somebody lightly on the bum and calling it rape. This is a throw-away society and because he's obviously a throw-away person he's going to make sure his bumper's replaced. Which means hundreds of dollars in excess for me to pay, which means poverty.

So I need to put myself through fiscal penance. Because this major collision happened when I was on my way to a city art store to buy a few hundred dollars' worth of canvas and stretcher bars, I'll have to start this fiscal penance as of now. I don't know how I'm gonna manage it; I'm already cutting back on chocolate because I spent so much on my new laptop. Will I have to cut back even further on chocolate? Fuck. I might have to give up on everything.

I do have a plan, though. If my friends were to invite me out to dinner and drinks about twenty times in a row, I could say *'No I can't, sorry'*, and by not having paid for twenty dinners-and-drinks I'd effectively be saving around five hundred dollars. More if I figure petrol money into my estimate. I just need to pretend I don't see the obvious flaw in the plan, being that it'd mean not-going-out even more than I already don't-go-out, which I don't think is possible.

What a particularly odious man he was. Cared way too much about his bumper, for example. Something very crawly about him, and instead of popping into the studios to visit my friends and tell them all about a fantastic protest idea I had today, I suddenly didn't feel up to it. Suddenly I felt like a very bad person. All because I made a mistake and some-bumper-loving-body in the world thinks I'm awful. Isn't that silly? And me being so lovely n' all.

Anyway, it's a good thing I bought so much canvas to keep me busy, because I can't afford to do anything other than paint for about another hundred years. Also, the good thing about tapping somebody's bumper is that it reminds you to drive carefully; I'd rather be reminded to drive carefully by tapping a bumper than by being killed in a full-on collision. That's gotta be the bright side, I think.

A Question of Verbiage

Not that I want to carry on about it, but anyway why do they call them "bumper bars" if their purpose isn't quite explicitly to be "bumped"? Especially useful these days when cars are designed in a such a way that you can't even see your own front end over the dashboard.

If I was a politician I'd make it against the law to care about your bumper bar being shiny and polished. I'd force the populace to change their mindset, by making it against the law to NOT have a bumper bar that's scratched to buggery. I'd force car manufacturers to factor in a scratchy design for all bumpers throughout the world, so that small bingles could be dealt with in a civilised fashion, with something like a polite nod of the head and a *'Sorry 'bout that!'*, before all parties disperse. Happily. Going off into their lives without having to curse the panel beating industry for making such a whopping profit from insurance companies.

Doesn't replacing bumpers that have no structural damage because the tap was so LIGHT just cause unnecessary harm to the environment, via industrial processing?

Maybe we have to start calling them fuck-off-get-away-from-me bars. People suck.

Monday, 27th July, 2009.

2009, A Domestic Odyssey

Oh it's not just a black box, I swear. It's an obelisk and it has special powers. It's sitting on the desk next to the computer, masquerading as a back-up device – aka external hard drive – but we all know it's there to spy on us. Ex-Husband put it there before he left. One of his little kindnesses, you get me? *Kindness*.

Even First-Born said, without prompting, just after he'd left: *'I know this is silly, but it's like he's got cameras all over the house and* is watching us'. Yes! I always feel like that after he's gone. When I go to the loo I even wave *hello* at the exhaust fan above my shower, in case there's a little camera planted up there.

I think it's got more to do with his patriarchal superiority complex than anything else, and his wrathful pronouncements about our vile character. His obsessive watching of everything we do. The shaking of his head and the saying of *tsk tsk*.

His intentions are good. But still, ya never know. So within two days of his leaving I unplugged The Obelisk, and now every month or so my computer gives me a little reminder that my hard-drive hasn't been backed-up since forever ago. So I should plug it back in again? What's the worst that can happen – it'll encourage me to make flint implements so that my intellectual evolution can progress at an accelerated pace?

It does look pretty evil, just sitting there. Waiting for me to succumb to its powers. If only I was happy being a mere primate, I could give the thing away. If only.

Thursday, 30th July, 2009.

I think I'm going to die soon. But I thought that earlier in the year and I didn't die, so I could be wrong.

Last week, a night out. First-Born going to a formal function, so I called Friend Girl A and asked her *are you free?*. She said *yes please*, so after dropping First-Born off I swept her out for dinner in Collingwood (where she lives), and it was so beautiful to be with her because I just love 'er to bits. I forget and I forget more how wonderful friendship is. Then last night a text from Friend Girl A, asking me if I'd be free on Friday (possibly no), and it reminded me of how she'd said that night that we should get naked because there's not enough nakedness in her life. I said *let's do the Japanese Baths?* She said yes, and so we might (friend-naked, not pervy-naked).

This simple memory makes me sad. (Doesn't everything, these days?) Because I travel along like this. Day after day. And that night out was so nice and I was so, so happy, until afterwards, when I picked First-Born and First-Born's Friend up from the formal. I said no when they asked me to stop at a bottle shop, because Son and I both had school the next day, so the idea of First-Born and Friend partying all night was too much.

First-born got angry. How strong does a person have to be to make it through this kind of thing?

By yesterday I'd forgotten about my lovely friend and our perfect dinner. The text last night brought the memory back. I went to sleep and started dreaming about being naked with her. Still friend-naked, not pervy-naked. Just that lovely friendship and trust and an innocent kind of intimacy. It was very intense and I woke up and cried and cried and couldn't stop crying. I cried violently. The utter contrast of who I am to my friends and how I'm not allowed to have that kind of happiness at home. I guess it had to come out sometime.

Since that night, what to say. First-Born was nice on Friday because they had friends over. They even called me *Mumsikins,* like they used to.

I still don't talk to anybody. First-Born has left school and is always here. There's nothing to do about it but sit it out. And hope I'm wrong about dying.

―――

Friday, 31st July, 2009.

Heart-Breakin' Deal Breaker

I wasn't going to write about this out of respect for Ex-H's privacy, but something he said has left me with a feeling of things being wrong.

He's in Peru again and has a crush on a woman. This woman was the "girlfriend" of one of his colleagues in the field. Apparently most of the men over there have temporary "girlfriends" that they sometimes call "wives". Usually these are men who have real girlfriends and real wives at home in Australia and yes it's all a bit tawdry.

Not so for Ex Husband, who isn't the tawdry type. He's the shy type, but he met this woman and she's warm and tactile and so beautiful, apparently. She paid him a lot of attention and wanted him to dance (he declined). She liked him because he's different. He had me convinced of her merits when we were on Skype a few weeks ago. I was happy for him, and encouraged him to practise dancing (he never dances) (singing into hairbrush optional), so that next time he could say *yes*, because his body would be familiar with movement to music.

Everything was looking groovy until I tried to end the call. He wouldn't let me go and eventually said *'Ask me how old she is'*. The answer was 21 [!!], and I didn't guess. While this amused him, I was alarmed. He's 46. How does a 46 year-old man of pretty high intelligence even begin to relate to a 21 year old Peruvian woman [girl] who struggles with her English? *Ex-H does not speak Spanish.*

I kept telling him to be careful, and he assured me that she's very mature for her age. With infinite kindness I even defended him to myself by accepting it as a crush, caused by his desperate loneliness and barely-existent social skills. And then I tried to block it from my mind, hoping he'd meet somebody older.

But this morning – and this is the upsetting bit – he dropped a bombshell comment. He's already told me about what he calls her *'sad past'*; how she has a seven year-old daughter that she's never seen, because the father took the baby away from her. That means she had a baby at thirteen. *Very* sad. Even sadder, she doesn't get to see the child. I know this, I'm a mother. But after explaining how their relationship might proceed in the email he sent me today, he wrote:

> *That baby business is the main stumbling block. Children are always ruining my life, even those that don't exist.*

What an awful, awful thing to say. To me, to the mother of a child that he rejected. There aren't many scenes where First-Born doesn't end up mentioning this rejection, so I have direct confirmation of how much he broke their spirit. He's devastated my child, run an axe through my family, and now he writes this.

On top of that, I find it difficult to accept that he has crush on a woman but detests something so important to her. That poor woman has no idea what he's thinking. This *sweet man*. I want to confront him over it, just to tell him that what he said was inappropriate to me, to First-Born, and to the new woman. But I can't, because I have to keep the peace and he won't take it well no matter how gently I point it out.

My poor child. How does he not know that saying those things is completely offensive? How does he not realise how much they *hurt*?

Still Friday.

Trench Warfare

Sweden is a heart-throb, I should have known. This heart-throb is the reason my child stays in their room without sleeping; they're awake all night talking to Sweden on Skype. I've seen the heart-throb and I've heard them. They sound like Abba.

I had to say no to driving First-Born to the station and picking them up later tonight. Because Son and I have to live with the messy kitchen they leave behind. I stuck firmly to my no, hoping First-Born'd just clean up and be done with it.

That was a mistake. Now the child's broken, the plates are broken, whatever else was in the sink is broken, the chairs are a bit more broken, there's a new gouge in the kitchen floor. So I ended up driving them to the station and will be picking them up later anyway.

The worst thing is First-Born's fighting somebody who's not fighting them. It's driving them crazy because they can't get a foothold on rightness. There is no rightness, it's just an unfixable mess that makes no sense whatsoever. I'm not aggressive; they were angry that night in the car because I wouldn't argue with them. They told me I should fight them back.

I don't have a battle in me. I just want them to be nice.

p.s. A text from First-Born a few weeks ago, just before I picked them up from a party: '*Just to warn u we are going to get me Maccas on the way home! =D LOVE YOU MUMSY!*' I want more of that, please.

p.p.s. I'm not depressed. I'm so glad I'm not depressed. A very pure sadness a lot of the time, missing the way it could be, but still capable of happiness. Just moseying along, waiting for time to pass and things to either improve or not. And no wallowing. Shit just happens, is all.

Still Friday, 31st July, 2009.

addendum

Okay so I'll eat my words – I e-mailed Ex-H and he says he didn't mean those words specifically, it was more as a general comment about children (which admittedly he does always make). I'm sure I read it as *specific* because of the way things are here at home = making me protective of First-Born.

So he's not insensitive, he's just plain old depressing. Good. Just as long as he remembers that *hell hath no fury*, n' all that.

August 2009

Saturday, 1st August, 2009.

A Tug on the Heart Strings

I went to see *My Sister's Keeper* and it was so sad I thought a woman sitting nearby was particularly heartless, because when I took a furtive look at her, her eyes were dry. I was relieved to notice on the way out that she sniffed good and hard. My face was so wet it was probably reflecting light.

I wondered as I looked around at the rest of the audience, trying to reassure myself that other people were also coming undone, why we subject ourselves to other people's sadness like that. As if we don't have enough sorrow of our own. This desperate need to be connected to other people in a really intimate way. Not so far from being hive animals, are we.

Tuesday, 4th August, 2009.

Death Knell

It turns out I *am* dying – or at least I *was* dying. I had the prognosis delivered by my hairdresser, who kept interrupting what would turn out to be a damn good cut to ask me *'Are you sure you haven't been really sick at some stage?'*.

Not something you wanna hear when somebody's examining the mechanics of your appearance, but all the same amusing. He even dated the inexplicable new hair growth that's fluffing up my head, back to a hair-dropping trauma that must've occurred 18 months ago. It was very forensic.

I don't remember being very sick, or traumatised, or losing a great deal of hair. But obviously I did, and obviously whatever it was = I'm in remission. It's a miracle!

Still; although I'm usually fit and healthy (not counting stress re parenthood), I think I should pay more attention to... well, to not being stressed.

I hope my hair grows quickly so that I can go back soon for a check-up. I had no idea vanity could be so diagnostic.

Friday, 7th August, 2009.

Last Time, I Almost Promise

So, let's get the unhappy bits over with, and then after a good day of painting tomorrow, let's do books.

I'd had a wonderful night teaching and nobody cried. Somebody usually cries, the class being a Circle of Trust and such a lovely group of people. We're all quite attached and open and they take themselves to the limit of deep, dark and personal with their writing. Usually.

After teaching I was driving along in a fug of this wonderfulness when I decided to meet First-Born at a train station a little out of my way, because the trains had been replaced with buses. I was doing them a favour, because train plus bus plus train = a shitty ride home.

On second thoughts, let's not get the unhappy bits out of the way – let's just ignore them and hope they go away.

Tuesday, 11th August, 2009.

Same Bat Time, Same Bat Channel

Almost every morning now I wake up to a message from Ex-H, asking me to Skype him. Which is good. We're friends, and I'm happy for him to have this new love interest. He's much more fun when he's in love.

Tuesday, 12th August, 2009.

The Up-Side

Painting's such a refuge. Home = hell in a hand basket = thank goodness I can paint. Used to be I needed a settled atmosphere, but desperate times call for desperate measures. Now painting's the thing that settles me.

Almost finished – maybe just one more session with it later this week and I'm done. Am holding my breath until then.

I wish Art School wasn't getting in the way quite so much. I need to be there to counter loneliness and find my people, but I work beautifully at home. Hanging out washing and even balancing, now, both writing and artwork. I think I need to accelerate things. My brain's ready but my life is not.

Thursday, 13th August, 2009.

So Much for Up

Tonight, after I left for work, First-Born first smashed a glass and then went downstairs to smash their portrait, which I painted earlier this year.

Got home after teaching my wonderful class, Son met me at door, led me to bedroom, describing what they'd done to it before I could see the portrait propped up on my pillow (leaning against the graffitied wall). They'd smashed it against a table corner. There's a big slash through the middle, and a hole. Next to the hole they wrote '*Your work*' in black marker of some sort. Across the bottom, in large caps lettering, they wrote '*I AM NOT YOURS*'.

I was fond of that painting; I'm not usually allowed to paint First-Born. I know it's a bit nut-jobby, but I talk to that painting as I pass it in my work room. Telling it I love them. Lamenting their loss. Wishing I could have them back. I managed to give them a soft look, an unexpected vulnerability that to me summed up what they might be inside at the moment. The painting was more real to me than the real First-Born, who's too buried in anger for me to recognise.

Predictably, the response of Art-Skool friends: First-Born's interventions make the painting more interesting. Hah.

Friday, 14th August, 2009.

There's a Hole in the Bucket

What to do. Last night Son said '*You need to put a lock on your studio door*'. This morning, as I dropped him at the bus stop, he said '*I think you have to forcibly evict them from them house'.* That from First-Born's calm brother.

This morning = vacuumed up the broken glass. And now, painting. It's called burying your head in the sand. Hopefully a brilliant solution will occur to me as I work.

Funnily enough, I thought it'd be the self-portrait I'm working on that First-Born would attack. I've been checking it every day, a few times a day, expecting to find it slashed. It's fairly large, and I thought the temptation to destroy me symbolically would be too great to resist.

Am supposed to be in my studio at school today, but can't leave the house. Bodyguarding my art work and keeping vigil over my broken child. Too late = I've been thinking about getting a professional photographer in to document more artwork in case this happened = there's a helluva lot there to photograph = there's a lot of work to lose. But one of my favourites is gone before I had the chance.

How do I un-break them? I don't like today. I don't like tomorrow and I don't like the day after tomorrow. What's life with one of your children missing? Bugger bugger and *fuck*.

Saturday, 15th August, 2009.

There's a Hole in Everything

I'm calmer today than I was last night. I hate to think of First-Born going through a private hell, believing we're ganged-up against them. Which we're not, except with our revolting and excessive concern.

I don't want them to go. I want them to get over the anger. Am trying to think of a way to love-bomb a child who can't stand the sight of me. Sent a text last night that I worded very carefully, to let them know that I love them and am not kicking them out.

My love probably makes them vomit. They wanted to go to Mum's, but confusingly, my parents must have said no? Maybe First-Born didn't ask?

It was gut-wrenching watching First-Born walk towards the train station with their friend, whose home they were going to for the weekend. Their body full of hatred, still connected to me through the words they left resonating as they slammed the car door. But worse is the idea that they feel unwanted – they said as much – and I can't help them not feel that.

Son and I watched *Dance* and then I lay awake last night listening. Eventually I slept soundly, but sadness is inevitable. Weekends like this become a pivotal moment in your life, where you hold your breath hoping that by the end of it somebody you love more than anything will come back to you. What a mess.

Sunday, 16th August, 2009.

So This is What's What
Fuck sadness. Sadness was for that beautiful calm yesterday. After First-Born left on Friday night I had a phone call from Friend Girl A. Was nice, the humanising effect of friendship. The next morning woke to phone call from Prodigal Friend, my closest connection to the mind meld. Also nice, and also humanising.

Then a phone call from Reformed Hippy Friend, who's been asking for painting advice and arranging drawing sessions again. Lovely people and their arts. These three friends are my closest connection to other people at the moment. I have other close friends, but these are every-way close. Right into the guts of everything worth sharing.

I didn't paint as planned but I read all day in the sun by the window, with GrandKitten by my side. I'd baked and iced the best biscuits ever the night before, so Son and I partook of domestic wholesomeness and chatted and dispersed to our own activities, returning occasionally to the biscuit plate.

The day was silent. Then Son went to a party and I was home alone. Storm raging outside, and the empty nest feeling creeping in, despite being busy with writing.

First-Born made their way home earlier than expected, because the party they were at was full of vomit. They sounded calm on the phone and I picked them up from yon distant station. They were half-friendly for about five minutes before the anger started to escalate (I hate it most when I'm driving). The *don't talk to me's* got louder.

Anyway. After sadness comes planning. Plans require decisions. Will a bolt on the studio doors be enough, or do I need to remove my artwork from the house? Probably the latter. Which is difficult, like sending a limb off to be packed into a crate until you need it.

Do I start patching up the house, ready to sell? Ex-Husband will want to anyway, if this new relationship of his goes ahead. I don't know where we'll go, or if wherever will be any better. But the history of this house is a history of my failure to love well. It's family gone wrong, all of the promise of a nice life together equalling a big fat nothing. Maybe *here* is the sum total of my sadness, and I have to shuck it off.

If I find a house with a separate unit attached, so that First-Born can live with us but apart? Will that help? At least they wouldn't be on their own. I can't imagine life without them.

And to do all of this and still write and paint, do I need to leave Art School? I'd have to leave for a whole year, and I don't want to. I love my people; I love that no matter how much emotional baggage I carry in from home, as soon as I'm there I'm human and alive again. And happy? So should I leave to get things happening, or should I take refuge in the Skool studios? Spend as much time as possible away from home? Bury myself in my work? It's only seven or so more weeks.

But don't I need to be here to guard our life? Who knows. Such a huge failure. I failed at my own family. The thing I wanted most in life, as a backdrop to everything else. Love just hasn't been enough.

Still Sunday, 16th August, 2009.

One Foot Forward

This morning, writing. Good work, soldier. I love that it forces its way out when it's ready. If I can get two hours in before I go to work, things will be peachy. Oh. Make that one hour. I just looked at the time.

Thursday, 20th August, 2009.

The Cove

I was practically holding my breath waiting for today, so that I could see *The Cove*. And I did. And it was worth holding breath for.

It's about: the dolphin slaughter in Taiji in Japan, September through to March each year. Beautifully presented, not overly sentimental, just straightforward with the history and the facts. And that's good, because sentiment is so easy to dismiss.

It's important that people see this film, and what never ceases to surprise me is that when a film like this – and like *Sharkwater* before it – is released in Australia, it goes straight to limited-release in arthouse cinemas. Yey arthouse cinemas and all that, but with issues that need spruiking you sit in the cinema moved to pieces, wishing *just wishing* you could somehow get it into the mainstream.

Moreso because the people involved in gathering the information and footage have put so much on the line. So while you're watching you're appalled by humanity and at the same time reassured by the potential goodness of humanity, because certain individuals will risk their necks to do what they feel is right.

Makes a girl feel useless, until she remembers that although she hasn't got what they've got when it comes to resources and opportunities to commit to something like this, she has her own contribution to make to the bigger scheme of things and is doing what she can. Quietly. I admire those people so much. Theirs are the only feet I'd throw myself at in awe and worship.

Anyway, busy day. I've only been to Art School once this week. Slowing things down, walking, painting, writing and reading. Part keeping vigil, part relaxing the freyed nerves, and part not letting School dominate. Anybody who's been to Art School knows that there's a part of your work you need to take seriously and independently, to keep it in perspective. Remind yourself that life is life outside of that institution, that you need to exist out here in the real world. Where sun shines and birds sing.

This morning I booked a flight to Sydney, then after the cinema went to Reformed Hippy Friend's in Coburg to draw her twin sister, who so kindly modelled with a squirming nursing baby on her lap. Then rushed to work, and only just now am home and wanting all of life to be this slow. Even though "slow" is sometimes still busy as all heck. The luxury of being able to work on real projects. Slow time and thinking. I love it.

Friday, 21st August, 2009.

Dishes is a Dirty Word

And funnily enough, dishes are as rare as they are dirty in our house these days, what with Mother being on strike and everything but the bare minimum still hidden away in a secret location. Not on strike in a recalcitrant way, but pretty much on the oh-I-can't-be-bothered front, I'm there with pickets and a megaphone. Or I would be, if I could be bothered.

Our dishes problem has gotten pretty serious. When I dragged my famished body upstairs to make a toasted cheese and mushroom sandwich this afternoon, after having worked on a manuscript until starving to death, I was about to start preparing the food on my broken half-breadboard when I noticed a clean plate on the rack. That's right, I had my lunch on a clean plate, and it felt like luxury dining.

First-Born's away for the night again, so I decided to be charitable and clean up. And I noticed, as I filled the sink with sudsy water, that there were hardly any dishes to wash. I couldn't find them anywhere (the filth towers so high on our benches you can understand how I thought they were there among it all), until Son walked into the kitchen and opened the dishwasher, and there they were. Dishwasher!! I forgot we even have one!!! That's hilarious. Now I have to think of a way to disable it, because they're evil things. I won't have us draining our reservoirs or contributing to global warming by using the damn thing.

Besides, it's cheating. They cleaned some of the dishes in the dishwasher, but left the filth.

If I can hold out for a little while longer maybe the offspring will realise the error of their ways...? I know I shouldn't have cleaned. How can they learn from their mistakes by succumbing to salmonella poisoning if they don't actually succumb to salmonella poisoning?

Monday, 24th August, 2009.

Truant

I'm calm because I'm not at Art School *again*. A nice walk in the rain this morning was somehow more relaxing than a peak hour train.

The house is quiet and life's quiet and I want to soak the quiet in. At first I was just staying home to keep vigil. But now, in addition to recovery, there's that ongoing craving for a slow life. I'm spending whole days propped up on my bed with my laptop and some books, alternating between reading and writing.

Isn't it a bitch that when you're working on a painting you can see it happen in front of your eyes, but with a novel you're as good as blind? I'm still unsure of myself as I write this one, the territory unfamiliar, literally. And I hate that school imposes time limits on your year, so if you whittle a whole week away on a single chapter (really, who would do such a thing?), it sets your whole year back. And at the end of that week, you still have nothing to show for it.

Thank goodness I'm popping paintings out here and there. Come to think of it, I'm lucky, being the jack and not the master. A positive note to take with me to the manuscript. Off I go, then, to make some more invisible stuff.

p.s. Am getting overwhelmed. At the front of my mind, instead of being tucked away and waiting their turn, are my new novel, an old novel that needs reworking, an old novella needing attention, a short story and a couple of poems, a few threads of art ideas that are slowly evolving, a few threads of art research, a review I want to write, and a craving for family time and fixing up the garden, and the house, and an also-craving to be entertained by *Glee* and *Pelham Whatsit*, both of which aren't available for my viewing pleasure just yet. I can be working on one and another will just pop itself forward and say '*ME – NOW*'. Not to mention the books I want to *read*. No wonder I want the quiet. So if I manage to squeeze some drawing in later, school can wait until tomorrow? I'm sure it's doing just fine without me.

Still Monday.

Hindsight

Art School is nature's way of stopping me from sitting on my bed for so long [with laptop and sleeping GrandKitten on my lap] that my back muscles seize. I should have realised this when I went to lift my leg to dry between my toes after my shower this morning, and couldn't. I didn't realise I'd chosen such a perilous occupation. I might have to do something radical from now on. Like sit at a desk to write. Hell forbid.

Friday, 28th August, 2009.

Welcome Back, Mojo

Today was a day was a day was a day. I wasn't going to write a review I've been wanting to write, because I've been keeping my focus on my novel. Said novel's been a motherfucker, whaling [still] so foreign to me [despite the research] that I'm nervous finding my footing. When did I become so chicken? Well, obviously when I started thinking that the footing could be found as opposed to created. Stone by bastard stone.

But last night I was driving along to work when the words for, and the arrangement of, the review just came pouring out. I scratched into my notebook at traffic lights, and by the time I got to class it was planned good n' proper. I was tempted to write it while my students read but refrained, because my manners are so good.

So I got up this morning knowing exactly what the day would be. It'd be a day for wagging studio [again], and started with a nice long walk. I was walking along listening to Robin Hobb's *Shaman's Crossing* instead of to music (which I don't usually do because walking is think time and my mind still wanders away from any story I'm listening to), and the novel chapter I've been stuck on evolved so quickly and with so much assurance I was bowled over. Robin Hobb was the mental laxative to my stoppage, and now just try stopping me.

I wrote the review in one hour and spent the rest of the day cutting it down to word limit. Which is a bitch of a job and reminded me that a review can be a cheap thing made to order, rather than to properly explore the qualities of a book. Maybe an essay next time. Something I can be satisfied with.

But anyway who cares; it was a day of such intense focus that I think all of the things I felt I'd lost have returned. No time for the chapter yet, but it's there and it's ready and I'm not nervous anymore.

This is the fun part, where you just get to love it and then love it some more. Until the next difficult passage comes along. And even that's okay – I'll just keep a vial of Robin Hobb on my iPod and take her as prescribed. If that doesn't work, seek medical advice.

Saturday, 29th August, 2009.

A Picture Tells a Thousand

It'll sound very dramatic if I tell you I was painting my sadness, but I was, in the most inconspicuous way possible. That is, not as an I AM SAD statement, but as a quiet lot of nothing. I wanted the most simple self-portrait, honest and natural-like. To everybody else it was supposed to be a face; only to me was it to have great personal significance. (I know! I'm a barrel o' laughs!)

But everybody who sees the portrait gets the *wow* over with and then looks at me smiling stupidly at them, and says *'It's you, but it's not you. You're always smiling and happy...'*. And then they look worried that I've painted myself empty of all of that. Sometimes I get a hug.

I laugh it off and explain to them that a person, when they're on their own, has a relaxed facial expression. The way a dead person looks if you see them in their coffin; you can tell it's them, but the life has drained from their face because their muscles aren't engaging with you or with anything.

You can imagine how inadvertently comparing myself to a dead person in a coffin really makes the conversation cheery. Then I just keep on smiling because they're right, when I'm with them I'm usually happy.

But today I was so surprised when I walked into Ye Olde Sister's house, and the first thing she said was *'Your painting's great, there's no doubting your skill... but I can see your dark thoughts and I want you to know that we don't see you like that – that's just how you see yourself...'*. Surprised is an understatement. It was very insightful; also, it was sweet that she was comforting me over a problematic perception of myself that I'd never expressed aloud. Perhaps she thought it was self-loathing? Anyway, I explained it lightly and then changed the subject.

It was at a café and between spoonfuls of an amazing pumpkin soup that she brought it up again, and I had to elaborate with the kind of personal honesty I don't really give to anybody. It feels melodramatic to tell somebody you've painted a profound sadness, especially if you're still smiling as you explain. She went on to say that it must affect my children (especially First-Born) that I've painted myself like that, but to tell you the truth First-Born's not very open to the idea of my right to soft emotion at the moment, so it's not affecting them at all.

What surprises me is that not only does my sister *get it*, but she gets it all the way. I feel very exposed today, and embarrassed that something so personal is much more readable than I thought. The fortifications around my privacy are down.

Mum was there during both conversations, so I hope they don't repeat my words to anybody. It's a good thing I'm not the centre of everyone's conversations, otherwise I'd be worried.

Sunday, 30th August, 2009.

Home Coming

Here We Go. Ex-Husband's back for the week, as of some time this morning. This could be a good thing; maybe a week isn't long enough for him to get thoroughly sick of us and our revolting family-ness. I hope it's a nice visit. We're good friends when we're apart; I'm sure a bit of not being apart won't hurt too much.

I always say that, but somehow it doesn't work out that way. So I'm houseworking and getting the room ready, trying to make everything Ex-Husband-proof. That involves moving artwork that he might bump, tidying piles of work he might disturb, and getting things in order so that I can work even though he's here and likely to be a big and potentially grumpy distraction. My biggest concern is not having headspace for my novel, given that I also have to spend the week in the studio and at work. Oh lawdy, it's gonna be a doozy.

The thing I'm most glad I remembered, though, is to plug in the obelisk so that he doesn't know I haven't used it. I have to remove my more personal files and then back everything up. The worst thing about this little job is that I didn't think of it last time, so I've no doubt he has copies of all of my things on his little whiz-bang gazillion-gigabyte external hard-drive. This only bothers me because I have reference photos galore of naked people (for painting, not for perversion). The kind of thing you think you'll use and then delete, not suspecting that somebody else will have copies of and probably never delete.

If I ever want a career in being paranoid, this is a really good starting point.

September 2009

Wednesday, 9th September, 2009.

Manuscript

A discussion. Sometimes this can be the point of change, leading to peace on earth and harmony among all creatures. But I was reluctant to be lured into it, because I suspected a trap.

Son, also lured by First-Born's manner even though he didn't quite trust it, sat in because he hoped this was an opportunity to make things change. He interrupted to get me to move to a different seat because I was sitting below First-Born, and he was disturbed by the dynamic this created.

Son defends me but part of me wants him to stand back from this because I don't want First-Born hating him. I want them to be there for each other. He's so sick of it all; I also don't want him hating First-Born.

Anyways, eventually the discussion led to First-Born's demand that I let them read The Manuscript, saying that they have the right to read it because it's their story. They feel they need it to complete their knowledge of their [life] history. But the request was delivered with hostility, so I'm sad for them, but to give it to them when they're like this would be like offering myself up to die.

First-Born thinks it belongs to them the same way they think the portrait they damaged belongs to them. It's actually my story. And it's fictionalised. First-Born's a big part of it, but until they're capable of understanding that they're not the only part of it, they're not ready. It's full of love, and I won't let them destroy that.

I told them they could read it later, when the anger has subsided and they have the respect for me that's required. To read it is a privilege, not a right. First-Born says I'm weak, and they're right, but that part of me is strong. Stronger than they'd be prepared for.

Questions in my mind about what it means to be a writer who writes this kind of thing. Questions of what it means to silence yourself to help your child. Questions of right or wrong. Assurances that my motivation for writing The Manuscript was to... protect them from the attitudes of men? From my own stupidity as a young and naive wanna-be mother? To scream at the uncertain situation we found ourselves in? To consider the sociological implications of that situation, which we've lived and are still living through? Is that really harming my child?

They don't know what's in The Manuscript, so I have to temper my fears that there might be anything that could harm them. I don't think there is? Aspects of the story are ugly; I let frustration have its head as I worked. In fact that was a lot of fun, and then it was hard work because I had to soften so much of it during the re-writes.

The mere fact that I've written it seems to be harming them already, however irrationally. So I have to ask myself, am I selfish? Of course I am. But what kind of selfish? I'd say I regret writing it, but I don't. I've captured something inside that story, and that thing I've captured is an approximation of our little family. I can't not love that, and I can't want to undo the act.

Anyway it can't be unwritten now. This is the mother they were born to, a mother who does these things. Some filthy compulsion that makes me feel ashamed, even while I try to defend it.

I hope they don't take this anger into adulthood, that they get over it and live well. There's no happy ending for me. I've lost my child, who told me I disgust them. I'll spare you the inventory of broken things.

Thursday, 10th September, 2009.

Freak Show

I was reading on the train this morning and my body was calm, thank goodness. It was later than I'd planned because of a rough night. I'd treated myself to a walk, because these days I'm worrying about stress and heart attacks and I can feel my body's very tightly wound.

Health first, punctuality second. So I was calm and reading, but I realised after a while that the man who'd squeezed in to sit next to me was twitching. He had a severe motor tic, the worst kind of coincidence. Unless he chose me to sit next to because of mine? Maybe I'm a freak magnet. Who knows. All I know is that it's the third time I've found myself next to a person with my own affliction, and like both other times I was kind of alarmed. If you have a motor tic and it's chronic, the last thing you need is somebody with the same thing sitting next to you. Firstly because seeing somebody else do it makes you do it more, and secondly because it's more likely to draw attention, shattering your invisibility delusion. Because what are the chances. We look bizarre enough on our own, let alone in gangs.

This time, though, my alarm was for him. He was really struggling, and even though some of his movements were different to mine, I could feel him wrestle inside his own skin. I wondered if he could breathe, because when it's that bad you often hold your breath, so consumed by the action that you forget normal functions.

I stayed calm and was quietly amazed that I *could* stay calm. I simply refused to feel stressed, and bafflingly I managed this successfully. (Well, I did have to breathe slowly to suppress it.) It was so weird watching the struggle from an external perspective without sharing it. Except for the memory of suffocating yourself as your muscles tense. The sheer psychological pain of it. I watched him channel it to his fingers and then back again. All the time I kept my body very still, not wanting to make it worse for him.

Poor man. It's always worse on a train, or anywhere you're surrounded by people, especially if you can't see if they're watching you. The desperation to be invisible, the awful feeling of being so exposed. Is that what I look like when I'm really tense? I trick myself into thinking I can do it without anybody noticing. But of course I can't.

That's a confronting thing to acknowledge.

So maybe the sadness wasn't only for him. Sitting there holding his head with his fist, trying to still the movement. Knowing he'd do it until he was either distracted or safe at home. Calm today, but mine's been bad like that lately. So hard for some of us, on some days, just to be out in the world.

Saturday, 12th September, 2009.

Chance Meeting

This is the second time I've been unwell this year, which is challenging my belief in my amazingly robust constitution. I think it's because I have to handle the goobiness of old people at work, them leaving tissues [etc] on plates that I have to clear, and often coughing in my face when I lean down to talk to them.

With my body thus invaded I dragged Son to the cinema to see *Up* with me this afternoon (not bad). I figured I could be weak and bleary and entertained at the same time. The funny thing is, I thought to myself last night *'Wouldn't it be amazing if we went to the cinema and there was Muso Friend with his kids'*, it being a kids' movie. But it was highly unlikely – we haven't seen them for about two years.

So we passed a boy sitting in our row, we got to our seats, and I was watching the guy directly in front of me thinking *no way*. I was about to turn to Son and ask *'Is that Muso Friend?'*, when he pointed at the boy in our row, because it was Muso Friend's Son. I was confused because I said Muso's name and he turned around, but I couldn't place the woman sitting with him; she wasn't his wife. Two years is a long time, and they've split. He was there with New Woman. They have eight kids between them.

Well, talk about warm welcome. He kept turning around to hold my hand and chat and we had so much to talk about, but also a movie to watch. So they're coming here tomorrow for a proper catch up and it's such a happiness. Just like normal people; I'm going to be a *normal people* again.

I'm nervous about having anybody here because the house doesn't feel happy. (Censoring re physical evidence of that unhappiness, even though it makes great reading.) I don't invite people over anymore, and can hardly remember how to just "be". But maybe this is an opportunity to change that, get back a bit of our old life. If filling our house with eight rowdy kids doesn't make it a happy place, then nothing can.

I think I'll bake for them. I wonder if mid-morning's too early to drink wine.

Vagina-Mite Was No More

Still Saturday, 12th September, 2009.

A Caressing of Ego

Recently I did a tiny drawing for a particular class at art school, drawing the way I used to, very tight and concentrated. It took me about three days and I enjoyed the calm of it because I was very much in need of zen. Just smiled at a friend who's pretty out-there, when she kept exclaiming over the time I was spending on one piece. Because I knew that nobody would be able to see what I was really doing until it was close to finished. I always think it's funny that people can't handle the idea of concentrating for that long. I like being lost in the zone. She's one of those vibrant people that're always taking the bull by the horns, is full of pep and makes spontaneous art that's engaging and fun.

So it surprised me when we got around to my piece in class and she said '*I think it's a little jewel*'. What a nice thing to say.

This morning I finally got around to reading my novella from way-back-when. I shelved it despite the good attention it received (from academics, publishers and an agent who called me to offer enthusiastic interest and suggest I lengthen it when I'm ready). For years it's been at the back of my mind, but I've dismissed it as unpublishable because it simply isn't long enough to turn into a book. Well it is, but nobody's going to publish the novella of somebody who doesn't already have a name for themselves.

For some reason I expected to find everything about it immature because it belongs to my past. But it's not immature, and I'm amazed that I was that strong when I wrote it nine years ago. Today I'm excited by it the way other people have been excited by it. Because it's a "little jewel", the words fit perfectly. Because of its vivid nature it's an artefact as much as it is a manuscript. Is it an upmyselfness to say I fell in love with it? The memory of writing, the surprise of the story, the sheer energy of the imaginative elements. It's powerful writing, no ifs or buts. Was that me? I've lost so much of what I was.

Crushed little person. Why have I put myself down so much, or assumed that everything I do is crap? So many lessons on the stupidity of self-deprecation lately. I feel proud of it now, and protective of the old me who wrote it. I wish I'd felt this earlier. On the other hand, maybe I wasn't mature enough to feel it earlier. Maybe I'm ready now in a way I wouldn't have been then.

So there you are. It's a product of love and pure fascination with the here and now of history, and I want people to read it. Even the Afterward, which I'd especially forgotten about. It's a product of wanting to share the fascination, give people an entry point to some very spunky elements of history. Things I love and *love*. I'm now desperate to prepare it for publication (i.e. it's not perfect), and then push. I've been cheating myself out of something, I realise. I need one more lucky break, and I have to make it happen.

What a piss-weak little giver-uperer I've been. It's like I've been absent from my own body for the past few years. *Wake up!*

Monday, 14th September, 2009.

Grumpy

Bugger happiness to hell. I caught myself thinking it was good to see First-Born happy, but fuck that. Them and their scumbag teenage friend, who also seems happy. Bugger her to hell, too.

Am holed up in my bedroom, making plans to leave home. Except, I don't think I'm allowed to do that because I'm not the teenager. Still, I wish I could rent another house, and live both here and there.

Trying to love this place, but the filth, I can't keep on top of it = I threw pots into the corner of the kitchen bench. Only a fifty-centimetre throw, but still.

These = my holidays = no peace. I'm not even allowed to eat in the kitchen = they say '*Get out of my space*'. I love working from home, it's one of the joys of what I do. Being ruined because they're here and they're noisy, being stinkingly happy all over the place. Kids nonplussed about the havoc they wreak, leaving me to stew in the detritus of what was here before.

I'm not being tricked into false happiness anymore. It was too easy in the past to make me laugh. Wrestle over radio = would have been fun once. First-Born thought I thought = fun. But I'm just playing a role. I go for the radio, but they're strong and have my wrists. I use my elbow. They make funny struggle vocals and I'm silent, playing along so that they can't tell I'm not really there. Like I'm watching from the outside. They grip me in such a way that my elbows can't reach the buttons, so I manoeuvre my foot up to the dashboard and still change the station.

Laughing in car. First-Born's so funny, leans the front seat back to squash Son's friend and they're all laughing hysterically. But I can't even feel the happiness anymore. It's not for me, it's despite me.

And talking to Sweden. At first he sounded like ABBA, but now he's just an annoying voice that represents the un-real. I don't like any of them anymore. They can all go. Away. From me.

Get off My Case, Toilet Face

I don't know why *Welcome Back Kotter* occurs to me in a free-association moment when I think of Facebook, but thanks for the memory. So anyway, Facebook. After being nagged for years and years I finally set up an account, and now I feel soiled. As soon as I joined there were these people I knew bombarding my space, and so (after marvelling at how Facebook knows who my friends are before I've even identified them) I clicked the request-friend buttons, and now I feel like a little kid in the playground who's just walked around asking '*Will you be my friend?*'. A touch of desperation in it. Because what if they say no? They won't say no, but they *could*.

I find this very confronting and in violation of my Invisibility Code. Because the yes-I'll-be-your-friend answers have been rolling in, and it makes me feel as though I've imposed. Kind of turned up for dinner without being asked. What an icky thing this artificial networking is. Why aren't they offended that I don't call them very often? Shouldn't they tell me to get nicked?

Thursday, 17th September, 2009.

Swimming, Not Sinking

I know I've hit rock bottom because I'm drinking hot chocolate from a Xmas mug with a teddy-bear-wearing-Santa-hat design. But because

I'm smiling as I look at the stupid thing, I think I might just be able to climb my way out of this little "depression" I've gotten myself into.

Funny how sadness can be such a gentle presence for a long time, and then suddenly it gets virulent like an illness, and you're so sick with it you can't do anything. Not even mope, which takes emotional energy. So all of these days I've had free to work in, I've spent doing nothing but walking and walking and walking and reading.

Reading might be part of the problem. Even if it's not, I'm happy to blame the book. It was recommended to me by the agent I mentioned, who asked me to extend my novella. The novella, to me, is like a – a what? I don't know. But its short length seems fitting to its nature. This other book was recommended as an example of what a longer book of that nature (historical fiction) can do.

When I first read it I was dazzled and humbled, but picking it up this time I'm really appalled. It's terrible, whole passages that just don't need to be in there, all of it trying too hard to be profound, so much of it so unlikely it's just a caricature of some heinous past. A theatrical child playing make-believe with all of the excitement of gesture, but without any of the substance behind it. She [the author] has taken the facts and given them a poetic narrative, but she hasn't looked into her characters with any credible depth. They don't breathe. I'm sickened by it, so much so that I'm not going to name it here because that'd be bad manners. (Much better manners to bitch behind the book's back.) It's like I can suddenly see the seams of the thing, and they're stitched all clumsy-like. (Was hers short to begin with, too? Did she force it into a longer and unnatural shape to satisfy industry standards?)

So the question is, am I depressed suddenly because I've been reading that book, or do I find the book so appalling because I'm depressed? It's a chicken and egg question. Either way, next time I look at my novella I'll be scanning it for similarities, which I know are there. I just hope the similarities are in the strengths and not the weaknesses.

This ongoing sadness is a bitch of a thing, and unshakable. I need to find something good. Something good has to happen. I need to find somewhere to be.

Prodigal Friend sent me an e-mail that opened with '*You are beautiful*' a couple of days ago, and it was the nicest out of the blue thing to hear. Read. Whatever. Point being that the love I get sent to me from friends keeps me going, and I wonder if they realise how lucky I feel to know them and to receive their spontaneous emotional ejaculations.

Do they know that when you're alone in the world and struggling with rejection from a child you love, the reminders of love you receive from these friends = like a lifeline to something good that's waiting for you on the outside of the mess?

Conversely, the I-love-you's from friends could be as much love as I'm ever gonna get during my lifetime. This could be it for me. If I think of it that way, do I still feel lucky?

Prodigal Friend, in the same e-mail, offered to pay for me to fly up to her little seaside town in Northern New South Wales this weekend because she's desperate for me to visit. You've no idea how much this kind of niceness means to me. And I wish I could, because visiting a friend up north sounds like something an ace person would do. But I have bronchitis again, am sick as a dog.

If I can just get myself to do the things I need to do. Maybe set a specific task for tomorrow, and make sure I do it. Even though everything seems so pointless. Used to be I didn't need a point. Used to be I'd do it all anyway. Gosh, what a big fucking empty it all is.

Friday, 18th September, 2009.

:-(

First-Born: '*Oh god in heaven if you exist* [we all know he/she/it doesn't] *please give my mother a fatal heart attack this evening and save me from the* [I missed this word] *I have to endure before I go to Sweden...*'

Ungrateful Brat Friend: '*Yeah... yeah... yeah...*' and '*Yeah*'

First-Born: '*She disgusts me..., I think other people's parents are mild compared to mine...*'

Ungrateful Brat Friend: '*Yeah... you'd think that somebody who writes something about you, somebody they supposedly love, you have the right to read it...*'

First-Born: *'She won't answer to anything truthfully, it'll all come out fucking distorted.'*
Ungrateful Brat Friend: *'Exactly...'*
Ungrateful Brat Friend kept feeding First-Born lines to call out to me. I want to tell First-Born that Ungrateful Brat Friend isn't welcome here anymore, but I'm scared of what they'll do. (I've seen *Heavenly Creatures*.) They have such a parent-hating culture. They all laugh together about what a doormat her mother is because whenever she asks for money her mother just gives it to her. She doesn't say hello to me when she comes in here, as though parents are nothing. And to sit in my house while I'm home and incite more hatred from my child is too far beyond the call of a supportive friend. It's rude and disrespectful. I don't want her here anymore. Ever. (I think that's very grown up of me, by the way. I've never rejected somebody like that on moral grounds before. Makes me feel like a Real Parent.)

The above dialogue started with First-Born asking me to drive their friend to the station (which I was going to do until I heard all of that), and to get them a chocolate Bavarian. I was sick and in no state to shop, so I said no. They also asked me to pay for some Swedish language tutorial software.

Now it always ends with First-Born wanting to read my manuscript, and me explaining that they're too angry to read something so sensitive. Plus they keep asking with such a negative bent, as though the manuscript contains evidence of my revoltingness.

I can't give it to them. I just can't. To give it to them like this would be emotional suicide for me. They're fixated with it, as though it's the problem and not all of the other things.

They went to see Biological Father, and then last night rang Ex-Wife, and I could surmise from First-Born's side of the conversation that Ex-Wife was agreeing with me, that they're not ready to read the manuscript. I feel so much gratitude to Ex-Wife right now, and so much love for her understanding. I wish I could ring her and tell her, but that'd be dragging her into a side-taking thing.

First-Born said after that phone call *'None of you are my favourites and you're all full of shit'*, which tells me that they both challenged them and they didn't like it.

I'm sad for them. They're suffering because their mother happens to write things down. My writing's therefore harmful to somebody I love. Which means First-Born's right; I'm intrinsically toxic.

The only way to undo the damage is to undo the writing, and as I've said before, that's like undoing the love that went into it. I can't destroy the manuscript. I need to stop crying. Being a whimpering, frightened mess isn't helping anybody.

Saturday, 19th September, 2009.

Sunday In Your Face

I might be turning into a snob. Just an art one, but really, isn't that bad enough? Today went to a gallery to see some art recommended by two friends who shall remain anonymous. One of those friends came with me, because she loved the work so much she wanted to see it again.

So there she was thinking it was it-and-a-bit, and I was finding it okay on the surface, but really as boring as all fuck. All about the skill and nothing about the feeling. (Yes, I do hippy-speak with art.)

I was trying so hard not to call it Sunday Painting, but in the end I had to sneak that phrase into a cleverly disguised analytical sentence. She got very defensive and I thought *alas, here we part*. There was nothing exciting in the paint application, and I think without excitement in the paint application you can't really have a good friendship.

Well that's not true, it's just I'll have to secretly think of her as a Sunday Painter Lover. Pretend to love shit art in her company. And introduce some condescension into our conversational repertoire, thinly disguised. (Art Skool has spoiled me for the real world?)

Oh My Word

Reading *Tender Morsels* – so smitten, but there's one sore thumb sticking out of an otherwise perfect book, where Margo Lanagan uses the adverb "ivorily". Whyfore? What the fuck? But what a giggle. I can just see someone sitting there as a writer thinking *should I?* And *will I get away with it?*

I'm so attached to this book in this particular moment, but every time I read it I flinch at that moment. I know it's wrong, but maybe I'm wrong about it being wrong, and most readers will get it, meaning it works? Well she obviously did get away with it, so good luck to her. It got past the editors. I haven't seen it mentioned in other reviews. I didn't mention it in mine. But I'll never forget it in there amongst the brambles. I'll remember it as much as I remember the gentle placenta slipping out of Liga's bits. Maybe I'll one day confuse them and it'll be *the placenta slipping ivorily out of Liga*. Hah.

Monday, 28th September, 2009.

Two Good Ways to Die

When First-Born told Ungrateful Brat Friend they hoped I'd die from a heart attack in my sleep, I thought about how my heart thumps at night, quite literally, and how they might just have that wish granted. Tonight they said they *hope I die in a car accident.*

This is great news, because they're transferring the agency of my death onto something else. Good on them for wanting me dead in appropriate ways. Maybe I've raised 'em good after all.

Anyway, the frogs. Every night now, for a long time. There didn't used to be frogs like this – so, so many, and they drown out the sound of traffic. I love them. It's not soothing, as in it doesn't stop the tension from humming in my body, but it's a distraction, and it makes me feel that there'll be happiness soon. It makes me love this place again, and makes me not want to leave, even though we'll have to soon-ish. I hop into bed and I listen and listen until I fall asleep. Wherever our future is, I hope there are frogs nearby. Noisy ones. Very nice.

I Suppose/Perhaps/Maybe This Went Over My Head?

I try so hard not to be a man-hater, but I've been reading *Dead Europe*. Christos Tsiolkas. Great writing. And yet...

It's depressing to read. I suppose the point, implied by the title, is that the grandeur of historical Europe disguises the lack of grandeur in today's Europe. And that lack of grandeur permeates all Western societies. And that this novel is a microcosm representing the reality of the macrocosm.

It just left me wanting to tell men to evolve. Grow up. Stop bringing the species down. But the species is already down, and his characters represent the secret norm.

Do they? Maybe.

I wasn't convinced by the eroticism. Sexuality like that = brutal and in your face = also boring. Proud of itself and strutting its wares. Tracking my progress through the story, these were my thoughts. But then I started to respect the story and got thoroughly engrossed. First it was grudging respect, and then it was Book Love.

Until – farken fark. Really, drop the machismo. The association of sex with violence and the desire to overpower with aggression. The will to harm, the repressed male, the glorified paedophilia. What was it all for – to reveal a sub culture that's there in the gutter of every city? There doesn't seem to be any redemption.

I was disappointed when the politics that gave the narrative steam got reduced to superstition. *What*, I want to ask him, *were you thinking?* Was it supposed to be a psycho-sexual form of magic realism? I suppose the story could have worked as representative of accumulative guilt (through generations) and human evolution. But how was that storyline supposed to excuse the violence and paedophilia? The dark perspective didn't seem to serve an observable purpose. Are there really people whose world view is so completely skewed by sexual obsession? I know there are. But still; to me this was a great voice attached to just another twitching dick.

I actually felt angry at the end of the novel, that so much skill was used to write such an empty story. The potential, dammit. He coulda been a contender.

I've no doubt this is because of my own shortcomings as a reader. I'm naive and have led a sheltered life, so a lot has probably flown right over my head. Just, the take-home is that with this kind of maleness in the world, the species is doomed. Perhaps that was the only point; that we glorify with philosophy what is often just primal urge. Somebody should invent a Sigmund Freud to look into that shit.

Chris Fontana

Thursday, 24th September, 2009.

Too Old Soon Too Smart Old Late

Despite being the last person on earth likely to pick up a self-help book, I went out of my way to buy a copy of *Too Soon Old, Too Late Smart* (Gordon Livingston M.D.). The worst title ever, yes? I can never remember it, and get it wrong when I try to name it during conversations, at least three times before I can get the word order right. I wonder if he did that on purpose, to fuck with our heads.

If you were to ask me why I bought this book I probably wouldn't admit to you that it's because I read that article about what footballers read in *The Age* a couple of Saturdays ago. Ha ha ha. Funny just thinking about it. But anyway, there was a quote (about the three things essential for happiness being someone to love, something to do and something to look forward to – not a new idea, belongs to some old philosopher, ironically first quoted to me by First-Born), so I looked it up thinking it might contain things that would help at home, and that maybe I could get First-Born to read it.

Isn't that arrogant of me – wanting First-Born to read a book because it reinforces things I believe. But really, most of it's good and will be helpful if they read it with an open mind. If they recognise my words in it I'm in trouble, but it's worth a try. I'm hoping it can change the way they live, help them choose happiness instead of clinging to narratives that feed anger.

I have to say, it's a good book and reading it made me feel calm. His is a wisdom that people could live by and be happy. So I have my fingers crossed. But there are two chapters I hated absolutely.

One is the chapter on suicide. His narrow belief that suicides have selfish motives is way off. He doesn't even consider that there's such thing as a profound inability to feel or foresee happiness, and that as a trigger for suicide that inability is very innocent. Then there are people who've convinced themselves that the world is truly better off without them, which is the opposite of a selfish motivation. There are a lot of reasons people might think about for suicide, so to claim that it's simple is just stupid. Especially given his history.

With that kind of writing, the definitive statement just doesn't work. Nothing in life's so clean cut, or so easy to reduce into pithy solutions.

The other bad chapter = I can't remember right now. Maybe I'll just tear those two chapters out before I pass the book on. I think an author getting that sort of thing wrong could be dangerous.

Wednesday, 30th September, 2009.

Things come together. A point where friendships start to get cemented, where you take them outside of their point of origin and they survive.

Had my first ever dumplings, out with young studio friends. Dumplings are a thing. I think I like them?

October 2009

Thursday, 1st October, 2009.

Noise

I'm happy at school, but my head's all over the place. Really and truly all over the place. I hate not focussing properly. I want to dig in and get dirty. This its-and-bits business isn't satisfying – I want to be doing more than I am, but am squeezing things into small amounts of time. That's not how I work.

Still Thursday.

Good Riddance

I felt protective of Odious Prat at work, on accounta he was being picked on left right and centre. Nobody liked him. I didn't like him. He was a knowitall and so stuffy he belonged in a much older body. He didn't get it. But I got along well enough with him so I travelled along, feeling sorry for him and his awfulness and the fact that nobody would ever love him.

Then it was his last night, I was rostered on, and I witnessed him refusing to help somebody with something. He was a prick, and I was so shocked by his prickness that I wanted him gone then and there. I realised some people can't be saved from their own revoltingness, and deserve what they get.

On another note, an old woman whose husband died. So frail and old and sweet and lost. They haven't put her in the dementia ward yet. Strange because he seemed healthy and alert, except for the rotten kidneys. Imagine knowing you could be gone at any moment. And then being gone! Leaving that poor sweet little wife behind! Sad. Life is sad.

Working in a place where people not only die, but are expected to die, takes getting used to.

Vagina-Mite Was No More

Friday, 2nd October, 2009.

Luke Warm

It's such a bummer when you look forward to a movie and it's a dud. Well, sort of a dud. I saw *Mao's Last Dancer* and it's okay for a while but then it's just a this-happens and that-happens kind of thing, and oh it was hard it was so so hard but here are your parents – surprise! – and now you can go back to China and we all live happily ever after.

All of the feel-good stuff and none of the drama. The potential for dramatic narrative was huge. If only.

[*Note from The Future: I recently watched this with Mum, and it was fine. A beautiful movie. What, exactly, did my younger self want from the world?*]

Saturday, 3rd October, 2009.

Somebody Else's Rain Cloud

It was a sad, sad morning yesterday, so I did a smart thing by leaving the house, counting on the theory that if I'm not happy in one somewhere then I need to relocate myself to a different somewhere. And it *worked*. I made my way into the studios but took a detour to ACMI to see the Cabinet of Anthony Lucas (which I didn't even know was a cabinet – life's very generous with its surprises).

I was happy before I even made it to said thingamy, because once inside the tv-history-ish exhibition I came across a little documentary about *Prisoner*. Memories, nostalgia. The right recipe. We weren't allowed to watch it when we were young so we snuck it on after Dad had gone to bed, and we almost always got sprung when he got up to go to the toilet.

I was in a good frame of mind by the time I made it to the cabinet, which is a little piece of perfect. It contains a 3D robotic animation called *The Faulty Fandangle,* and the display/aesthetic = the kind of thing you wish you'd invented yourself. This forces you to accept that you'll never invent anything significant because all of the ultimate things have now been created and there's no more to be done. The world is *complete*.

So off I went with my double happiness to the studios, which were so barren I had to track friends down in tiny crevices. I found two and we had a lovely catch up. If I hadn't found them I would have had to create imaginary friends because I had no intention of doing any work. (I was there to make an appearance, and couldn't even find teachers to make an appearance to. Fridays at the end of the academic year are clearly bad for business.)

But then I made the mistake of finding another person who I'd been meaning to meet properly (as in, speak to without mutual friends around to see if we had enough in common to be friends ourselves). She was drawing. I started talking and she dragged me outside so she could smoke, and do more and more talking, and after a while I realised [too late!] that she lives a dark life. The kind of life that's full of seriousness and struggle and not caring, with little joy in it. Seriouser and seriouser. She loves to talk the seriousness. *All* the time. So we talked and talked very *seriously*, and then she made noises about us having to catch up not just next week and not just the week after, but regularly over the holidays.

I've accidentally attracted a dark people! I know I've had my unhappinesses lately, but I'm not a dark people. I have an inner Faulty Fandangle. I don't want to be dragged into darkness, but I'm in Darkness's Venus Flytrap and must [*must!*] escape.

———

Alas. I looked up more of Anthony Lucas' work online and discovered some of his work is very dark. Too dark. Everything dark. Who turned out the lights?

———

Speaking of Serious

Teacher B was seriously cunty at the beginning of the year. Always angry at his students, for no apparent reason. Maybe a bit elitist? So I'm relieved that he got better. I think our engagement with the subject helped. But mostly (at least in my case) it helped that he'd visited the studios one day when I wasn't there, and when he passed mine he saw the giant painting of Reformed Hippy Friend leaning up against the wall, as nude as the day she was born, and said out loud *'That's my neighbour!'*. A good conversation starter, handy for starting again on better footing.

He's since been so friendly, as in friend-friendly. Overtures of friendship are nice, and I wish I could make the leap properly. Unfortunately, I think that because I'm close to Reformed Hippy, he's mistaken me for one of The Beautiful People. I'm not that.

I've gotten used to the friending process on Facebook, though, and now have a small collection of people. Still, am close to saturation point, and can't go onto the site without squirming a bit. Or a lot. Seems so unnatural? Why does being in the world have to be so hard?

Thursday, 15th October, 2009.

Best Hyperbole in the World!!

It's everywhere – there are so many bests, greatests and most magnificents that I don't think there are any average achievers/celebrities/places left. Tv's getting very difficult to watch (the most difficult thing to watch ever!).

Is it just dumb enthusiasm, are Australians expecting outrageous standards, or are we forgetting how to use a wider variety of adjectives?

After watching some show I was too tired to move and got exposed to *Getaway*, which was okay because the scenery was nice. I coped okay with the *mosts* and *bests*. But then *Rush* came on and I stayed in my stupor, more by accident than on purpose. Not impressed that the episode was giving police AND taxi drivers a bad name for the sake of drama. In a society renowned for its pockets of police-hating culture, I wondered *couldn't you maybe not go for the cheap storyline and show the complexities behind police stories instead*?

I had to draw the line when that damn Industry Super ad came on and belittled the original meaning of *From Little Things, Big Things Grow* (Paul Kelly). Who let them use that song? Some days you just don't wanna look into the world's ugly face. Successfully disturbed out of my stupor, the tv got turned off.

Chris Fontana

Wednesday, 21st October, 2009.

Wanton Bloodshed

I'm probably not supposed to think this, but when Son comes out into the loungeroom and I'm in another tv stupor in front of a tv show I don't even want to watch, and he says *'MUM'* and I say *'Waitaminute'*, so then he says *'No really, MUM'*, and I say *'Wait until the commercial break'*, and then he says *'No Mum, REALLY'* and I look up and see him pacing around clutching his hand, which just happens to be dripping bucket-loads of blood, it's all very funny.

Blood is a very pretty thing.

Anyway, I got the story out of him. He'd been fidgeting with his pocket knife while he was on the computer – as ya do – and accidentally almost severed the top of his thumb. Cut it through to the bone. *Didn't realise it was so sharp*, he said.

Son's a pacer – always pacing, never sits still during a phone call, does boredom on foot, thinks on foot, handles digital dismemberment on foot. He did his usual route around the kitchen, all the time clutching his thumb, and instead of wondering what to do next Mother followed him with a stack of tissues, cleaning the dripping blood from the floor because he was getting it on his bare feet and spreading it around. So much blood, gosh did Mother have a job to do there.

Nice to know that in a panic situation, Mother will clean the blood off the floor first.

'Could we maybe go to a doctor?' asks Son. (Oh yeah. Okay!) So I took him to Emergency and after a two hour wait he was stitched up. It was then that I realised I was going to have to teach him how to swear properly [again]. I mean, he knows how to swear, but in public decides that he needs to be polite about it, so as the local anaesthetic was being skewered into his hand he was calling out revolting religious things like *J%#$& Ch#*@!!* and *Holy Mother of G@$!*, and more along those lines. I was so ashamed that when the doctor left while he numbed up I tried to tell him he needs to call out normal things, like *'FUCK!'* and *'FUCKEN FUCK!'*.

Tomorrow's work is cut out for me – clean blood out of Son's SHINY NEW school shirt, and scrub religious filth out of Son's mouth.

But not the floor. Thanks to my ability to keep a cool head while Son was bleeding to death, that bit's already been done.

Sunday, 25th October, 2009.

Radio National Anonymous

The buying of a transistor radio has gotten me flat out addicted to Radio National. But it's not a problem, really. I can stop any time I want. If it was a problem, hypothetically speaking – such as, if I was painting away in my studio and people were coming up to talk to me and I was nodding my head and saying *yes, yes,* without really knowing what they're saying, because I'm 90% listening to the daily book reading – not that I would but say that was happening, I'm wondering if there's a twelve-step program to wean myself off it without painful withdrawal...?

Who would I apologise to? To whom would I make amends?

But anyway it's not a problem. I can stop. Any time I want. And when I reached for the radio this morning to listen to the Sunday morning story, I fully intended to turn it off afterwards. I didn't mean to get alarmed by Noam Chomsky's wonderful voice of reason, which was offering opinions that contradicted this week's piece on Ronald Reagan and his pacifist stance on nuclear proliferation.

A contradiction! *Oh no!!* It's not because the edifice of an addict's world is built on a singular faith in the goodness of their addiction, but say if this was my church, it being Sunday morning, how would I be able to keep my faith in anything when the fabric of what I'm listening to crumbled so suddenly and unexpectedly?

You mean there's not one single answer to each of the world's problems? You mean RN can't source the definitive stance on any issue because there is no definitive viewpoint? You mean diversity's okay even if it means the world's as out of control as I thought it was before I started listening full-pelt to Radio National again?

Doesn't matter. I can walk away from it. If I need to. I've given it up once before. Maybe tomorrow.

Saturday, 24th October, 2009.

Being Everywhere at Once

I wagged an artist's talk today. I would've loved to have seen this artist again just because he's inspiring, but decided not to = giving my body a break from running around into the city. Ish. In fact, I did no work. I did great things. For a day I emptied my life of all responsibility; it was very, very productive. As it should be.

This time last year I was lonely, and now I'm not. Now I'm where I wanted to be. On this side of the fence it gets crazy, being invited to so many events and finding so many others = how do we do everything? Actually, outside of semester it'll be much easier because the events become the human contact time. I'm looking forward to that. I've spent years learning how to live well and slowly, so for the next four months (after assessment) I can slip into that mode and just live. So much work to do and I can't wait. From now on, work is pure pleasure.

Thursday, 29th October, 2009.

Cool as a Cucumber

The day was lovely. In the olden days I would've organised it myself, but there's ageism afoot at Art Skool and I no longer have the confidence to follow through on ideas. Young Studio Neighbour is cooler than me, so a few days ago I said to her *'We should all have a picnic in the gardens while they assess our work, yes?'*. It's like being a puppeteer; I said it, she organised it, and there ya go, our whole year was there for a picnic in the gardens. I love that I can do that (even though technically I didn't do it). I guess these are my people; I was looking for a people and these are it. Such a nice thing to belong to.

That done, and my body soaked through with sun and bonhomie and such-like, Kitchen Nazi came in for a studio tour, and to help me bring my work home. Afterwards we took the kids to the Pancake Parlour for... pancakes. First-Born met us there. Me plus Son plus First-Born plus Friends equals just like a normal family.

But there in this perfectly friendly situation, First-Born kept making derogatory comments and generally putting me down. I thought nothing of it because everything bounces off of me (willpower), but Kitchen Nazi was appalled. I whispered an instruction to her: *do not react*. Lesson One in the school of parental shock-absorption. Times like these, I have to radiate a force-field to protect my friends from missiles that are aimed at me.

First-Born will grow out of it. In the meantime, *harden the fuck up, Friends*.

Friday, 30th October, 2009.

Set Adrift

I was in the Skool studios this morning to clear the last of my paintings out and our upstairs floor was full of the beautiful shadows that precede a hot day. There was nobody else there. It was quiet and calm, and it was gut wrenching to see the studios empty.

But look at me at *home*. By only 10.30 am I'd already been for a long walk around the hills, driven in to the studios, gone to Readings to buy more books than I can afford, done some shopping for fresh fruit and vegetables (*What are these? Apples? Ah, I remember those...*) and now I'm doing class prep and sorting through my tax receipts, and reading and enjoying the sunshine and soon – the garden!

Big are things happening in my garden, some in my head and on paper, but mostly involving me sweating it out in the dirt on the hillside. Plus I bought Stephanie Alexander's *Kitchen Garden Companion* so that I can live again the way I used to live. I'm not a complete beginner but I'm starting again from scratch. The book's big and heavy and I've kissed the cover, which is dressed in a coarse woven red cloth, which you have to love even though it's not the nicest red in the world.

So today's my first day off and the peace is everywhere. Somebody's burning off in a yard behind the trees below our property and I can hear the branches crackling. A happy sound.

Plus, cats everywhere. A nice kind of calm.

Plus I'm blowing three balloons up at a time and leaving them on Son's bed so that he comes home to a balloon-filled room, because he made a comment when we were out about us not ever buying balloons anymore. By the end of the day my lungs will be burning. Worth it.

Chris Fontana

Saturday, 31st October, 2009.

Thunderstorm
Not up early = no garden this morning = bereft. But rain all week = good for weed pulling and getting vegetable planting ready.

So, can't go out there, but looking, looking. Yearning a little. All of the peace on the outside of the house. Pass the day so that I can get to evening. Even if it's raining I'm going out there. Make life good, that's my job.

November 2009

Sunday, 1st November, 2009.

A Book and Its Cover
Two books, actually. First, *Things We Didn't See Coming* by Steven Amsterdam, which is as good as they say. And interesting because it's less apocalyptic than it is rationally imagined, in that the downfall of human society isn't cataclysmic but a steady result of environmental and bureaucratic failings. And it reveals the hopeless drudgery of managing human beings. Sad, that we've evolved in such a way that we need managing. Something I think about quite a bit. I wish he'd taken it further – it left me with the sense that it wasn't finished.

The point: great cover. So simple but oh so clever.

The second is Sarah Blaffer Hrdy's *Mothers and Others: The Evolutionary Origins of Mutual Understanding*. Cover not so sexy. Nice photo, yes yes, but wouldn't you want your spunky evolutionary theory dressed in the right clothes, so that people actually want to read it? I ordered this book and waited by the mailbox for it to arrive, but I was disappointed when I ripped open the packaging and held in my hands this drab thing with brown internals.

Brown – I mean really, why would you? The whole thing just doesn't seem inviting. You need to be able to hug a book to love it. So I'll be reading this one with a serious face on, and using its contents only after I've put it down and moved away from its ick-brown visual contamination. A blight on my eyeballs; yes, am still shallow.

Monday, 2nd November, 2009

I've Walked a Mile in His Moleskins
I've been reading *Beaten by a Blow* by Dennis McIntosh and am gripped by the way he tells a story. When he's been shearing all day I

start believing that my back's aching. I have to look up from the page and blink myself awake before I realise that *no it's not*. In fact, he's allowed me to experience the shearing life so well that I think I should put sheep shearing down on my resume.

So be warned, if you're going to read it, by the mourning you'll have to go through when you get to what happens to the dog. SPOILER: Smokey, who's like a son to me. I cried and cried, because how could he? And looking the dog in the eye, and it pawing for mercy. And not letting somebody else do it, so that the last thing Smokey knew was betrayal from the one person he loved. It killed me, so much so that as I was reading I had to seriously consider never reading again. Because look what I was putting myself through. And why? Why would I subject myself to things like this?

There's a short story by Peter Goldsworthy called *Shooting the Dog* (In *The Best Australian Stories 2006*) (Black Inc.) that's just as well written and just as traumatic to read. I read it once and swore I'd never read it again, but then picked it up again a year or so later *BECAUSE I FORGOT*. It's just like childbirth = I only learn the lesson properly after going through the experience a second time.

The emotional pain those two stories provoked was intense. There are so many awful things that humans do, and chances are I'm going to come across them in books. And what if I write some of them myself? No, reading is bad. I really need to give it up.

I like the house in the morning, and tending to its needs. A bucket of water around the fruit trees, patching the splits in the compost bin, opening windows to let the cool air in and then keeping an eye on the sun so that I know when to close them. The cats enjoying the cooler shadows, everything gentle.

Tuesday, 3rd November, 2009.

Quaint and Parochial Us

What an extraordinarily self-indulgent thing from a writer whose name I won't mention, talking on a radio station I won't name. About being an ex-patriot, and bringing her children to Australia to live. Why am I irritated? Perhaps because she sounded so sheltered, and patronising, or just so stupid. Even stupider to think that the viewpoint was worth expressing. (And yet, I admire her writing. With clauses in the fine print.)

Turns out she's written a book, and was promoting it [oh dear]. I want to hope she's used it to make observations about cultural differences (between Au and EU) without exposing the narrowness of her affluent life and the immature[?], naive[?] and/or culturally ignorant[?] nature of the reasoning behind the decisions she was making. Instead of some gooey maternal gush. Might as well squirt your breast milk in public.

I'm being hard, I know, but maybe it's just that in the past I've thought of her as at least a little down to earth. Today she came across as a princess with a privileged or private-school perspective that seemed entirely out of touch with the world. Bothered me a lot. Also, it's just weird that somebody would make an observation about the Australian light as though she's the first to have noticed the difference between here and Europe.

I don't know. The whole thing was flippant and self-absorbed, and frankly not that interesting.

Wednesday, 4th November, 2009.

Don't Go There

For a long time now I've thought of Scary Woman (who no longer scares me or anybody else) as the ants pants at work. We larf, oh how we larf, et cetera. But there comes a time in every working relationship when somebody broaches the subject of politics.

Can I call it politics, if it sounds too much like 3AW talkback radio? Well anyway, we were working away over the luncheon meat [yuk] sandwiches when she said '...*and how about those refugees*'. I answered with a tentative '*Ye-es...?*', because there we were embedded in the burbs and we hadn't done politics before. Whatever she said was going to be representative. Has the world changed post-liberal government, or has it not? I had about five seconds to wait before finding out.

It has NOT. Within those five seconds Slower-than-Slow Worker came along behind us and said *'Well they said that it's possible trained terrorists are sneaking in as refugees...'.* What was there for me to think? Something along the lines of Holy Fuck. Because all a Liberal politician has to do is drop the crumbs out there for the seagulls to pick them up, and those seagulls will swallow anything.

How to have this conversation? I realise that asylum seeker issues are a tricky area and have learnt to back off on my opinions, because I'm simply not sure about all of it. But what I am sure of – now – is that bigotry is alive and flourishing and *in people I actually like*.

So I tread very carefully, not wanting to blacklist myself from future conversations. I gently raised the possibility that complicated issues can't be dismissed as simple, and that actually the two governing powers are playing you – the public – off against each other. I told them about immigration statistics versus asylum seeker statistics, and about how small the comparative percentage actually is. I also told them about the fact that most of them are proven to be worthy of asylum and then explained that the Immigration Department have a bummer of a job because they're the ones who have to transcend the cold politics AND the blind compassion to find the rational middle ground, and therefore everybody hates them. The hardest thing for you to find, in the media, is the whole truth of anything.

Ex-Scary Woman kept saying that most asylum seekers are rich and the first thing they do when they get here is line up for the dole. (Did I mention talkback radio?) Said *'Then they bring their relatives'*. You see what I was up against. I did some more explaining and she compromised with *'Oh well the African's are loaded with money...'*.

She might be close to right in one sense = only middle to upper classes can afford to get here...? Anybody could be right about anything. BUT – where's the critical analysis in how people receive and process information like that? How does anybody form a concrete opinion in the mess of the greater whole? How, when caught in this kind of conversation, do you encourage others to open their minds and then step back from what they don't really know?

I managed to squeeze in *'We're a stinking rich country'* somewhere along the way and suggested that rational compassion is a noble quality. I tried to get them to consider what it might be like to be so desperate that you'd risk your life to get here. Plus I threw in the Very Important Perspective that the people smugglers are the ones we need to be angry at (although they, too, are performing an inadvertently humanitarian task). COMPLICATED.

Anyway, that was me doing my bit to un-demonise the asylum seekers themselves. Then I lightened it up and changed the subject so that they wouldn't be scared of my tendency to rant. Did I manage to make a difference? I doubt it.

Now I have to wait for Reformed Hippy Friend to get back from Christmas Island to fill me in on what's-what lately. I'll tell her about the state of the suburban mindset and we'll shake our heads about the world being so stupid and ugly. All part of being so hopelessly wise. [!!]

Still Wednesday, 4th November, 2009.

Evil ScumBaggery

I feel a bit mean, but not much. I don't hate First-Born's close friend. In fact, in many ways I think she's quite ace. For one thing, she rips her own hair out from the side of her head because of anxiety, and has dyed what's left of it blue. She looks like a smurf with a mohawk, and like First-Born and their other close friend she dresses all weird-like in tartans and chains. They're all very cool. Plus they're smart and funny.

But with me being the designated enemy in their parent-hating culture, at the moment I don't like her being here. She comes in without knocking and makes herself at home. If I weren't their designated enemy, I'd think this was wonderful. *Mi casa è su casa.* I used to believe in the-more-the-merrier, and we've always had visiting kids stay over.

These days when she stays over, they take over the house and I feel like it's their share house and I have no place in it. Tv loud, kitchen filthy, always cooking mi goreng noodles and leaving the rubbish on the benches and floor. Rude comments all over the place, no friendliness whatsoever. She sleeps on my couch and sprays deodorant in the house even though I've asked her not to, because she has that sweating condition. It's particularly strong and I can't breathe when its particles have sucked all the oxygen out of the air.

I once walked through the front door after work as she was walking up my staircase and calling out to First-Born '*Oh I can't find it, it's usually on the shelf...*', and then stopped as she saw me. What was she looking for? I didn't ask, but it disturbed me that she knows my house so well that she's wandering around in rooms that belong to me (downstairs = my bedroom, my bathroom, my work rooms, and nothing else but the spare room), looking for something she's obviously taken and used before.

Today she used my shower, and afterwards asked me if she could borrow a spare toothbrush from the packets I keep. She offered to look for it by herself so that I didn't have to stop what I was doing. I gather from this that she knows the contents of my bathroom cupboard very well, and the mystery of why my new toothbrushes disappear so quickly has now been solved.

I replace my toothbrush every few weeks (I wear them out quickly), and at over three dollars a pop I don't like the idea of careless teenagers WHO HAPPEN TO HATE ME helping themselves to my stash. So I said '*I'll just see if I have any*' and then rummaged about in the cupboard, hoping she couldn't see me pushing the packets to the back as I called out '*I don't have any – sorry*'. (I hope she didn't look into my cupboards when I went to work yesterday, because if she did she knows the inventory and the jig is up.)

That was mean and scummy of me but really. She's the one who feeds lines to First-Born and oversteps boundaries. There's a heartlessness in their attitudes. I like her when she's nice, very much. But bugger them all to hell. Until they start treating me and their own parents well they can buy their own toothbrushes and keep the hell out of my space. I'm tired of being *nice*.

———

You know how you look into the mirror while you're washing your hands and you see this thing on your nose and you think '*Ohmigawd!*

A skin cancer!', and then when you rub at it you realise it's just a smudge of hot chocolate from the rim of your glass?

Must remember to check my face before I leave the house.

After a night of processing, First-Born repeats what I say back to me the next day, as though it was their observation. It's bizarre, as though they've somehow linked their mind to mine and have the two confused. As though they can't distinguish my thoughts from theirs once they're in the open arena.

Son noticed and said so today. First-Born got angry; I'm the last thing they want to be linked to.

Thursday, 5th November, 2009

No Show

I'm not going to Sydney. The plane tickets are booked and paid for. I had great plans to see the Portia Geach and the Dobell Drawing Prize Exhibitions, so I don't know why I don't feel like going. I'll regret it later. But you know how sometimes you just want to be home? With family?

I could pay for another ticket (the first ones were outrageously cheap) and do a day trip, which sounds like a very swank thing to do, popping up to Sydney for a quickie. But I think of my kids and their needs and I suddenly feel uncharacteristically responsible, as though I shouldn't really spend that extra money. Not at the moment. Because shouldn't I spend it on feeding my children? What an idiot.

Saturday, 7th November, 2009.

Hard Workin'

It's not nana-napping, it's cat-napping. Just making sure we get that straight.

Chris Fontana

Monday, 9th November, 2009.

Breaking Point

Every night this week = somebody here. Not friendly somebodies, but ugly teenage angsty somebodies.

When they finally left it was a relief. Then, a surprise. As I was gardening I heard them coming up the path I was [ironically] clearing to make people feel more welcome. Instead of passing by to get to the house to see First-Born, they both sat with me and talked while I was pulling weeds. It was good. They're nice and they're reasonable. Understanding, even.

But then they stayed over, and they made noise and I didn't sleep and the day I'd planned with Friend Girl A – who came here to write with me in the calm and quiet – was suddenly ruined.

I went ape-shit. I woke them and asked them to leave, including First-Born. I demanded the house to myself. Nut-job, ape-shit, it's all the same. I screamed. I said if you hate me like that then I'll hate you back. Can I really remember what I said? Just, it's much easier to love my angry child when I'm hating them.

No more taking it lying down – I'm fighting back.

———

After Breaking Point

Today they asked for permission. I still don't want them here, everything being too raw and me clinging on to a day of real peace. But for a while I can manage it, and I do like the friends, and I'm impressed that First-Born asked. Not impressed that my watermelon has gone before I had any, but still. Nice and friendly.

This is good life, yes? Obedient children and their friendly guests. I like.

———

Bugger

Well that was short-lived. But look at me kickin' arse. Isn't being assertive supposed to make you feel good? Then why do I feel like shit?

Because yes the extra teenagers were here for a little while. And then they were still here. I went to the garden, leaving them all upstairs, my lovely quiet day gone but everything still okay because of all the respect n' stuff.

Only, when I got back up from the garden, dripping with sweat but very happy, they were still here. I went for my walk, and when I got back, they were still here. At 10 pm. It was then I realised they wouldn't be leaving, and the peaceful repeat of today that I'd planned for tomorrow was completely down the toilet.

First-Born started being rude about me being in the way, and was then rude to Son, and I asked the girls *'What's happening? First-Born didn't say you were staying'*. Hint. In the ole days I wouldn't have been able to be so direct. Those poor kids. I hope they understand, I can't do stress anymore.

Have to remind myself; I'm not putting them in this position – they're doing it to themselves.

It's hot again tomorrow and extra bodies in the house = hot hot hot. The house was so quiet this morning I could cry. I can feel my personality slipping away, but I like this peace and will do anything to protect it. I'll break teenage hearts and make them feel unwanted. Apparently.

p.s. I still feel like shit, but at least tomorrow I'll be feeling like shit peacefully. Assertive people must be so calm.

p.p.s. Afterwards: I said *'Sorry for kicking you out, Friends, I just have to be firm'*. One of them said *'That's okay'*, but I know it's hard. I'm an ogre; a pigeon-feedy gardening old ogre who talks to her cats and her plants and doesn't go to the parties she's invited to. My conscience isn't cut out for this assertiveness thing.

And then it was the next day and I felt even WORSE. So I've vowed inwardly to get stinking rich (just enough rich for kindness) so that I can build a share house for them to live in. The vow has made me feel so much better. And it's working out; they're still friendly, still here, but not overnight. So far so good.

Thursday, 12th November, 2009.

Ego Stroking

Being a legend in my own lunchbox is tiring. I've had teacher fatigue for a while now. I'm not looking forward to the classes, the frustration of knowing you've taught them everything they need to know and are now just spoon-feeding them tidbits that you yourself find fascinating. I'm aware that if they wanted to they could find these things for themselves. Why aren't they finding these things for themselves? So you know how it is, having taught but knowing they haven't learnt.

I could teach them forever, and it's a joy, really, and a lovely community. But am I doing a good job, or am I whipping a dead horse? I'm suddenly self-conscious, as though I'm not doing enough for them. And then one of my regulars said reading with analysis like this was all of her dreams come true. She said: *'You are it, Girly. It and a bit.'*

Another finished his long project, and although he lacks ambition the guts of his work is fascinating. I'll read over his copy later to see how it sits together as a whole. Then consider how to help him publish (hilarious, seeing as I'm having no luck with that prospect myself).

Then I find out one of my students knows Mum through her volunteer work. Suddenly I'm not fatigued anymore. I received the results of our formal course feedback forms and they all say my teaching is *'Excellent'*. Yey? I hope they weren't just being generous.

Friday, 13th November, 2009.

Pancakes in Suburbia

It's like being on the breadline, turning up to the Pancake Parlour with shopping receipt vouchers and only ordering the freebie. We even snuck in our own strawberries, which earned us a few shitty looks but nobody stopped us. Maybe they remember Kitchen Nazi Friend has a mouth on her. Maybe sometimes it's not worth the effort to enforce proper business practices. They were right not to say anything – just turn a blind eye, people, it's easier that way.

My focus is on the garden and the novel, the latter being slow-as. I dread my day being interrupted, so much to catch up with in life, which moves much faster than I do. I should be catching up with school friends, and writing friends, but instead I'm [mostly] only managing this hello with Kitchen Nazi. We have nothing in common but good company and that's all you need for a nice afternoon. She's here in the burbs with me and happy making her way around out here. I'm here but also half in the city, torn between two entirely different playgrounds. Which one I belong to I don't know. Neither. The noise of traffic. Same here as it is in there.

It's overwhelming thinking of even the small things.

Prodigal Friend coming from interstate – how do I get the house ready? Is one day enough? All of my thoughts are outside. Aside from the times when I grow vegetables, I've never dedicated myself to a garden like this before. It's an aberration.

I think I'm trying to simplify life. At the moment I just don't want to have to be so many different things at once. And the truth is, I *never* feel ready for visitors. Everything's always a mad rush. I'm overwhelmed all the way up until they arrive, and then I enjoy them so totally I'm baffled by my own overwhelmedness.

That feeling of needing to be more than one person, so I can have my friends and eat them too. I'm glad nobody can see inside my head.

Tuesday, 17th November, 2009.

She's Gathering Moss

I'm enjoying having Prodigal Friend here. Although, bit-work isn't as satisfying as ongoing hard slog, and it's hard to give up my hard-won routine. The reward is the strange niceness of having her there in all of my spaces – including novel and garden – with child.

When I went to the movies with Ye Olde Sister the other day she made a comment about each of us being a bit hermitty. I now realise she's right, and I'll do anything to hold onto quiet space. Especially when I'm using that space desperately against so many social odds. But I've resigned myself to the lost working time, and salvage what I can by disappearing into my room with my laptop here and there, squeezing writing into small crevices of time. That bit she understands.

She's meant to be leaving tomorrow, but has changed their flight to Saturday. That's nice. I know that what I'm providing for her is an essential break from a real struggle to exist alone with a baby. I've been through the same thing, and being welcome in a household that's stable and warm is a thing you dream of. She's very vocal about how happy she is with us, and I can see why. It makes me realise just how nice the life I've built [and worked hard to maintain] for us is. We've all survived First-Born's [self-]destructive streak; the edifice still stands.

Now; I have one hour. Can I do a big chunk of the killer chapter in one hour? Please yes.

Thursday, 19th November, 2009.

Pillaged

Prodigal Friend came out of the shower and told me that she's borrowing my hair clip thingy, she hopes I don't mind.

Of course I don't mind. I don't use it. I didn't even remember owning it, until I saw its slender end sticking out of her head. Except, I don't know how she could possibly have found it without going through the box of stuff in my bathroom cupboard.

What is it with my bathroom cupboard? I don't feel the need to go through other people's cupboards. Should I hang a sign in my bathroom saying '*Guests please mind your own fucking business*'? Or offer them my underwear drawer as well and tell them to help themselves?

Oh yes, the teenagers have spoiled the act of rummaging for all of my future guests. I don't actually mind that she went through my cupboard – I love that she feels so comfortable in my home. It's even funny. But maybe I should build an en suite and hide it behind a secret panel. Or just get the hell over it, maybe I should do that.

Monday, 23rd November, 2009.

Just Quietly

I'm reading the boringest book on the planet. I can't name it because it's a work of fiction that sits in a similar niche to the fiction I'm writing at the moment and I don't want that to come back and bite me later. It's really bugging me, because it's full of the right ingredients but with NO PERSONALITY WHATSOEVER. How are these books getting published? I'll tell you how – the author has authority. What a pity authority doesn't make a good writer.

I wish I could give you examples of the appalling writing. The emphatic descriptions of one of the female protagonists' *'natural beauty'* are so clunky and romance-genre it's spewy. *Natural natural natural.* ARE YOU GETTING IT READER? YOU ARE SUPPOSED TO BE IN AWE OF HER. The constant descriptions of her body, the way she focuses upon remaining slim despite being heavily pregnant. All of it shallow and simplistic. Almost halfway through I hit a paragraph that describes one female studying whatsername's *'naturally attractive face'*, closely, and the jealousy this arouses, and wanted to scream ENOUGH WITH THE NATURAL ALREADY.

Don't get me started on the sensitive male character's contrived monologue-ish asides on the plight of marine life. We get it, can the sentimentalism. The insight into the truly poetic nature of the Bad Guy is so badly done it's ridiculous. Without being clever it can't be effectual. If you wanna show both sides, then don't resort to romantic notions. Such a waste of a literary opportunity.

I'm so mean! She meant well, kudos for trying.

But I have to also be mean about *Monster Blood Tattoo,* which I will name. (I'm so sorry, D.M. Cornish.) It seems to be less a natural telling of a story than the product of an idea written the way the author thinks a fantasy novel should be written. All construct, no voice. I'm not very far in and I'm labouring. I'll force my way through it, but suspect that the review that made the outline of the story so attractive to me might be better than the novel itself...? Even the glossary's a little overkill, the whole thing like an object designed for the big sell. I hope I'm wrong.

Not everything in Book Land is joyful. Sometimes pleasure is hard work. And yet, another book I bought recently came with a one-cent novel attached and parts of that one-cent novel are so much fun. It's a bit vacuous story-wise, but the voice takes you right to the inside of a person's brain. That's what we want, yes? Yes.

Sunday, 29th November, 2009.

Cupid Missed

I slept in. Clearly this needed to be announced. I hate sleeping in; I start early with a walk and if I miss my walk I feel all wrong.

Luckily I'd planned an easy day and so went to a gallery to see some good stuff, *and* got chatted up by a man [!!]. The sad thing is that you have to have a long conversation with somebody to get a feel for whether or not you really connect with them, but to commit to the conversation is to lay yourself open to them thinking they connect with you [being so lovely n' all], and then when they DO seem to like you and keep you talking when you're trying to walk away, and they somehow extract your e-mail address from you and express interest in seeing you again, it's *too late*.

Such awkwardness. He was nice, but when I realised this was a little beyond gosh-we-could-be-friends, I kept looking at him and thinking that I don't even know how to find a man beautiful just because he's there. Although I did find somebody interesting lately, and I'm curious about that somebody, when I look at men I usually just think '*What is there to love?*'.

This is only because I need to know them first (hence the conversation, which was purely friendly and how was I to know it was going that way?). Had I found more to connect with I might have found him attractive. But *meh*. It's a tragedy, because meeting somebody at an art gallery is an ideal situation. It would have covered a lot of how-we-met dinner table conversation ground.

I think I'd prefer to fall for a man right now. If only they weren't so stupid.

So no love today, but with a bit of thank-fuck about it. I don't know. Maybe I'm just rusty.

December 2009

Tuesday, 1ˢᵗ December, 2009.

These Books, Those Books and the Mysterious HKs
The pile of books next to my bed has gotten out of control. In fact, everything's gotten out of control. Thing is I'm catching up with friends and not getting much else done. Good, yes, but the euphoria's making my head spin.

Yesterday, Friend Alice in Wonderland and I did the paper sales and the love affair has reignited. So much paper to roll around on, so little time. She gave me one of her editioned artist books (printmaking), and I'm understandably swooning.

And last week catching up with Studio Neighbour Friend, who just happens to be the ants pants. We trawled through Melbourne's galleries, cementing what must be actual friendship? Our first time alone (as opposed to being in with the group). I'm cautious with friendship these days, so just as well re the reassurance.

Anyway we did the Hare Krishna's for lunch, my first time. Forgive me for generalising, but I couldn't help noticing that they don't smile. In fact something seems to upset the Krishnas and I wonder if it's just that they have to work in that steam during this hot weather, or if it's the incessant noise on that kitchen level?

We went upstairs to sit by the tree at the window and it was surprisingly calm, except for the chanting video blaring out into the room. Perhaps they look haggard because they never get any quiet. Perhaps they should incorporate a bit of shut-the-hell-up into their philosophy. Or Maybe they're sick of giving and have learnt that humans are arseholes who aren't worth the subservience. (I'm not judging them, I'm judging us.)

They also don't acknowledge thank-yous. And they shoo the sparrows back out the window. The ones we were accidentally feeding because we didn't know they weren't allowed in. Not our fault the milk of human kindness doesn't extend to birds.

So in this world where thank you means nothing I'd really like to know what makes them laugh. The restaurant is so beautiful I want them to be happy. Do they laugh? If only I were a fly on the wall.

p.s. Today First-Born re-enrolled in school, *oh thank goodness*.

p.p.s. Today I discovered that Readings Hawthorn is close to the station. This is not only fuelling my impending poverty but also, am I ever filling up on things literary. The famine is over.

Wednesday, 2nd December, 2009.

Neighbour Cam

My neighbour did a kindness, so now I feel guilty for having egged his friend's car oh-so-long-ago. But not that guilty. What he did was call out '*Hello?*' while I was lugging things green around, ready for green waste collection, and when I looked up he offered me the use of his green waste bin.

This made me stupidly happy. I couldn't stop smiling, but *had* to stop smiling because I didn't want him to see me smiling, not with that stupid quality attached. Just, you know. The little things.

He also said '*You've been carting things up there for weeks...*'. Oh hallelujah, somebody's noticed what an absolute gardening legend I've become. Problem is, I now know that I've been watched while I work, in all my sweaty, grunting glory. The sweaty grunting bit's literal, by the way; I've worked my guts out. And on this hillside visibility is optimum because of the slope, and because the properties open out with very little fencing.

I'm a veritable specimen, now, and have to worry about whether or not my experimental garden bed's going to work. I planted my spares on the slope. What if he's secretly a horticulturist and thinking '*What an idiot, planting tomatoes there!*'.

Well for your big fat information I *know* it's stupid planting tomatoes on a slope, but they were leftovers and I thought the experiment would be interesting. The slope's bastardly challenging. I can't mulch because of the fire risk, and the water just drains away. I have to come up with a plan. In the meantime the pressure is on to save face. *Grow,* tomatoes, *grow!*

Tending the risotto; a gentle act, if not for the butchered-onion thumb.

Thursday, 3rd December, 2009.

Snail's Back

Friend Girl A and I are doing a seaside town for a weekend, as an intensive writing thing. Usually I dread going away. Something about me being a homebody and boring old fart. I love day trips. Maybe even overnighters, but anything more than that and I usually just want to be back here, working and being peaceful.

It's harder this time because I'm leaving the kids on their grown-up own. I had to trick First-Born, who's being lovely lately. Lovely because every time they're in a bad mood they go out of their way to explain why, careful not to hurt me specifically. They're growing more aware of their own impact. This is *nice*. But I lied to them so that they won't know I'll be gone overnight, because I don't want them organising a small but destructive party while I'm gone.

On the other hand, I told them to invite their two closest friends over. I'm not so bad.

It's funny; Friend Girl A only has to leave her partner, and it's made me think about how we outgrow our own comfort zones. A partner in the house is easy because they're furniture and no big deal to leave. But teenagers who invite friends over = the threat of invasion. They're termitic. Their friends burrow through your personal spaces, violating your privacy. You lose control of your space because you don't trust the people who're guarding it to care the way you yourself care.

So getting ready to go is difficult. Such baggage upon my mind. And when I'm gone, will I feel free? I think so. I'm really noticing the distractions lately and it'll be good to work on the novel without external pressure. The timing's perfect; I need peace to re-establish my cut-throat project-prioritising instincts.

Plus it'll be fun. Mornington Peninsula = wine and nice food, and we'll see *Where the Wild Things Are* at the local cinema while we're there. We'll live like single people with no responsibilities. Regular check-up phone calls and garden watering instructions aside, I'll try not to take it all with me.

Sunday, 6th December, 2009.

Jjjjjjjjj
There's no phonetic way to make a grinding-nerves sound and in this way language is inadequate, because I need to make this sound. Here. Now.

Not in a bad way, seeing as it's only because after a weekend away I expected to come back to a quiet, empty-except-for-us house, and instead First-Born's friends are still here and they're staying overnight. This equals no peace equals day of writing tomorrow is in jeopardy. I need peace, I need it badly.

And yet, First-Born's happy and their social life is important. The friends are nice again so I just have to toughen up. Frazzled nerves are for pussies.

Plus I need to kick them out early. Better make that clear tonight.

Monday, 7th December, 2009.

[SAD CONTENT WARNING]
Oh Dear
It's not nice to talk about your students, I think? There are etiquettes and possibly laws involved. I've held off for half a week. But one of mine's a strange one, the kind of person who drifts through the world engaging with people but not-quite. I can't get below the surface. Is there anything below the surface? She's not cruel, but she seems to experience the world without emotion. A cold functionality about her personality. I've felt an aversion to her, like she's another species altogether.

Usually I'm weirded-out when a new person enters our group, that whole stranger danger thing. But with this one I never stopped being weirded-out, and today was the icing on the weirdness cake. Because she wrote about a rabbit.

When she announced the rabbit bit, I thought the story was gonna be cutesy. I wish it had been.

I wouldn't do this under any other circumstance, but it was really traumatising, so I'll summarise it here knowing that it'll never be published anywhere. The story goes; she had a neighbour, and the neighbour had rabbits. The rabbits were a handful and eventually one escaped but the other didn't. Neighbour went away and asked her to look after the remaining rabbit. She looked after it alright. She'd seen rabbits killed before and thought it was easy. A grip on the neck and a bang on the back of the head. Except, it's not easy. Because of her incompetence the rabbit died a slow and painful death after multiple attempts. And then it was skinned, and then it was eaten.

The neighbour returned to a sad story about her remaining rabbit having escaped. The lie is as awful to me as the act.

My intuition was right about the student being all surface and little depth. When she told this story, the thing that stood out for me was her inability to really connect. To people and to rabbits, who are very beautiful people. And her inability to anticipate or recognise our reaction.

What a bizarre thing. The rest of the class kept making eye contact with me. We raised many a distressed eyebrow, which was the polite suppression of *holy fuck*. I was really upset but had to hold it in. Humans shouldn't be let loose in the world. It was our last class for the year and most of us felt all warm and fuzzy and emotional, and then this. It ruined our night/year/lives.

Thursday, 10th December, 2009.

Harvest

I was going to pick three apricots from our tree last night but decided against it, because of all of the inherent dangers. Such as, if I put them on the table a burglar could break into my house overnight and STEAL MY APRICOTS. A fire could start up and BURN MY APRICOTS DOWN. Aliens could visit me and ABDUCT MY APRICOTS.

Plus it was too dark to find them once I'd finished planting the last of the sunflowers for the secret making of happiness for my children.

I picked them this morning, and because there are strangers in my house I had to eat all three. Those are the apricots I remember from my childhood. Apples and apricots = I can't find nice ones in the shops. But this morning – bliss. I need to plant more and more and more apricot trees. I need that orchard. And weeds growing already = it's time to find a way to get it. I have to fall in love, which is a problem because I'm now a grumpy old misanthrope. But for the apricots, I must.

———

I really regret not sharing those apricots with my kids. I mean, there were *three*. Do the maths, Mothah. This selfish eating *cannot* be undone.

———

Saturday, 12th December, 2009.

Mow Mow Mow Your Boat

It's not that I'm so tragic that I'd mow my lawn on a Saturday night, but while I was mowing my lawn tonight (which coincidentally happens to be Saturday), a man somewhere yonder across the hillside kept calling out '*SHUT THE FUCK UP*' every time the mower blades stuck and it got quiet.

It's pretty scary when somebody yells like that, but I kept mowing because *fuck you, Bogan Mofo*. Then when I finished and Son and I were potting around the yard (he's so much fun to pot around with), Yelling Man started up again and seemed to be yelling at somebody else. I can still hear him, an hour later.

Why has somebody put a yelling man on our hillside?

I've spent the last few days attending a portrait master class. It was fun. Models and drawing and euphoria and going at it non-stop = so, so tired. But not too tired to mow the lawn. How good do I feel to have that done? So good. Doing is a good thing. I should do things more often. Oh waitaminute, I already do do things. And yet, so many things don't seem to get done.

Tuesday, 15th December, 2009.

Crisis Averted

I accidentally invited another friend into the tight Circle of Us. "Us" includes myself and my two closest studio neighbours. We make up a sacred triangle. Only I was at a portrait workshop for four days with Other Friend last week, and happened to mention I'd be catching up with my studio neighbours, and then what could I do? Not invite her? Well yes, I should have not-invited her. Because there's us, and then there are *other studios*. And well it's foreign over in the other studios. We're xenophobic about our studio row. And if I invite one extra person, doesn't that mean we should have invited everybody? And then what? Global studio pandemonium and no "us" left [!!].

I'm *so* lucky she pulled out at the last minute (I suspect anorexia, actually) and I didn't have to tell anybody I'd slipped up. When Pregnant Friend pulled out presents for us both I was even more relieved, because imagine the awkward moment for the non-present-receiving friend had she been there.

So, another present from a friend; I keep being given presents and I feel bad because I just don't buy presents. I'm not stingy, I just don't shop. I don't think in terms of stuff. I do nice things for people so I guess it evens out, but probably not enough. I should go out of my way to give things to people so that they know I value them just that little bit more. To make that stand-alone moment of acknowledgement happen. Not so much for Xmas but during the year, at any given time.

Afterwards = I dread coming home and finding an extra pair of shoes in the hallway by the door (never neatly arranged – why does nobody have neatness impulses?). Extra shoes means that my house is being taken over for the night by teenagers. I hate it and have said no, but here they are. I'm mean in front of them; I would never have done that before. They're turning me into a hermit, and if I could grow a beard I would. I'd guard my property with a hound dog and a shotgun and say *'Get outa my gosh dang house'*. A lot.

I shouldn't complain; First-Born's still being friendly. The only thing bad about them at the moment is the smoking. It's just, please, no more friends. Friends are bad. Go away. Go away so that books and garden are foremost on my mind. Art and family. Everything else is too much else.

Wednesday, 16th December, 2009.

Void

There's a big empty space between my ears. I've missed my Churchy Friend. Really. I noticed I was missing her during the year, but didn't think much of it because I thought we must have drifted apart. Maybe I thought I wasn't cool and dope-smokey enough for her at one stage, but it didn't bother me because I was having a nice little breather. The sort where you enjoy missing somebody because frankly you need a break every now and then.

Anyway it turns out it's got nothing to do with me not being cool and dope-smokey (although true, I'm not). It had more to do with her being busy with her new boyfriend and him being perfect and then not so perfect, and then whaddya know he's a real shit, and her not wanting to burden anybody with it. Which is so uncharacteristic it's almost scary.

Then we're on the phone for two nights in a row and a little during the day here and there, and it's just like old times, when she used to ring me every second minute. Only I like it this time. I don't mind that she repeats herself, and that the conversations have gone for hours, and I have to say I find the awfulness of what her now-ex boyfriend is up to so hilarious I can't help laughing even while she cries. Because she describes him so well he's like a caricature. A horrible, hypochondriac caricature who's so revolting I practically wet myself laughing. I call out *'Good! I'm glad to see the end of him!'*.

Now. The phone calls will start again and that's good, but after I got off the phone tonight I couldn't remember who I was. It was bizarre; all of the plans I'd had were gone, as was the evening. So I wandered out to the garden and reacquainted myself with what needs to be done. I perused the nooks and crannies. Assessed the weedage. Made a mental list. And now I have to make sure that if Churchy's back in my life (not that she was really gone), I accommodate her without my brain evaporating in the process. Control the phone times, be careful of time commitments. Squeeze her in where she fits comfortably so that I can enjoy her and still work. Easy peasy. Good.

I think what's happened here is that I didn't have to watch the decision-making process, I just got the tidy end of it, where she walked away. That's why I'm happy. I'm protective of her. Because she gets a bit intense every now and then The Men in Her Life tend to dismiss her opinions when the crunch comes. I'm worried about her inability to be happy, but proud of her new ability to walk away from something bad.

Friday, 18th December, 2009.

So Simple it's Complex

I took Son to see *Avatar*, and am confused because I really really enjoyed it. It was trippy, but when I thought about how I might describe the experience to anybody, mashing together a quick summary of the story, I realised that the storyline is far too dorky to speak aloud.

That's what the reviews had said, so I went to the movie in a sceptical frame of mind, ready to be disappointed. And yet, it wasn't dorky. It suited the movie perfectly and didn't need to be anything other than it was. Despite all of that Gaia hippy shit. Which is totally acceptable given the current climate. Despite, you know. *Hippies*.

So do I agree with the reviews, or don't I? Yes! No!

The only thing I didn't like was the shallow Americanism of his character (by "his" I mean *Whatsisname*). There are too many of him around and they're so similar they're generic. Allegedly spunky [but not really spunky]; testosteronic, rugged, et cetera. His character wasn't as entertaining as it was meant to be, just sad.

Therefore I declare the movie brilliant, yet dorky, yet brilliant. What a thing to experience.

Wretched

I made a phone call to Old Uncle in the nursing home today. I don't visit him nearly enough, but after today I think that's probably a good thing. He had a negative answer to everything I said. Not because he's trapped in a nursing home and therefore miserable, but because of his dementia. I tried to turn him around by asking him about singing, as in *'Doesn't singing make you happy?'*, but he twisted what I was saying and used it to reinforce his conspiracy theory. He said the reason people are out to bring him down is because he's happy and people resent him being happy. (*So ironic.*)

Today my charm and cheerful disposition couldn't win him back. The worst thing was that he started telling me how Deceased Wife doesn't love him anymore. He said she's run off to have an affair with a man in Africa, and I feel even more sad for him because he's ruined the memory of somebody he loved very much. They were in their conspiracy theories together. Peas in a pod.

It's bad enough that his dementia's gotten in the way of his dying from grief (because he's continued to think she's still alive), but to spoil her memory completely? Not that I want him to die from grief, but how do we believe in love if they don't obey the plot? He's outlived her by two whole years now, which is outrageous.

Anyway, I try to tell him that she loves him, but he's not listening. He also thinks he's about to start a new job in America. Everything he says is a product of his younger, arsehole businessman days and that's not the part of him I love. It was a really unpleasant phone call.

So back to my theory that in demented old age you become the product of how you live when you're younger. Which means that if I end up that way I'm gonna be roaming the nursing home saying *'Why are all of these people in my house? I just want to be alone, I just want some peace! I hate people! I love people! But can't you see I need to paint? How am I going to get any sleep?'*. Things do not bode well.

Two days later = went to visit and he was lovely. Still in arsehole-mode, but lovely. We're lucky he recognises us, and that he hasn't tainted us with evil conspiracy stories. If only the affectionate side of him was dominant, he'd be much happier. Poor Uncle.

Saturday, 19th December, 2009.

Do Drop In

That slapping of feet down the driveway, them raucous voices booming out, them five seconds I have to throw on some respectable clothes and answer the door.

People dropping in who haven't dropped in for a long while. It was Muso Friend – one of my few male friends – and his very loud and very many and very wild offspring. So visitors galore, and hugs and affection and another friend arriving with a gift of a water tank and a trailer to borrow, and therefore somewhere to stow the water I collect in buckets every time it rains (I love to collect water!) and some-how to cart more green waste to the tip.

But with all of this house-being-alive-and-friendly, I ran late for a drawing date with Reformed Hippy, who I'm dying to catch up with, so I feel as though I had my day railroaded. We've had to postpone. Still, it was nice. I just feel very bad about that.

I'm overwhelmed by things-to-do even though I've been enjoying it, believing I can fit all of it in. But now I'm starting to feel anxious because the time and focus I've given to the garden could have been spent painting. This is no small thing. It's time to get my shit together and do it all.

Too much too much too much too much too much too *much*.

p.s. I'm not attracted to Muso Friend. Kitchen Nazi Friend is because he's a bit of a spunk, but he's more like a goofy brother to me. Still, he hugged me an awful lot, full body hugging, so I felt my breasts against his chest and it was the first time I've hugged somebody like that and felt it for a long time. Suddenly I realise what I'm missing by not being in love. I want that. Not with him, but with somebody. It's time.

Wednesday, 23rd December, 2009.

Relax?

I have discovered [again!] my balcony. A stupid discovery, seeing as it's been there all along. But today there was shade over the chairs in the corner after I came up from putting bird netting over the plum tree, and I hung the washing out with that blissful feeling of bare feet on the boards, and I stood looking out over the rail but was so tired I couldn't stand up and look out there any longer, and it occurred to me that I didn't have to stand. That I could, if I wanted, sit down and stay there for longer. On cushions n' everything. It was an epiphany, so I sat on the chair in the shade and did nothing but enjoy the warm air until the shade disappeared.

I just don't *do* that. Sit and do nothing. It was nice! Everyone's still in bed so it's a beautiful, silent, gentle day. So rare. Why shouldn't I be allowed to sit? How did I forget that I can? Why do I think that to be anywhere I have to also be doing something? Do I need guests here to enjoy the place? Because that's the only time I sit like this.

I hereby promise to arrange life so that I can sit in the shade on the balcony on days like this. Slow down. Today I catch up, the void is over with. I have well developed themes to work with. That's what I wanted, and now I have them.

I'll buy a swinging chair and put the hammock up, fix this no-sitting-peacefully problem once and for all.

Thursday, 24th December, 2009.

Fish, Water

I haven't swum laps since earlier in the year, because I had bronchitis TWICE and in my decrepitude was scared of getting it again. Today I overcame the fear because it's Xmas Eve and it's raining, and Xmas Eve means an almost-empty pool, which means a wonderfully peaceful swim which equals irresistible.

It was like a homecoming. Even though I went to a different pool because my local closed early, and this one was salt-water chlorine. When I first went under the salt on my lips made me feel as though I was drinking in other people's body fluids. And the pool is older and has tiles that look like they're lining a rental property bathroom that hasn't been cleaned since the last tenants moved in six years ago.

But I loved the salt water, so even though it's further away and usually so busy, and the water surface is so choppy it makes you choke, I might swim there more often.

I loved that I could see where people most often walk along the pool edges, because of the dirty trail of foot soil on the tiles.

I loved that *Poetica* was on Radio National on the way there. They were talking about eroticism and read aloud a short piece by Yamabe no Akahito (Japanese poet from the 7th Century):

> *I wish I were close*
> *To you as the wet skirt of*
> *A salt girl to her body.*
> *I think of you always.*

I loved that those lines occasionally said themselves over in my mind as I swam, but in an abbreviated form: '*I wish I were close to you/as the wet skirt of a salt girl*'. I loved that my novel likewise began to re-form; that no music played through the centre, so as my head bobbed above water there was nothing to interfere with my thoughts.

And I LOVE that this particular pool complex has a sauna, so after my very long swim I lay down on the hot wooden bench and was suffused by the cedar smell. I could hardly breath, allowed to sweat until my body was limp and relaxed and *ohmigawd*, I love the heat.

More. More of that. If I was rich I'd have a 50 metre salt water lap pool and a sauna and I'd swim without crowds and feel wonderful *all the time*. But I'm not rich, so if there's a quiet time at that usually-busy pool I'm going to find it and claim it for myself. And never go for so long without swimming again, even if it kills me.

Friday, 25th December, 2009.

Doom and Gloom

What is it, peak suicide day of the year? Or is that New Year's? Well, *happy whatever it is*!

Things aren't bleak like that, but they are kinda sad. In fact, I felt like crying, until I noticed GrandKitten poking around under the very spunky shoe cupboard. I climbed down to dig out her rubber ball, so that we could play soccer around the kitchen.

It's hard to rally the troops to stave off emptiness; no wonder people crack. The kids aren't very interested in things festive. Although, they came with me to see a street full of Xmas lights last night. That's all a mother needs, isn't it? Company when looking at pretty lights?

It'll get better. I'll see Churchy Friend and I'll see my family and it'll be downright jolly.

Wild Thing

I want to see *Where The Wild Things Are* again, but wonder if it's the sort of movie you should see twice within a short period of time.

I think it's the visual beauty of it I'm craving. And the clever simplicity of the storyline. And the profound telling of the impossibility of happiness. The impossibility of peace between factions. People and their compulsion to destroy what they love. The clashing pathways of destruction and creation and the sheer and brutal rendering of the emptiness of the world.

It's bleak and beautiful, and that bleakness might be what's deterring me from the second viewing.

When you're writing there are certain movies and books you turn to because they offer a positive influence on your work, because their structure or their imaginative qualities or their atmosphere are aligned with your own. But you need to steer clear of everything else because the influence will distract you or poison your voice.

I don't think this one's poison. Is it? No. Just sad. That has to be what I'm avoiding. I wonder how kids respond to the movie. So devastating with its simple, grown-up truth.

Waiting, Waiting

I did wait. Gosh, how I waited. And I got sadder and sadder when I realised that First-Born wasn't going to give me a Xmas present. Really

really sad. Normally they steal something for me and then promise me they didn't steal it. Normally the present is really thoughtful. Alas, not this year.

I went to our family dinner running on half-steam, lugging my unloved body and my sunken Xmas cake (not my fault – the recipe said four hours) and bags full of presents. It's just as well my family kicks arse because I love it when we get together, so I was able to forget how unloved I am in no time.

And then First-Born left early to host their teenage friends here, and sigh, sigh and *sigh*. I wasn't sad again until I got home. The scumbag teenage friends are really nice so instead of moping and having them think I'm shitty, I went out to the kitchen and announced *'I'm sad because First-Born didn't give me a Xmas present'*. That was their cue to give me pity, but they didn't give me pity because First-Born didn't give them presents either [!!].

That's actually funny, so should I continue to feel bad? First-Born made such a big deal about the ordering of their own present [from me], and I didn't even get a thought from them. Should it matter? Parenthood can make you so invisible. Love is so easy, I have no idea why teenagers get it so wrong.

Saturday, 26th December, 2009.

Aftermath

I'm not doing too badly on two hours of sleep. It's the euphoria you feel when scumbag teenagers leave your house; it's almost worth having them here in the first place, just so you can feel the relief.

They're good kids, really. I seldom meet a friend of First-Born's who I don't like because their people are very decent. Two new ones last night, one who does art, so I stayed up way past my bedtime to talk to them. I have a feeling he's gonna go home and dig out his old paint brushes and resume painting. I inspired somebody. *Again*. My work here is done.

Now if I could just inspire myself a little....

Chris Fontana

Monday, 28th December, 2009.

Gadget-Fest

Ex-Wife's world is a foreign country. It neighbours the past, kind of thing. And yet, it's in the whizbang future. We did breakfast yesterday, and I didn't realise until I walked in that I hadn't been to her home for over a year. Trees were bigger, Young Son was bigger, and the designer house has finally been home-ified with the scatter of childhood mess.

I got the feeling I've missed the point when it comes to the meaning of life. Could all of the things I abhor really be what it's all about? House filled with stuff, and every contemporary gadget you can think of. And within this: entertainment. Black boxes that play movies, Wii's that play games at you, race tracks and train tracks and a big tv and a small tv and computers and a pool and a trampoline and a ping pong table.

The ping pong table I loved. So simple, so boring, and yet so much fun. We played ping pong while we chatted. Doing. Doing doing.

That's when it occurred to me that I don't do entertainment properly. No trampoline! No pool! No stuff!

But then, enter Younger Son, who I love, and I noticed his childhood shape. Alert to everything, social, but he seems profoundly lonely. *Watch me, can you please watch me,* he said. Constantly. Of course I'll watch you. But watching somebody play Wii is dead boring. Choosing a single player game when you could choose a double seemed wrong, even for a 5 year-old. As though he's in training to be the centre of his own universe. *Watch me play cars*, okay. But I joined in. *Watch me play my new DS,* yes I watched. All of it insular and unsocial. Stimulating but personally unsatisfying. The DS going, the Wii on and the tv blaring. Every movie and show you can imagine. Noise noise noise. If boredom ever threatens to take over the world, their battlements are ready, a veritable activity fortress.

The kids' home life there seems dependent on external stimulation. They're a prototype for the consumer family model. Sad.

Then we brought Other Son back home with us, to where there's no stuff. Prodigal Friend, when she was staying, congratulated me upon our lack of materialism. Nice home, nice us, equipped with computers and functional things, but not stuff. I didn't realise until today just why she was so surprised.

Other Son's sleeping in my spare bedroom, and I'm thinking of waking him up. It's the first time he's stayed since forever. He used to stay much more frequently, but because he hasn't lately I feel inadequate. He's into basketball and the stuff of mechanical entertainment. Are we enough for him? We watched a movie last night – that's technological, isn't it?

I wonder what we are. The sum of what manufactured components? Our house has silences he may never have experienced. Here's me wanting to buy a swinging chair. And now a ping pong table. It could be I'm very boring.

Tuesday, 29th December, 2009.

Food, Glorious, Et Cetera

Ex-Wife would have to alter the lyrics if she sang the *Oliver* food song to Her Younger Son. It's not my business to be alarmed, but I am, because my spies tell me that all he eats are chicken nuggets, sausages and chips. Although, when we did breakfast he did eat a piece of toast. Still, that makes for very limited verses and not much rhyming, song-wise.

I asked conversationally if Ex-Wife still cooks a lot, and was surprised when Other Son told me she doesn't. That he cooks his own food, and what he cooks is pasta and pasta with beef. I tried to find out if this meant real pasta or packet pasta, but having seen the insides of her pantry I'm scared to know and didn't push the point.

So today, with my maternal instincts ebbeth and flowething, I made him a roast for lunch, thinking I could send him home full of wholesome goodness. He didn't eat overly much of it. I'll try not to take that personally, seeing as First-Born was hoeing into it, saying *'Mmm, I love meat'*, and I know I make a nice roast, succulent n' all. Other Son made me heat his up in the microwave, before it was even cold. Anyway, it's not my business, but Ex-Wife seems to have let everything go. She was a great cook. For all my crappiness and limited repertoire, I at least make sure my kids eat decent-like.

What's happened to them? Somebody waved a modern wand over their house and they've become a product of the product, processed food and processed intellectual stimulation? Computer games are the MSG of the entertainment world. Her Younger Son wants to stay here for a long visit with us, but the truth is he'd hate it. Because I'd draw with him and take him to parks and make him eat real food. Could somebody like me entertain a child who's been raised on condensed stimulus? (Actually, Son's addicted to computer games, so we're not that pure.)

Anyway, it was lovely having Other Son here, but I'm awkward with lack of familiarity. Asking myself again if I'm boring to him. First-Born's been keeping to themself, and instead of sleeping in the room with Son, Other Son's been sleeping in the spare room on his own. He hugs me, which is nice. Hugs me from the front, puts an arm around me from behind, and I jump on him whenever I catch him lying down on his stomach. (Son and First-Born don't hug me anymore, so this is both really nice, and really sad.) But is it all okay, this quiet? I'll never know if we're boring, with our antiquated time-spending. Or if it's a nice home-away-from-home for him.

Also: I'm very conscious of often saying "your mum" when I'm referring to Ex-Wife (which is too much like saying that I'm not also his mum, when technically I'm supposed to be), and saying "my kids" when I'm referring to Son and First-Born (which is the same as saying he's not also my kid). These possessives disturb me and once I've said them I can't take them back. I do it all the time. I don't mean them, it's just habit of speech, compounded by the fact that he's not even nearly in my every-day life. The exclusion in the nature of the words makes me panic because I know what I want to be with him, but I'm aware of what I'm not. Is our relationship all talk/no action? Does that hurt him? What?

Thursday, 31st December, 2009.

Friends Who Stayed-Over

Another writing intensive, but I find I can't write with other people around. It's a solitary activity, I think? Or maybe it's just because one friend was always eating, and when not eating she was planning what to eat next, or thinking out loud about our next meal. She ate at least five meals a day, plus snacks. I feel physically like shit even though I didn't eat what she ate. Just the thought of it = unhealthy and unpleasant.

And yet, we had a nice time. I really am turning into hermitic old bag. A clear-cut case of *careful what you wish for*; why on earth would anybody wanna be so alone?

One of the friends lives a sad way of life that I don't often get to witness close up. Thinks of herself as a prey animal and acts like one, is one. Abuse survivor. Fierce intellect, but easy to startle. Always on edge. Mobile phone often turned off, very hard to catch, and yet conversely very needy. I bet her cats leave their mobiles switched off as well.

Another one whose friends are rostered on to visit, a steady stream of interesting people entering our home. I love how she wants to share her friends and gather community around her. When she introduces them, these friends are prefaced by their intellectual credentials; '*She has a PhD, you'll like her*'; '*He's incredibly intellectual*'.

I wonder what my intellectual credentials amounted to when she described me to them. Something like '*Has the potential but doesn't quite cut it; perhaps avoid using big words with her*'.

January 2010

Friday, 1st January, 2010.

Reasons to be Happy
Yesterday I saved my row of pumpkins. Looked down onto the garden and saw that those fat, happy leaves – as big as umbrellas – were wilting. So I ran to the garage, grabbed the water I'd saved in buckets from the last heavy rain, and tipped it down over the balcony. Again with the medievalism, tipping slops down onto the street.

Son watched. Then we waited. And nothing happened, so we went away and came back later. *Lo! The pumpkins wuz saved!*

It was good to be staring at pumpkins through the window, instead of staring into space. I've done that quite a bit this week. The new year's irrelevant, and yet, what a good excuse to pull myself out of this. DAY ONE.

I grit my teeth after going crazy two nights ago (extra teenagers constantly in the house), and told Son he could have two friends over last night. I made them turn off the lights so we could watch the lightning and thunderstorm in the distance. We didn't go up the hill to see the city fireworks this year, because of the storm, but the boys were happy. With First-Born and I not so much happy, the balance was tipped in favour of joy. The one thing I can do is make sure that Son doesn't suffer, and I do an okay job of that.

All going well I'll swim laps today. I'll paint, I'll write, and I'll bake. Please pool, don't be full of anybody.

Then I'll wait for *First-Born's* leaves to stop wilting; I should've saved some of the rainwater buckets for them. Oh look, a crappy analogy! Beggars can't be choosers, that's pretty much all I'm good for right now.

I hate the sound of my mind as I write this. Because it's not the little, whiny details that make the situation, it's the bone crushing sadness of having a child who won't love you. Palpable animosity and the impossibility of happiness, despite my being hard-wired since the womb to create just that.

Enough. When I'm painting and writing again I'll be happy. While the rest of the world was partying I was cleaning paint brushes last night, getting ready. Transcendence is the key; if I let myself sink I can't help them. I have to think *superhero* and *nemesis* and overcome the odds. New Year's resolution: lead by example and *kick arse*.

―――

I love that when rain is promised, rain happens.

―――

It's funny having to text to communicate with an offspring that lives in the same house and is only a couple of rooms away. '*Please turn your music down*', and '*Can you please feed Kitten*', et cetera. We really could survive the rest of their upbringing by never having to speak or interact. How did the human race make it to now without this?

―――

Still Friday, 1st January, 2010.

Never Too Early for Philosophy

I was listening to a repeat *Life Matters* program on Radio National as I cleaned those brushes in the studio last night, and heard Alan de Botton talk about work (his book = *The Pleasures and Sorrows of Work)* and the problematic symptoms of a perfectionist society.

The part that interested me specifically = he said that an idealistic and individualistic society leads to higher levels of suicide, which result from feelings of failure. In a possibly-gappy nutshell, he gave an overview of notions of work between classes. For example, the working class might see work as a way to make money, whereas the middle class might see work as a way of achieving meaningful occupation and personal fulfillment. Similarly marriage was once a practical agreement, whereas now it's idealised as a product of ongoing romantic love. When individuals fail to live up to the ideals promoted by society at large, they attribute the failure to personal inadequacy and voilà, depression and possible suicide.

I recognised these feelings in relation to parenthood. I always feel as though I'm doing it all wrong because I'm not the right person for my children; because I'm not socially connected to the right kind of people, don't cook the same sort of food, stay home and clean paintbrushes instead of partying with friends at Elwood beach on New Year's Eve. There's no end to my inadequacy, I know that deep down in my bones and feel sorry for my kids all the time.

I use the word failure in this respect, even though the benchmark I measure myself against is so foggy it's indefinable.

Because First-Born would be happier if I'd been a more socially oriented person? If I was a pub-goer and followed football and other things that lead you into social communities that aren't obsessed with introspective things like books? How would I even know that?

The germ of a thought process that'll help me somehow. It's as simple as recognising that the perfection we fail to achieve doesn't really exist. Did I not know this already? Since when did I subscribe to singular ideas of perfection? How did I get so stupid? Overactive emotions. And being told I suck for five years in a row doesn't help. But still, the grinding down of confidence can be undone with a little bit of pragmatism, and I'm therefore glad I heard him speak.

———

They keep changing things at work, even though everything flows smoothly. Why is everybody always *improving* things? Why not just *be*? We're now using whiteboards instead of books; a thumb print instead of signing in; email instead of speaking; and nobody's being paid after clocking off.

———

Wednesday, 6th January, 2010.

I Did Good

No stewing in my own misery, which is just emotional filth. I finally felt settled enough to write, having convinced myself that burying myself inside a story is the best way to escape domestic unhappiness.

Novel-writing's my saviour, I have the power n' all that. Once I'd decided this was how it was going to be, I leapt in and *behold!* I opened the most recent file thinking I'd find a half-written chapter, but found instead an almost fully-realised chapter, which only needs tidying up. Not only that, but the descriptions are fulfilling and poetic, they're everything I wanted them to be, and the chapter fills in some of the background exactly the way I wanted it to be filled in. The whole kaboodle holds what I'd call "my vision".

I love it when I've forgotten how much I've done. This must be what it's like to have dementia [hell forbid], where every memory's like a little gift.

I'm now officially writing a novel [again]. This one = I had doubts about my ability to be the narrator I needed to be. But I own the story now; I made it, it's there, and simply needs to be told.

———

I've been worrying about my direction with visual art and it's making me hesitant, not helped by the struggle for priority between the two (art versus writing). The art will fall into place when I'm ready for it? Notice = I'm avoiding the studio – if I can get myself in there and start again, I won't stop. Fuck misery; it's a bitch and I won't be its slave.

———

Thursday, 7th January, 2010.

Empty Nest

After getting the act of whining down to a fine art when it comes to my longing to be alone, I feel sad now because there's nobody here but me.

I dropped Son at a friend's house for the night, and First-Born's away. Isn't this what I wanted? To know that my kids are safe but more importantly safe *somewhere else*, so that I can finally be calm and just work? Yes, but this morning Son made a comment about leaving home after he finishes secondary school (he's starting Year 10). I'm stupidly surprised that he wants to leave me. Surely I'm a joy to live with?

The crazy thing is that I expect him to leave when he's ready and am not the smothering type, but here I am alone and suddenly I'm worrying about them leaving for good. What if he said it because he doesn't like me? Can you imagine a more irrational question? I need to slap myself out of this.

It's just, tonight's what life will be like, and it's *empty*. The "empty nest" concept is *apt*. I'm being an idiot. It feels empty because it's not a happy break and I'm having my guts ripped out so often I don't have time to grow them back. If life's empty now it's because I've allowed it to be that way. I have a lot of people to be with and I don't go out of my way to be with them, so it's up to me to change that. And I will. And by the time kids leave home things will be happier because they'll be older and First-Born'll be less hostile.

Reminds me, though, that I need to provide an environment worth living in. In the meantime, write. Because look at this big, empty house. I've done research today, will convert that to story tomorrow. After this quality Pep Talk, I'm not gonna squander the time.

Saturday, 9th January, 2010.

Empty Nest II

This is how you do empty: you get up early, you go for a long walk, you pull the weeds from your main vegie garden before the sun's even finished rising and voilà, you've started the day with a sense of satisfaction.

Then you mimic Friend Girl A, who writes like a maniac when she's sitting at a table, and discover that writing at a table is fun. When you write at a table you don't even *fall asleep on the job*.

Piece o' cake. I tackled the difficult chapter yesterday. One I was avoiding, forgot to mention. Not really avoiding, I guess, but looking at and poking with a stick, because it was like a dead thing you find washed up on the beach but can't quite identify. I was unsure about turning a non-event chapter into an eventful chapter, but I'm so pleased with what I've done. That unfamiliar little world I'm creating is coming together so well I'm walking inside it without tripping.

Doesn't make me any more interesting outside of the novel, even though I had a bit of serendipity because of it. When I picked Son up from The Friend's house, The Friend's Mother told me about The Husband, who works in shipping. She told me how the financial crisis has affected shipping, which makes the landscape I took my characters through that morning so appropriate I had trouble not squealing.

Then I brought First-Born home and they were grumpy and I plummeted, but when I dropped them back to another friend's place they were so sweet they even kissed me goodbye.

Son's also at another friend's house today and they're both not back until tonight. It's quiet. I'm set up on the couch with my notebooks and the air conditioner, and life is good. Ish. Good enough.

———

Tuesday, 11th January, 2010.

The Answer is "Not Very"

How nice am I really? The impulse was there to do a monumental niceness, but I made myself wait-and-see. The old me wouldn't have waited – she would've jumped in and saved the day. Everybody loved the old me. Thank goodness I'm new and improved.

First-Born's Friend has nowhere to go. I like this friend. She lent me *The Kite Runner*, which I read a few days ago (it depressed the hell outa me; humans – bad). She watched *Sharkwater* with me when it first arrived, and I give her copies of *Whale Wars* and *The Cove* and other oceanic documentaries as I get them. She reads Chuck Palahniuk and we talk books. All of the things that I can only half-do with First-Born. Half? Quarter. Less.

This friend left her soak of a mother because she didn't get along with the mother's boyfriend; that sad scenario, where a mother lets her daughter leave and her boyfriend stay. Couldn't go to live with her father because he's a reclusive, pale, gangly, hepatitis-riddled man with a methadone lifestyle. First-Born confided something to me about that but I promised not to tell anybody about it, so let's just say, if you have stockpiles of methadone in your many fridges, HIDE THEM FROM YOUR TEENAGE DAUGHTER.

She went to live with her twenty-something brother, who has Asperger's and bought a one-bedroom flat in Carlton. She's had to share his bedroom, one curtain serving as a wall. Enormous amount of board to pay. Not a good story. Lately he's been difficult, partly because he can't stand couples, in fact would like to kill all couples, and First-Born's Friend has a boyfriend but has to hide the fact. Has to hide many things. Which would be a helluva lot easier if Asperger's Brother hadn't used his Asperger-Brilliance to hack into her computer and read all of her msn thingies, causing a great deal of trouble.

Long story short, with nowhere else to go, she came here. They all come here. The residual parts of the old me love that they do this, but only in theory. So I held back, overcoming the raw impulse to say *'Come and live with us'*. I confided the impulse to Son and he said *'Please, no'*. The smell of that crappy tinned soup she eats polluting our kitchen. I braved the fumes and made salad sammiches for dinner and made her eat one. Again, as with the roast, she was amazed by how good real food can be. The most normal salad sammich you can imagine, not even fancy. Of course I want to take her in.

I could have fed her real soup while she studied all year for her VCE. I could have nurtured her, it would've been like having three children at home instead of two, and she might have made First-Born more family-friendly. Just like I always wanted.

But anyway, fuck orphans. By *'Come and stay here for a few days'* I did NOT mean come here and party all night. They all know my struggle with sleep (CAUSED BY THEM IN THE FIRST PLACE – I'M A NERVOUS WRECK) and they know the rules. But they stayed up. I used earplugs, but was stressed. I had to make them go to First-Born's room because they were making too much noise. First-Born smoked on the balcony; it came in through my bedroom window. I called out *'Are you smoking?'* [nicely]; they answered *'Would you just PISS OFF'*.

They'd promised to go to bed at 1 am, but First-Born's Friend didn't make her way downstairs to the spare bedroom until 4:20 am. I know this because she woke me up. My alarm was due to go off in less than an hour so I didn't go back to sleep. I got a grand total of less than 4 hours' sleep. Every time she stays, I don't get to sleep. *Every single time*. If that didn't happen, I'd welcome her with open arms.

No way in hell am I gonna be nice now. I worked hard to get a good rhythm going. My body can't do this. How do you help teenagers when they're just so damn revolting? Maybe I'm hard-arsed, but I think being on the streets might make them so much less selfish.

Still Tuesday, 11th January, 2010.

A Bit of a Jog and a Spray Bottle

I don't want to alarm anybody [namely myself], but the above title is Son's bushfire evacuation plan. If there's a job for a Panic Merchant going anywhere I'm absolutely not going to get it, because I can't raise panic in anybody. When I drill them with the facts (i.e. *we're all gonna die!*) my kids just shrug it off and tell me that if a fire comes through they'll escape down the back path. On foot. Carrying a spray bottle to keep them cool and ward off flames.

And here's me spending a good part of every warm day with even a hint of breeze sniffing at the air for signs of smoke.

What does a mother do in the face of such lack of fear? How do I scare the bejeezus out of them so that they'll take the threat seriously? *WE LIVE RIDICULOUSLY CLOSE TO A FOREST!*

It doesn't help that I've been a bit lax. It's just, you wouldn't think the sun could burn an ant through a magnifying glass, it's been so gentle this summer. January already and today's our first Extreme Fire Warning day.

The truth is I've been only almost-ready since before summer. I read the run-for-your-life bushfire guides and know exactly how to evacuate. It's all there in my lists – so many lists. What to take, what to do, what to buy to be prepared. If I haven't gotten beyond the list stage it's only because... just because.

So a few days ago I finally took all of our photos and one of my [sold] drawings down to store in Mum and Dad's bungalow. (Last year I only got around to doing this on the evening of a day when I'd watched plumes of smoke rising from the Upwey fires on the other side of the Dandenongs, as I rode the train home from the studios. This year I consider myself more advanced.)

Last night, when I read the warning, I started to really plan. Not the plan I'd already planned, but a tentative plan that relies upon fires coming through not today, but some later fire-day when I'm more ready. Today's like practise. I've packed clothes, made piles of my more valued and hard-to-replace books, and have only to grab my boxes of old diaries [pre-blog], which I'd forgotten about completely.

The cats are all inside, ready to grab and shove into the car if need be. I might have to leave the kids behind to see if their on-foot plan works, because it seems I want to save more than I thought I would, and they just won't fit in the car.

I promised myself that on Extreme days we'd leave regardless, so I hope I'm not being stupid by thinking an Extreme day that hasn't been book-ended by other Extreme days is a gentle kind of extreme.

The funny thing is, the morning was calm and beautiful, and after a walk and getting the bird nets over my vegies (just in time before the tomatoes turn red), I had a shower and lay down on the balcony to enjoy the last of the shade before the day hots up. I lay down with a book that I'd grabbed from beside my bed, and that book just happened to be *Things We Didn't See Coming*. I'd forgotten about the first story being about a father panicking about the Y2K bug, in which the loading up of the car, and the family's scepticism, resembles my fire evacuation preparations just a little too closely. I sit here with a large packed bag at my feet and feel a bit stupid.

Please world, if you're going to burn do it some other time, so that we're not caught off guard. If you give me time to buy proper boots and goggles and gloves for the kids, that'd be lovely. Give me time to sell the house first and move out of this death trap, even better. Ta.

Wednesday, 12th January, 2010.

Catch What?

Recently Son was being his saintly self and helping me break branches up to put into the trailer for a tip run. He did his usual thing, all neat and tidy-like, and his technique plus my technique = we now have such a spunky arrangement of branches in that trailer it's gonna be a shame to throw them out.

Anyways, not the point. He was more reluctant this time. Bored shitless. So I gave him my iPod, so he could listen to *Catch 22* while he worked, thinking he'd love it. I was so excited!

But then a strange thing happened. He didn't *get* it. He kept pressing *Pause* to ask questions and I had to explain to him that it was meant to be funny. But he still didn't get it, and I'll tell you why. Because the humour's *mean*. He took everything literally. He couldn't find the censoring of letters funny because it meant people wouldn't receive their letters. Why would anybody do something mean like that?

The way I was raised is, the only time you're allowed to be mean is if it's *funny*. Mean is good! Mean is hilarious! Maybe I need to make him watch a few series of M*A*S*H*?

Son gets brilliant school reports, being a smart little chicken, but his English teacher this year suggested he read alternative kinds of fiction, to expand his reading experience. He reads and writes like you wouldn't believe, but it's all fantasy genre-ish, often the same Robin Hobb books over and over. So now I have to source alternative books, but I have to choose them carefully. He can work his way up to *Catch 22*? An emergency situation if ever there was.

Thursday, 14th January, 2010.

Pest Control

Ah, the whinging and moaning going on inside my head. I try to get up early, they stay up stupidly late. I try to sleep in, they get up early. The nervous-wreckness comes from not being able to determine my own schedule, having no routine, and not being able to predict when or how seriously I'm going to be interrupted.

Time to accept [again] that you can't win, Mother. You sacrificed your life the minute you gave birth. You didn't think it'd be literal, but there ya go. Even though you're not dead yet.

I don't know how I'm squeezing the chapters out, but I am. Yesterday's was written during a quick morning session before the House Guest got up at 7 am and broke my concentration. But I read it this morning and again, it's what I wanted it to be. I'm glad it's done, even if it is skeletal. The cheery-uppy approach here is *Something's Better Than Nothing*.

The problem is that after I've been interrupted, I do nothing. I waste hours and hours a day trying to negotiate the problem of wasted time. I don't mind if the time's being used for something like being with the kids, but when I spend it just completely lost because I've got too many things to choose from and no mental space to work in, I mourn the loss of it. Giving up early yesterday, I was downright depressed so I went to the video shop. I hired videos. I watched.

Synechdoche New York won me over before it even started – I was in film love as soon as I heard that little voice singing about worms eating their head. What a strange and funny film, the kind of funny that makes you laugh so deep inside that by the time it's bubbled up to the surface it doesn't break but makes you smile all over the place.

Beautiful Kate: made me cry.

District 9: I had no idea that this was such a seriously funny film. So politically beautiful. Awful and stunning and psychologically astute. Was it marketed like that? Why was I not paying attention? So clever it cheered me up.

Anyways, this morning the babes were up early again. Bye bye writing time. And House Guest has the TV on [in the morning!] which is like a crime in this house. But because I'm big spirited I'm going to use the time to rearrange the house a bit. Something I've been thinking about doing constantly, but have been too overwhelmed to do. I just stand in doorways staring at the space, trying to work out how to do it. From the outside I must look like a mannequin.

When rich people renovate they shop and design and hire cabinetmakers. All I can do is fiddle the atmospherics. No problem, that's all I need. Plus an exterminator for the teenage-guest problem. Who I wish I could accommodate, I really do. It's just, you know. If I could feel happy again it'd be okay. Maybe rearranging the space will make that happen.

Friday, 15th January, 2010.

When Good Chick Flicks Go Bad

Well, I've worked hard, and rewarded myself with a crappy chick flick tonight, with Son. I have a rule about crappy chick flicks – I'll only watch good crappy ones, not bad crappy ones. So I'm confused. Son promised me that *The Ugly Truth* is a good movie. He said it's funny.

We're talking about Son here, who has a lovely soft and protective side but is also archetypically male, in that he doesn't do schmaltz or care about some of the things I – archetypically female – care about.

We normally have similar taste in movies, and love comedies, but as I watched this movie I was more amused by him than by its bad-crappy jokes and overact-ory performances. It's so clichéd and sentimental, but he laughed, I tell you, and really did find it funny. What an insight into Son's mind. I think I'm stunned.

———

My workroom and studio space isn't looking like a glorified storeroom anymore. Pluralise that, seeing as I'm referring to four rooms. Had to overcome guilt at wanting to use the spare room, but in the end built some painting racks (more hard work; I hurt my finger with a hammer!), and that was the only place I could put them. I've now officially taken over the whole of downstairs. A despot, no less.

———

Was going through the kids' old school books and found a journal First-Born wrote for school. Yes I read it. Don't judge me, it's not like a real diary. Anyway it said:

> *While dropping off mum's friend at the station I saw the MEANEST bitch from primary school her name is Nikki and her & her friends were laughing at mum's clothes & her messy hair. that [%#$@]! At least my mum doesn't leave me at a train station to go to st Kilda with a few friends! I'm proud of my mum & at least she cares about me! I'm glad she doesn't let me go far away without an adult, it's too dangerous!*

Gosh, remember when First-Born loved me? Even though I was [was?] so daggy [!!].

———

Saturday, 16th January, 2010.

The Purge

Still cleaning things up, only this time I've been going through every loose pile of crap in my studio and work rooms and throwing things out. More out than I've ever thrown things before, and most of it's so personal it's like skinning myself alive.

I've been ripping up some of the notebooks I wrote into when I was young, saving others. Hating what I was. Hating the stupid, rapturous voice of hope and the ridiculous sunny outlook. And I've realised I've always gotten things wrong – what a dick.

But also, I've been reading through old diaries (I found them!), things that are retrospectively painful to read. Skeleton in the closet-ish. Not dramatic like an uncle who shagged his goat, but serious stuff, like First-Born's small pleas for my company during times when they were pushing me away, and my inability to do anything about it. Happy things, too, but still. Reading through my diaries is like sticking needles into my own eyes.

I know I need to keep these things, but I also hate that I have them. Because after reading bits of them it feels unnatural to wear the past so close to your skin, to let it clutter up the present. I'm repulsed. And yet, I know that at other times I'll read them and be fascinated. So I can't chuck them.

What to do? This compulsive writing thing I do seems really wrong at the moment. It's like not letting yourself forget what needs to pass into nothing. Maybe that's what's wrong with humans, this keeping of stuff.

It's like I'm punishing myself, but it's good to clean up the cluttered corners. Soon everything will belong somewhere. Some of it on the scrapheap. By the time we sell the house, some of the hard work will already have been done. Pat on the back for all the effort.

Wednesday, 20th January, 2010.

Them Streets, They Smell Like Ocean

I rescind the feeling of guilt about having too much space to myself. Pregnant Friend (who needs to be defined than by something other her breeding status, or I'll be sent to feminist purgatory) has the perfect house. If I could steal and plant it on a property full of fruit trees I would. Her house has attic storage spaces and enormous floor-boardy rooms and offices, and a studio, and room upstairs for tenants that she feeds and waters, which just happens to include something I'd call a very pretty and sunny writing room, even though she doesn't write.

I want her life. Because of its calm, its happiness, its bright future and its security. I love 'er to bits and she deserves it. Maybe I'll have that kind of life when I deserve it. When I can make things go right.

Anyways, after a beautiful lunch inside my friend's perfect life, I picked the smelly boys up from Luna Park and took them with me to visit Older Ethnic Friend in her tiny flat in Balaclava, thus transcending class boundaries aplenty in the space of mere hours. Here we forget houses and focus on their produce, because that's what all good houses are; glorified studios where we produce work, and don't you forget it.

Older Ethnic Friend is the ethnic-est person I know. It's in every sensibility she spills into the world, so that her stories and poetry, her plays and her art all have this vivid kind of beauty, but because of the way she structures things they wouldn't be palatable to a contemporary Australian audience. It's like a cabbage covered with chocolate.

Also she smiles without knowing her teeth are chock full of carrot pieces.

So I had to laugh when she was showing me her new paintings (hundreds of them – I haven't been there for a while), and she got to a series she produced as illustrations for a children's story. So well-intentioned, but so wrong. The storyline's not mine to give, but let's just say it's something about a cute dog belonging to a woman who has her body mutilated by thugs, who then opens a sanctuary for tortured cats and is visited regularly by a little girl who was raped by her uncle.

Ideal bedtime reading for children! Funny! But also strangely inspiring. She works and works and works, shut away in that world of hers. I love it. I love that I saw her after hours of long conversation with Pregnant Friend, who's also an artist. It's nice when you step outside of your suffocating own life. What a good, beach-smelling day.

Friday, 22nd January, 2010.

Sweet Captive

I'm bunny sitting. I don't mind this, apart from the fact that the distinctive smell of rabbit urine is *not* a welcome element in this household. So I hope the emergency *'just for a few days'* beggary holds true, although I suspect it doesn't. I suspect he'll be here for weeks, and that'll be difficult because I'm against rabbits being kept as domestic pets, and it breaks my heart to see this proud animal in a hutch as much as it does to see birds in cages and fish in tanks.

He's a rescue bunny, not a general pet, and he needs his humans. This I remind myself. Still, as a conscientious objector, don't be surprised if I sneak him rose petals through the prison walls. Bake him a cake with a nail file in it, so he can escape. Give him a spoon so that he can dig his way to China?

Monday, 25th January, 2010.

This Morning

It was a beautiful hot chocolate. The powder had spilled onto the cup rim and made a crusty trickle down the side of the mug.

Yesterday morning. I sought and found old stories, ones I'd forgotten I'd written. I was a busy little thing back then, wasn't I? So many. Some of the firsts surprised me by being something other than crap. Things I'd chucked onto the never-send-anywhere pile, which maybe should have been sent after all.

Except, there were even firster firsts, the ones I'd really-really forgotten. The ones I *should* forget. Or not really, seeing as they were the cutting of teeth. Something to be buried away on a dark shelf.

But still. Such a busy little thing. And it's not just the stories; it's art and everything. During the big clean up over the past week or so I've come across records of so many activities, and I realise that I was very go-gettem. I must have thought everything was possible [before life crushed me].

For the past few years I've been too afraid to be that busy. Not trusting my instincts. Or actually, that's not true. Just not having time to develop instincts. Doing other things, like painting and drawing and writing novels. That has to change. Something like back to what it was before. Except, also with painting and drawing and writing novels.

No more fear, is the point.

Tuesday, 26th January, 2010.

On Reading

People who start their poems with "oh"; people who use "oh" anywhere within their poetry [unplayfully]; people who write poetry "after" somebody else; people who quote inside their poetry; people who write bland prose and disguise it as poetry with frilly line arrangements; people who think poetry excuses age-old syntax; people who think rapture requires ancient reference and antiquated voice; people who think every single moment of rapture deserves capturing.

Please, stop *doing* that. Or at least, *not quite so often.*

Friday, 29th January, 2010.

Is Long, Less Travelled, The Long and Winding

I recommend reading a negative review about *The Road* before going to see it. I went last night and went reluctantly, because I had a movie ticket that was about to expire and couldn't waste it. Plus, free popcorn.

I even regretted it when the movie started, because I'd been working hard all day (two deadlines down, two to go) and was hungry for story. I sat there and thought *oh no – nothing happens, I have to sit here and watch nothing happen.* That's because I believed the negative review, which claimed a) bad acting on the Big He's part; b) great acting on the Little He's part; c) brilliantly imagined landscape; and d) a failure to utilise the novel's more dramatic moments.

Wrong! It was very dramatic, and very moving. The acting was wonderful, the story fully realised, and frightening, and I cried all the way home. Most effectively, it conveyed how cruel it would be to subject a child to that kind of life, exaggerating fears we carry about our children before they're born and well into their lives, to match the extremes of the imagined circumstance. (I'm assuming, here, that everybody's instincts are like mine; you won't have waited for bad things to happen to be worried, you'll have wept over all of the possible suffering your children will ever undergo IN ADVANCE.) It taps into the empathetic thread that binds you to your children so directly.

Not just that; it's an exploration of the suffering people can/will undergo at the hands of other human beings, just one more recent work that's successfully dug into the dark animalism of human nature. (No offence to animals.)

There were elements within the novel that I questioned, mainly to do with its simplicity, but those elements didn't surface within the film. Read the book first, then get ye to a cinema and be satisfied.

February 2010

Monday, 1st February, 2010.

Signs from Ye Gods

First day of school! Not for me, but for my kids, as in kids *plural*. I knew it was going to feel good, but I didn't know it was going to feel *this* good. Up early having their breakfasts and making their lunches, a bit of hilarity on the way to the bus stop – it all stinks of normal.

It's not that I get the house to myself, but that I get the internal peace and quiet that comes with knowing that both children are out in the world doing something productive. Four days a week. For the first time since June last year, my kids are safe and where they belong.

Plus the five-thirty bird is back. No offence to kookaburras, but it was a bit rude of them to displace the five-thirty bird, who I much prefer waking up to (at 5:30 am). Kookaburras are for afternoon and evening, and it's probably their fault First-Born wasn't going to school. Now that the five-thirties are back, things will go back to being as they should be.

I'll just temper that with a realistic thought: I should suck this up, because it may not last. Here's to today, then. [*Whoo!*]

Thursday, 4th February, 2010.

Land Down Asunder

I won't express an opinion because I'm not as informed as I'd need to be to justify one. But. I will say I'm disappointed to discover that *Kookaburra Sits in The Old Gum Tree* was composed/written by an actual songwriter/composer (Marion Sinclair) and wasn't, as I've always thought, something discovered in the landscape. Kind of there, always was there, in your face, never wasn't there.

Disappointed also that *Land Down Under* – which is like a cross between an anthem and sacred hymn for anybody who was alive in the eighties – has been soiled by a legal battle that declares it less than original.

A question: even if the flute section was referencing *Kookaburra*, was it doing so as a malicious act of theft, or was it there because *Kookaburra* is as quintessentially Australian as *Land Down Under* has become? Doesn't it honour the tune, by incorporating it into an original song as an essential rhythm, so much like a heartbeat that we didn't even notice it was there inside the song until now?

It's not good to not-acknowledge a source, but still. Motive has to count. Motive and a counter acknowledgement that the song is an artefact that contributes such a happy feeling to our national identity that it shouldn't be punished unless the alleged "theft" can be shown to be malicious. I want to believe it was good natured. I heard somebody mumble something about it being accidental – yes, that's what I want to believe. It could easily be more a case of art *interacting* than art *being stolen and peddled* under a trenchcoat, with evil intent.

Litigation's taking one of the most fun things about us and making it not fun anymore. As for Mr Simpson's '*It's a big win for the underdog*', followed by a pledge to suck as much money from the situation as possible, well. I'm biting my tongue. But try laughing now, kookaburra, without sounding just a little more sinister than you did yesterday.

On second thoughts, let's not bite our tongue. '*It's a big win for the underdog*', he said, but wasn't the copyright bought by somebody else? Define *underdog*.

Wednesday, 10th February, 2010.

Me Tarzan, You Jane

It's my humble opinion that female bodies can do really good things, other than being penetrated by a penis and giving birth. So it strikes me as odd that the female opening dance displays on *So You Think You*

Can Dance Australia are so hip-swingy and coquettish while the boys' opening dance displays are spunky and acrobatic.

It doesn't stop there. The female group dance tonight was about as interesting as an empty speech bubble, with all of those come-fuck-me hand gestures and cheap sexual tempters that, ironically, are too far from sexy to be taken seriously. Kids playing grown-ups? So what's with the choreography? Apparently it's a common belief that female dancers en masse are worthy of nothing more than superficial tripe?

The boys, in what Son described as gay porn costumes, got to do back flips! They break/broke danced! Aren't they clever! No sticky-outy do-me-up-the-arse poses!

I'm wondering if there's an unwritten law stating that women are only allowed to do those things when flung about by men. I don't know why we don't just stick them in a frock and stand them in a dimly lit window with a sign saying '*Sex for Sale*'.

I'm also wondering if it's always been like this, or if it's getting tacky and over-confident. The show. Because I tape it so that I can fast-forward through the monotonous and ostentatiously weepy talky bits, I wouldn't know. All of that revolting *caring*. (Can't we care with dignity? If writers told people when to care so sloppily we'd be raked over the coals. Rule #something-or-other = let your reader work it out for themselves.)

It could be I've had enough of reality tv. (Which is amazing, considering I hardly watch it.) It's just – dance, you know? How do you not like watching people dance? Social evolution on many fronts is just an illusion, granted, but evolution *has* happened. So if they're going to honour the human animal and emphasise female flirtatiousness, then they need to do it intelligently. Please.

Saturday, 13th February, 2010.

Assertiveness 101

I had to complain. Not the whiny complaining you get away with behind somebody's back, but the confronting type that leads to resolution of a whopping big three-hundred-dollar problem. It was supposed to be a one-hundred-and-fifty-dollar problem, so you can see that I had problems on top of my problems.

I felt and still feel sorry for the photographer because our air conditioner was broken and it was one of the hottest nights of the week. I could measure his effort by the sweat patches on his shirt; first just on the small of his back, then half way and all the way up his back, then those revealed on the front when he turned around, and finally the all-over dripping wetness of him. Really, he needs to fitten up, maybe walk more, eat less cheese.

He's such a nice guy, but I've used him before and am loyal to a fault, so when he started doing things less than perfectly I expressed concern but let him continue. I thought that maybe he – being the photographer and me just the artist with the paintings – knew what he was doing.

Bad call on my part. He took so, so long (hence double the cost) to line up each painting, and I could see just by looking at the images that the tonal detail was obliterated by reflection. *Shouldn't we do this and that?* I suggested, but I'm just the artist, what would I know[?].

I was almost in tears when I later looked at and then tried to fix the images with Photoshop. I wondered how somebody could be so careless with detail. The reflection was a nightmare, and that's something he, as the photographer, was supposed to be able to deal with. Could he not see? To sum things up, there was no way I could use the photos, and I really need them for portrait requests and gallery submissions. So I waited over a day, and then pretended to be an assertive person and sent a complaining e-mail. It was blunt. I spelled it out.

It seems to have worked, so I can now tell you that the way to be blunt in a complaining e-mail is to apologise for being blunt in the first paragraph. Then you can go hell for leather. You can be the person who sends their plate of food back to the chef in a restaurant. Haven't you always wanted to be that person?

No! But sometimes you have to be, or you get ripped off.

It's been excruciating because he returned for a fix-it shoot. I felt really really mean, and was very aware of being the Difficult Customer. If he was a waiter he'd have spat in my soup. But it was good, because at my suggestion he used the polarising filter, and lined them up where

I said they should be lined up (no indirect reflection from furniture), and in the end Son and I held up black curtains at the side to stop the glare from flattening out the surface. It was so easy it only took 40 minutes, and now I have properly documented paintings. Also I have a bigger ego, because I know nothing and yet I solved the problem.

And I fell in love with painting all over again, just being able to see the tonal subtlety of my work as he struggled with it. Made me want to paint. More ego – this could be good for me.

When I finish with feeling squeamish I'm going to feel really proud of myself. This'll cure me of my loyalty problem, because I know I'll be too embarrassed to use him again. And actually, I can put that exorbitant amount of money towards lighting equipment and do it myself from now on. (Famous last words.) It cost me about $75 more than it should have and I haven't triple checked the images yet but still, a happy ending is a good ending. I'm so relieved.

(Air-conditioning = was just the fuse! There's no end to my problem fixery! That poor man.)

Sunday, 14th February, 2010.

Bill Loves Ben Loves Little Weeeed

The weirdest thing. The sunflowers I planted in a row at the top of our back garden to make my children happy are in full bloom, but nobody seems to be any happier. I watched them grow sturdy and then bud and then open, and then I waited for the kids to bat an eyelid, be surprised, and smile.

What a crazy anti-climax. Perhaps I should have planted them in the lounge room? On the kitchen bench? In the doorways to their bedrooms?

They were supposed to make me happy, too, but I guess I was taking a risk because my happiness is filtered through my children. I'm happy when I'm allowed to be. Which makes the last week or so a tough call, because First-Born's in a particularly bad mood. Self-esteem issues, I know, but more than that.

Another manuscript argument, another me agreeing that they should read it (I didn't change the terms – has to be on my laptop with me in the room and no way of them making a copy), another week of them avoiding being at home and therefore not reading the manuscript after all, another forgetting-of-manuscript altogether and being so hostile that any possibility of me letting them read it is again obliterated.

And then the ultimate in happiness crushing; First-Born stayed home from school on Friday because they didn't think the classes they were supposed to attend were worth it. So by the time I was up on Friday morning my stash of happiness had run out. Friday was, to me, a signal that this year's going to be exactly the same as last year. I can't do last year again. Emotionally, physically, psychologically, *cannot*.

I skulked away in my now not-empty house, tried to motivate myself to do some work. Failed, just like my sunflowers have failed, and they try so hard with their happy yellow faces.

Now I wait to see what happens. Wait for First-Born's hostility to abate, for some sign of friendliness which I can't see coming. Have made myself draw, but have only managed it slowly. Easing my way in. It's hard to learn that life and happiness are too complicated to be managed by the blooming of a flower. We're entering our sixth year of hostility. Not that I'm counting. But please don't do this for too long, child of mine. *Please*.

Wednesday, 17th February, 2010.

I'll Tell You Where to Go

If you feel like slashing your wrists and are looking for inspiration, go and see *Precious*. (Was it based on real experience? Don't know. Are there really people like that in the world? Yes. Maybe. Yes. Should fiction like that be closely linked to real experience for the sake of integrity? I think so. So was it? Is it? Must find out.)

Unrelated matter = *So You Think You Can Dance* is getting better. But how boring sitting in front of the tv. Just, boring.

Get Over It

The person who goes to the booking site after falling for the offer of a cheap fare, then realises the cheap fare sucks because it's for an unnecessarily long and complicated flight, so searches for the next best thing and then it's *gotcha* – the airline sucked you in and you forgot that there are other airlines and didn't compare prices until it was too late... I am that person!

I just paid over eighty dollars more than I needed to and I can't forgive myself. Not thinking, trying to please other people and what's the point anyway? First-Born will pull out last minute.

Makes me feel alone. Nowhere to express my stupidness. I hate myself right now.

Friday, 19th February, 2010.

Burning Twice as Bright

I tried to consult the oracle, but not enough people talk about sunflowers, and when they do they don't say anything useful. So when I google about the falling petals and find that somebody has asked '*How long do sunflowers last?*', it guts me to read that they last '*about five days in a vase*'.

People cut them?

It's a good thing I sucked a lot of happiness out of them after all, because most of the petals have fallen off. I need a sunflower advisor to tell me if this is normal. Does it mean they won't seed? What's the point of happiness that won't go to seed? You see what I'm getting at, yes? Everything's so transient!!

I have some beautiful photographs and they're going on the wall. They're going everywhere. But I'll hesitate before growing them again; as far as symbolic things go, it matters that they didn't stay in bloom for very long. I don't think I can handle loving and losing like that.

Ten down, six to go.

Saturday, 20th February, 2010.

C'mon Aussie C'moffit

Was it ever a possibility that Mary MacKillop wasn't going to be canonised, d'ya think? Was the Catholic Church really going to risk alienating their patriotic Australian followers?

Of course not, this one was in the bag. The deliberations went along the lines of: *let's perpetuate fairytales; let's bring a colossal amount of tourism to Rome for the festival; let's inject some hysteria into the masses; let's distract people from the shitfulness of human nature; let's not spend the energy this will take on practical things such as, say, fixing the planet; let's buy souls and sell Mary merchandise.*

This kind of delusion makes the whole world and Real Life as fun as Japanese Disneyland. You know the actors performing the characters there aren't allowed to tell people what they do because it would break the illusion?

Oh lawdy, what a pain in the arse the Catholic religion's going to be this year. Like one big military sign up. Celebrate the woman's life by all means, but by encouraging the Catholics you're going to be ensuring that this is at the forefront of current affairs, and I predict we're going to see an enormous setback in human intellectual evolution.

Thursday, 25th February, 2010.

Many Hats Maketh a Warm Head

I've been juggling, but so gently this time. Art school resumes next week, so the juggling has to be faultless. Because *look at this calm. Look at this sunny day.* I'm juggling eggs, not bowling pins, so if I drop one the sunny goes splat.

I'm outrageously happy, sort of, because I've been locking myself away to write. And I've been swimming. Alive and all that. The whole world's wonderful when you're twisting your body to turn at the end of the lane. All of that gliding through water.

Now I just have to add drawing to the sequence of Things I'm Doing Now and I'll have perfection.

So anyway where was I? Things happening all over the place. But this writing hat is what has me so happy. After speaking to Secret Agent a couple of weeks ago I've revised my paternity manuscript again, and this time I went that step further, cutting the passages I knew I should have cut in the first place but didn't want to.

Feedback has been consistently positive but also suggested that the voice is too confronting and prevents reader empathy from happening early enough. And I know what they mean; when I wrote the first draft it was like I'd just discovered a secret power and I let it loose. I've mentioned already spending the years since then trying to rope the beast in, but this time I had to tame it once and for all. I love the way Secret Agent expressed it; he said, '*I love her by the end of the novel – now I think we need to love her at the beginning as well*'.

Love? I can do love. Love's my specialty. I feel as though I've just done the last bit of growing up that I needed to do for that particular work. You can hear the maturity in my voice, yes? And I promise I didn't squeal when Prodigal Friend rang me to tell me she read the file I sent her and said '*Awesome... unbelievable... phenomenal... I want to read and then reread it*', which is just what the middle manuscript appraiser had said.

I'm not quite up-myself, but I am glowing with the praise. Also though, I have to be realistic. They said it'd be hard to find a publisher gutsy enough to take the risk, but that it *would* happen. I'm the only one who doubts that; I don't know why I feel so happy, because I just don't think I'm that lucky. Prodigal insists [always] that I'm on the verge of being discovered, but that's because she's naive about the industry. That's the way we imagine it'll happen when we're young and stupid. I know better (as in, that only happens to Other People).

Still, happy happy. Maybe it's just the feeling you get when you complete a Job Well Done? Or maybe it's because I've spent the last week or so inside that world, and have managed to make that world cleaner?

I want it out there – the more I read it, the more I want it to happen. What a bummer that I'm the child who always wanted a bike for Xmas, but each year was given a new doll. So I'll send this draft to Secret Agent, let myself feel proud, and then it's onto the next thing. No looking back.

Still Thursday, 25th February, 2010.

Why I Don't Need Dignity

There's a golden rule I have: wait a day or so before you write about something that makes you angry. As in, calm yourself down, so that you know what you write is measured and rational. That same golden rule applies when you're excited about good things people have said about your work. It's a gush-prevention strategy.

Usually by the next day I don't want to write about it anymore, because by then I'm embarrassed. Like when you're a little girl and somebody tells you you're pretty, and you want to tell everyone else that so-and-so said you're pretty (because it's so rare for you to hear it when your little sister is the pretty one), but you can't because that'd make you sound stupid. And kinda desperate. Because everybody knows you're not really pretty, and that so-and-so's opinion must be the exception, not the rule. Telling people about it isn't going to make you any prettier than you were before so-and-so opened their big fat mouth.

That's probably it, isn't it – this thing I'm so close to, finished but unpublished, so allegedly publishable but nobody will touch it. Sounds like a good excuse for desperation to me.

March 2010

Sunday, 7th March, 2010.

Awww

I love 'em when they're a drunken. I love 'em anyway, but drunkenness becomes them especially. At first I said no when First-Born's Friend asked me to pick them up just when I was about to hop into bed, it being horrible driving weather and late and me wanting to teach them that they can't just go out and then expect me to drop everything on a school night. I thought a night of sleeping in their own vomit might do them some good.

Mother of the year!! (They're in a safe place, I should add – I wouldn't just leave them stranded if they weren't.)

But then First-Born got on the phone and said *please* and said that Swedish had slept with other people and that they felt like crap and suddenly they were my baby again, so I braved the roads (really – horrible driving weather) and there they were in the gutter, waiting for me to pick them up. With their friend. Which could have been a nightmare, seeing as I'd only brought one bucket with me, but luckily they'd emptied themselves before I got there.

Gory details aside, it gets lovely. (Just, overlook the smell.) During their drunken ramblings and promises to themself to never drink again, First-Born looked at me and said *'Ya know, you're my mother and I don't even know you – isn't that ridiculous?'*.

Their friend got dibs on the severing of Swedish's dick, so I gracefully took second pickings and got dibs on the skewering of his eyeballs. That's when First-Born took me into a headlock hug and said *'Thanks Mum'*, and then didn't let me go. It was so sweet I kept driving like that, my head sideways and my nose scrunched up.

They haven't exactly been going to school, but it could be that this year's salvageable after all.

Chris Fontana

Wednesday, 10th March, 2010.

Under My Umberella-ellah-ellah

I'm not in the habit of stealing from children. It's just that when one of them leaves their little black umbrella in your house, something like THREE YEARS AGO, and after seeing it floating around for a long time you eventually claim it for yourself, it becomes very difficult to give it back.

It was ages before I even realised that it belonged [formerly] to Son's best friend. And only then because he started asking for it back. Which I thought of as audacious, actually. Kinda stupid, I know, but this kid's here almost every weekend – often overnight – and over the past eight years of their friendship Son has only spent a day at their place about seven times, and only once overnight. Doing the maths on that, I've spent a lot of money feeding that growing, hungry boy, and as the umbrella would have cost them diddly squat in comparison, I think the gracious thing for them to do would be to just get over it.

Especially because by the time he asked for it, I'd grown fond of it. I might even love it. My own umbrella had broken. I walk every day, rain or shine, and this "new" one became my trusty companion through the rain bit. On hot nights in summer I flick it to its full extension without opening it and swing it around in front of me whenever I pass under a spider-potential tree. I need it. I don't even like its stumpy, ugly little handle. But you wouldn't see *me* leaving it in somebody's doorway and then not remembering to ask for it back for so long that it grows attached to its new owner.

Still, the weird thing is that every time I pick it up I think of it as having Other People Germs, so every time Son says (as he did yesterday) '*We still have Whatsisname's umbrella somewhere in our house, by the way*', the full extent of its grubby past makes me squirm. It starts screaming NOT MINE NOT MINE NOT MINE. It's like an *out damn spot* thing, only I don't think it's my guilty conscience speaking. It's the umbrella that seems soiled, not me.

Do I need to buy myself a new umbrella? Other people buy their own umbrellas, and theirs are always nicer, but my dishonestly acquired one has had its advantages. I know, for instance, that as soon as I buy a new one I'll leave it on the train or lose it at the studios or something. This one will stay put.

I really don't know what to do. I can't give it back, because that'd be admitting failure. To have spent three years on a prolonged theft and then just not succeed in pulling it off would be pathetic. I've managed to conceal its secret identity for this long, right? So why's it bugging me? Could it be that I don't want to hide my umbrella anymore? That I want to be able to hold my umbrella up high, knowing that I won't have my claim to it challenged?

Who knows. It's just time, is all. If I can bothered going shopping. Which I probably can't. Moot point, then; the umbrella stays.

———

Saturday, 13th March, 2010.

Get With the Program

Doesn't the idea that women are sexually passive belong somewhere back in the patriarchal fifties? As far as I know, women in our society fought off the imposition of lying still in the missionary position for sex decades ago. Hate to be the one to break it to the writer of a certain article on the subject of that tv show about cougars, but if you're surprised by the proactive sexual streak in the mature, married woman, then you're doing something wrong in bed. Plus you might want to consider that a woman who goes nuts over the younger man is probably monumentally disappointed in the man she's with. He's probably something like your age? Yes, tuck your ego back into your pants.

A couple of my friends fit the cougar profile, and they're not what I'd call representative of female sexuality. They're boring, actually. Simply, most women break out of repressive lifestyles at some point (as men do; it's called waking up from the rut that is modern life and taking measures to free yourself from self-imposed day-ins and day-outs), but some break out with less class than others.

No big deal, but if you're going to analyse it as a social phenomena you should at least get historical and sociological about it, rather than drooling over Courtney Cox's throbbing vagina. Now, excuse me while I go off and do my housework.

Wednesday, 17th March, 2010.

Stupid Day 1
Yesterday. Insomnia-style stupid. A body don't function without sleep. Great plans laid waste could make same body weep.

Tension in the household, too many ideas trying to resolve themselves into words and images, and a 12:32 am phone call from my mother, who was panicking because she got up to go to the toilet and found that my niece had left her house in the middle of the night with nothing but a note saying something about having remembered she had a dental appointment to go to the next day.

Teenagers! They wreck my sleep! I'd had one hour, and after that lay more awake than I've ever been in my life. ALL NIGHT.

Screwed = the day I'd planned. Went to studios in the afternoon only because I couldn't stand being at home. Long story.

That was yesterday. This time I'm lying awake still, full-on insomnia. Because of teenagers, who should be locked up in training camps until they're twenty-one.

Wednesday, 17th March, 2010.

Stupid Day 2
Today, which is technically still yesterday, because since my mother woke me with that phone call at 12:32 two sleeps ago I haven't slept. Golden Rule: DO NOT WAKE ME WITHIN AN HOUR OF MY FALLING ASLEEP or I will have to kill you, unless you're my mother in which case I'll forgive you and just torture myself with insomnia for nights on end.

Not Mum's fault. But now it's still me versus the darkness and a fully wired brain, too many ideas racing and unresolved. Plus there's still too much tension, as of Sunday morning, when I held a house meeting and discovered that First-Born still thinks the things they thought last year. Thinks them with swear words. Long story.

Downhill is so fast, innit? Two weeks ago everything was good and possible. Now I can't imagine good. What the fuck is good? Are you pulling my leg?

First-Born finally went to school yesterday (after over a week of no school), only then they didn't come home. Being WIDE AWAKE I heard them sneak in at 3:34 am, and within minutes received a loud text that started with '*Why the fuk did you turn the internet off...*'. And yet, they were considerate enough not to come downstairs to turn the internet on themself.

So anyway, Wednesday's dead now. How to go to studios? Alternatively, how to stay home? Can hardly string a sentence together. Can't stay home with them, can't go in to studios without sleep. That's just the kind of dilemma that could keep a person awake all night.

On the other hand – life in all its glory. I go into the studios, am excited like you wouldn't believe, and in my studio I get hugged and kissed and visited and talked to and talked at and you wouldn't know by looking at me that I go home to this.

Monday, 22nd March, 2010.

And Then What
I did Sydney. And then I cleaned out my fridge. What more can I say? It needed to be cleaned out. It's swallowed all of my miscellaneouses.

A girl can get swamped by all of these happenings. Perhaps a mental reckoning some other time.

Wednesday, 24th March, 2010.

The Broken English Incident
There were two student presentations during a seminar, and the first one went off with lights and bells. She had speed, she had eloquence, she'd done top-notch research. Then the lecturer did some talking, and

then the lecturer did some more talking. Which is why he's called a lecturer and not a teacher, and it's okay because he's fascinating. He bounces around on his seat like a little kid, riddled with excitement. Personally, I think he's ace.

But then Second Student started her presentation – more tea-light-candle than lights-and-bells. Even that's okay; we just waited patiently for her to get to the meat of her research. Only she didn't get the chance, because Lecturer took over. Not just a little; he took over everything but the turning of the slides.

When he started I wrote a note on my page to a friend asking '*Is he being racist, or does he always do this?*' (the second student's Asian), but within a few minutes it became obvious. After forty minutes there were no doubts; he *did not let her speak*. He said some amazing things and was as usual a joy to listen to, but we were all squirming because we wanted to hear what she had to say, and there wasn't a person in the room who wasn't shocked.

When he was about to finish he politely asked her '*Is there anything you want to say...?*' and she just looked around, held her hands up in what-the-fuck surrender, and said *No*. So he said '*Well I'll just add one thing then...*', and off he went.

That's what I call taking the words right out of somebody's mouth. And we were complicit, weren't we? Because none of us said a thing. I wanted to, but don't know the teacher well enough yet. Just not something I expected to see happen in this country, in that particular institution, and in this day and age. Wow.

———

Thursday, 25th March, 2010.

Little Black Rain Cloud

I'm not a bad person. (Honest! I have witnesses!) But First-Born appears to be running away from home. Which is funny, if you think of how a couple of weekends ago I was threatening to run away from home. They're trying to beat me to it.

The deep and meaningful crux of it is, I can't work them out. I was going to be a party pooper and not go to Sydney again, because I'd planned that trip as an event for First-Born. Quite a few of our family were going. I wanted to take them there and show them *fun*, get a bit of "us" back. Because we were getting along, and there was an opening for goodness between us when I booked the flight.

But then last Sunday happened. They started accusing me of tricking them into the trip when they were asleep. So right up until the last minute I didn't expect to actually get on the plane. Wasn't happy enough for a holiday. I was going to say to Mum and to First-Born, *'Youse guys go, I'll just stay here and pick you up afterwards'*.

But I went. We all did. And once I was there I had a ball. I managed to ditch my family a hundred times so I could walk the streets and visit galleries. I did all of this while First-Born set about proving that Sydney's a shit place. They did this by hardly leaving Niece's apartment.

I'm angry, is what. I really am. The rest of us had so much fun, especially seeing each other. We larfed, *oh how we larfed*. It was one big memorably-happy family event. But I'm also worried because I didn't see First-Born's laugh once. I can't remember them smiling.

And now they're gone. I'm kind of dazed. Was it Monday night? An argument at bed time. Some unfortunate words spoken. Guiltily, I still love their way with words, which would shock other people. They're just so powerful with language.

Anyway, those powerful words resonated all night. During the last-Sunday discussion, where I tried to fix our household with a meeting, they said they can't do any of the things I suggested because I'd ruined them, by asking for them to be done. That says it all.

The dazedness comes from First-Born being away like this as though it's some kind of emergency. Am I something a child needs to run away from? The baby bird's supposed to fly out of the nest, not fall with a thud to the ground. Despite all of their anger, this isn't what I expected. It could be that I'm about to be a mother whose child has left home. *Before they've finished growing up.*

Saturday, 27th March, 2010.

Don't Get Sad, Get Busy

I wish I could be properly depressed. You know, the way some people are so depressed they can't even get out of bed. That's how depressed

I want to be. I want to sleep through everything. I don't want to wake up sad, and face the sadness, and have to trudge through the days with nothing ahead but more sadness – the sheer relentlessness of the great undo-able wrongness of everything. And the memories, the incessant wondering of where I went wrong.

First-Born's gone, for now at least. So I'm sad, then I go to the studios and am distracted, and my friends make me happy, and then I leave and am sad some more. It's probably a bad thing that I think of ten-year-old First-Born so much, but that's the one I miss, from before they started hating me, from before they rejected everything that makes [our] life fun. I keep remembering their laugh. The eye contact. Us.

So I cleaned the laundry out. It took hours, because I accidentally scrubbed the cupboards and the floor. We had new neighbours move in last night, and when I thought of the big emptiness of their fresh new house I wanted that. I think sadness hides inside dirt and clutter. It sneaks out and bites you if you let it fester.

Also I've been reading *The Geography of Bliss*, by Eric Weiner. I heard a few of the chapters read aloud on Radio National and was attracted to the summaries of place and national personality. The whole concept of the book. Nice. The writing leans towards tacky and the sense of humour's sometimes so clunky it makes me cringe, but I don't care. I like it. It's dopey and funny and insightful. I remember happiness and while I can't feel it I can pass the time by finding out how it happens elsewhere. It beats scrubbing laundry cupboards. You can only scrub so many of those.

Also I went for the most beautiful, long swim in the empty Saturday evening pool. I love that other people have a life, because it empties the swimming lanes for those of us who don't. I could stay in the pool forever. Maybe if I turn into a fish.

Anyway, maybe I'll draw, maybe I'll read some more, maybe I'll just go to bed. Maybe I'll wake up and First-Born will be ten years young again, and we can start over. Maybe if I make them some nice, wholesome soup.

April 2010

Friday, 2ⁿᵈ April, 2010.

Ghost of Them
This morning I woke from a vivid dream, so sharp and apt. We had to make it to the top of some stadium steps, and I was typically all energetic enthusiasm. Once I'd reached the top I noticed First-Born was struggling, and I went halfway back down so I could carry them the rest of the way. They were still young, and I did carry them, kissing their head, because I was such a head kisser back then, kissing *I love you I love you I love you* into their little skull.

In the dream I couldn't gage their emotions, or they weren't showing any, or they weren't overcome, they just didn't want to do the steps, not complaint and not exhaustion, not grateful, just *meh*.

So First-Born's not here but they're always here, and still this sadness, all inside my head or inside theirs, or both. Is First-Born depressed, or just angry? I don't know. At least I'm sleeping again.

Monday, 5ᵗʰ April, 2010.

Signs n' Portents
It's heartening to know that a person can be buoyed, even in these sad times, by the cut price of Humpty Dumpty eostre eggs. And if that person has acknowledged that the tradition of the Humpty Dumpty eostre egg goes way back to her childhood and is therefore a symbol of hope for happier futures (that she should by now be experiencing) in the way that all things lead to happier futures when you're a child, then telling herself that *if she fails to get bargain mark-down Humpties this morning she fails happiness forever* makes perfect sense. Her buying eight of them, therefore, can be seen as a triumphant sign of

proportionately happier futures to come. (One per year was clearly never going to be enough.)

Tuesday, 6th April, 2010.

Cloak n' Daggery

Or more cloak and plastic baggery, I think. This year, for days, Mum's been telling me about the plump and neglected state of the feijoas under her neighbour's tree. I've drooled as she described their firmness, on the brink of turning ripe. And the shame – oh the shame – that that man just leaves them under there, to rot.

So this year, instead of saying it'd be wrong for me to go in there and take some, she's telling me to do it. She *wants* me to. It's like that nice little old lady is the devil on my shoulder. Medieval scholars were right! Woman is the root of all evil!! And a complicit old woman is Her in Her Purest Form!!!

I've been receiving emergency phone calls all weekend, from Mum, who says things like *'He's mowed the back lawn today, you'd better hurry!'*, and *'He doesn't mow under the tree anyway, but you'd better get here before he mows the front!'*, and *'It's just such a shame!'*.

And now there's a huge pile of open feijoa shells on a plate on the kitchen table. Son likes them harder than I do, so I need to make sure he lets some of them ripen more for me. But the smell – that alone could keep me going. And now that I have Mum as a co-conspirator, this year's going to yield a bumper crop.

(If only First-Born were here to share the loot.)

Wednesday, 7th April, 2010.

Portraits Everywhere

Lipstick's such an awful thing. It doesn't make sense to slap colour on your lips to attract people to the sensuality of the mouth, as though the mouth's inherent sensuality isn't enough to draw attention to itself. It's also very inflatable-sex-doll – the round suck-hole that advertises *'THE ACTION HAPPENS HERE'*.

It's a shame that women feel they need it, because in my humble opinion it makes the mouth look flat, plastic, and anything but sensual. I don't like kissing it, and I don't like the idea of kissing it.

But even beyond that, it gets in my way. Last week Young Studio Friend and I spent an afternoon on a portrait sitting (drawing Pregnant Friend) and plaster-casting a pregnant body (also Pregnant Friend). I arrived early for the sitting, and was shocked when I saw Pregnant Friend wearing make-up. I hadn't ever seen her wearing make-up before so I didn't think to ask her not-to for the sitting. Plus she paints portraits, so I assumed she'd already know what to do, as in do nothing. I had to negotiate my way around it. The lipstick was the biggest problem; lipstick will both flatten your lips *and* reflect light, so that in the end you can't really see the lips.

Stupidest invention of all time.

Anyway the plaster-casting was fun, and I got a decent drawing done, and there was merriment and good food and friend-love all around. I'll be drawing her again this week, though, and can't really say *'Please don't wear lipstick'* because then she'll feel embarrassed that she wore make up last time.

More importantly, though, the sitting with one of my formal portrait requests has been arranged for Very Soon, and I was surprised when Subject expressed something close to self-consciousness in one of her emails. Was it self-consciousness? Either that or an outward request that I don't expect too much of her appearance. It then occurred to me that – knowing she'll be scrutinised – she might wear make-up, and I'll now have to carefully request that if she wears it she wears it lightly, with no lipstick.

The email made me worry for women generally, the way they feel about themselves and how they try to remedy their self-consciousness with such an overt disguise. But it also made me think more about the process of portraiture, and about what I see when I look at a face that a person who doesn't paint or draw doesn't see.

How do you explain tone-lust to a person who doesn't draw? The excitement that happens in your brain when you see the shadow in a lip corner that can define a person's whole face. Things that have nothing to do with the quality of a person's appearance – it's all just the meat of them, and "looks" are irrelevant. In fact, the friends/acquaintances who consider themselves attractive are the ones who most often offer to model, and they're so generic I struggle to find a way to make them interesting to me, sometimes succeeding but most often not. I just avoid making a commitment to those ones. Makes me feel mean.

In the end it's between their physical self and my perception. People are so self-conscious it probably doesn't occur to them that while I'm looking at them so intently, they're also looking at me, so the scrutiny goes both ways.

If I was nervous about the formal sitting my nervousness has been erased by that small comment. She's made herself human beyond the public persona, and in doing so has done me a favour. I love that a person can be the biggest kind of famous in her field, with success upon success and more success coming, and still be so small. She knows she's going to be looked at realistically, and not in the way she's looked at in controlled publicity shots. I'm going to enjoy this.

Tuesday, 13th April, 2010.

I Have a New Toy

I did enjoy it. Sat in the car for a brief moment beforehand and thought about how stupid it is to want so desperately to paint somebody you haven't even met. But then I met her, and that took care of that problem. I like her. I enjoyed every minute of her. I think because when I gave her chocolate, she said she'd just run out, because she'd eaten her last for breakfast. Yes! Somebody else who eats chocolate for breakfast! Every day! You see how it is.

I hated my drawing but that didn't even bother me, especially because she offered to sit again.

Which means I get to enjoy her again. Isn't that strange. Well to me it is. And it gave me a whole new angle on portrait sittings and what they entail; a person letting you sit in their life and watch them exist for a short time. Being allowed to play with things about themselves that you didn't expect them to offer so openly. It influences how you see them and what you want to do with them on the canvas.

I love it. I don't know if it's because not many of my friends are really my age, and she is, but I felt very easy in her company. I stood and listened and listened and spoke and spoke more, and almost found myself doing what I do so often these days, which is try to say too much in one hit because it seems so important to talk about everything instead of about one thing at a time. I'm glad I didn't give in to that – I mostly listened because it wasn't about me, I'm just the onlooker. It's comfortable being silent during the pauses where you would normally speak, swallowing back thoughts as they happen.

So there you go, it has to be the age. She listens to the same music, only she arranges her playlists better than I do. And when she named her love affair I nearly died, because he happens to be one of the few other people in the world whose portrait I want to paint. When she described how she fell for him after first impressions I understood because my first impressions were the same, except that I'm not as red-blooded because whereas she wanted to jump his bones I just wanted to paint him.

Same thing. There has to be a word for this somewhere, this intense desire to paint particular people. A visual attraction to the shape of them, or the presence of them. It's not sexual. I don't know what it is. I wonder.

In any case, the sitting's been and gone and now I'm allowed to play with a face I've wanted to paint for a long, long time. I'm stupidly happy. Maybe it's because it's an activity that involves enjoying a person without any complication, something purely positive? My first real n' proper stranger portrait sitting (as opposed to awkward, timid sittings), just like a grown-up. I hope they're all this good.

―――

Friday, 16th April, 2010.

Quiet

I'm a bit teary tonight, and I don't know if it's because First-Born kissed me on the cheek as I was dropping them off at a friend's party, or if it's because my body's so tense I couldn't go out to be drunk n' debaucherous with my bitches the way I'd planned.

The kiss surprised me, given that they've officially run away from home (except, they've been home a lot this week). They're very soft, I think that's what got me. Such a soft kiss. I don't know what it means. That they know they've broken my heart. That they're maybe sorry. That they know I'm not the evil thing they accuse me of being.
?

Anyways, I'm not stressed anymore so I wish my body would settle down. In fact, I'm quite calm. A few weeks ago I was devastated, but now I've accepted that this is the way life is and I'm quietly waiting to see what happens next. My motor tic's bothering me no end. I can't sit on a train for too long, which means extra driving. And now I can hardly drive, so I'll have to park somewhere half-way when I go to the studios, which means using the train after all, which means no relief.

I've started staying home to work whenever I can.

Being home tonight = I realise I'm gonna have to take proactive measures to get rid of the stupid thing. I thought being calm was enough, but apparently my subconscious isn't buying it. The jig is up. I have to slow down and not get excited by anything. Too much stimulus = stop reading books? Stop looking at art? Stop doing research? Live in a cave on a cliff face in a remote desert? One with a fifty-metre lap pool? AND a sauna [of course]. Also an early night. Starting now.

Monday, 19th April, 2010.

Bogan Watch

At first I thought there was a bit of Toorak in my street, but then I realised it's actually just a little bit of McMansion. And it's next door. Where my new neighbours live.

I've been keeping a bogan-watch going ever since they moved in, ticking things like bottle-blonde hair off on a list and sending it to Ex-Husband, who happens to be in Ethiopia at the moment. I'd hate for him to visit on his way back through and get a shock.

They were standing at the end of their driveway when Son and I arrived home on Saturday, and we finally saw them in all their glory. We were all smiling at each other in that *'Oh look, there's my new neighbour'* way, like little kids who're about to make new friends in their street. She waved, I waved, she waved again. The smiling! The joy! It was a sunny day, and I happily reversed down my driveway and disappeared into my house. Best to leave it at that, in case speaking spoils the illusion.

It was later that I realised what they were doing at the top of their driveway. They'd just put in a new letterbox. Not a Toorak letter box, but a big McMansion job – a cream-coloured pillar with shiny big numbers on the side. So now when you drive up our narrow street you come across our big earthy stone letterbox, and then get distracted by the stately not-stone pillar a little further on. Because it looks odd. Incongruous, even.

So were they being friendly, or was it just letterbox pride? I'm not being a snob here [?], but I hope when we finally meet properly, and have each other over for drinks, that it's wine and not Jim Beam on the drinks menu. No football conversation. That they don't have row upon row of Reader's Digest volumes on their book shelves, and tacky abstract paintings that were thrown together to match the cushions.

I don't mind bogans, really. It's just, it'd be nice to have close neighbours who have more in common. People I can feel guilty about neglecting, the way I feel guilty about neglecting Whatsername from over the road.

Doesn't matter, I guess. Maybe we can bond over the garden, open up the path between theirs and ours. It alarms me that they bought a house with such obvious neglect in its outerage, but maybe they bought it with a vision to improve. Maybe we can make this place what it used to be. And if a truck were to find the road too narrow and swipe that pillar letterbox over, maybe I could be there for them, kind of pat them on the shoulder and say *'There there, it's for the best'*. Because it would be.

———

Wednesday, 21st April, 2010.

Finis

I'm steadily using up my quota of woe-is-me, but it can't be helped. First-Born's officially gone now. It went something like this:

'Okay Mum, I'm ready to run away from home now. By the way, can you give me a lift?'

I'm allowed to laugh about this, aren't I? I'm okay with it because it seems to be working out in good way. They've enrolled in a catch-up program for their schooling, and this will make them feel good about themself, which will make them less hostile, which will make them love their beautiful mother again.

The even-more good thing is that First-Born's living in a caravan at my sister's house for a while. Which is like living in a cubby house, and when I dropped them there last night I secretly wanted to live in the caravan myself. Because it's nice; the caravan's theirs, but they're also being taken into my sister's family. I stayed for a little while but I felt like an outsider, kind of pariah-like.

When I dropped First-Born off elsewhere on Friday night I pulled over to ring friends I was supposed to see then, and as I hung up the phone I saw First-Born walk behind my car (through the rear vision mirror). In the dark. By themself. It was awful, because there was my child and I had no knowledge of what they were doing, no jurisdiction over their care. They could have been anybody's child walking along that street. They didn't know I was still there; I was just nobody and First-Born was everybody and I felt like a ghost. Or like they were a ghost.

Then on Monday night they wanted to be dropped at the station because they had to visit a friend who just found out he had cancer. When I was dropping them off I found out they weren't actually going very far. Two suburbs away? Three? Up the hillside. And it was dark. And people get stabbed on our train line. *All the time.* So I told them to be careful and dropped them off, and then wondered why I didn't just drive them there.

Was I even allowed to drive them there? Why didn't they ask me to? Would they yell if I did? Would my motor tic allow me to drive home without crashing? I didn't know what to do. I was shocked that it'd occurred to me to worry [a lot] about them travelling on the train at night, but that it hadn't occurred to me to drive them to where they needed to go. Until it was too late. Because I felt like it wasn't my place to do that anymore, the rejection by them is so complete.

I got home and was wondering if I should call and offer to take them, when my sister called me. Asked me if I knew the guy and was he safe and should she check him out. She asked me this because she was going to pick First-Born up from the station – where I'd dropped them – to take them to that suburb up the hillside. Because it's not safe to travel at night. Because my sister's a better mother than I am. Which made me get off the phone and cry.

Am I so confused by First-Born that I don't even know how to look after them anymore? Last year when I needed help and finally asked my family to step in, nobody did. They worried, but they couldn't find an entry point. Now they're all there. Mum and Dad wanted First-Born to live with them for a while, and now Ye Olde Sister has taken over with great gusto, and it's so nice. That makes me cry, too. Because this is family, and I love that my child's going to be embedded within that. I love that they're going to be safe and looked after.

But last night, as I was delivering First-Born to their new home, I was giving them gentle advice about the volume of their music at night et cetera, and I said something about my sister. First-Born said *'Yeah, she's good, she's really caring'*. Being happy about this I joked around and said *'So am I – I'm caring!'*, and First-Born said *'No – no, you're not'*. A cruel thing to say to your own mother.

So I settled them in. Their cousins (who're now grown-ups) were there, and everybody was happy. That's why I felt like an outsider. A not-caring outsider who doesn't belong in their own child's life. Then Ye Olde Sister asked *'So when are you two going to see each other?'*. She told us we had to make a date to see each other for coffee at least once a week. (I love my sister; she knows what's what and how to make things happen.) I looked at First-Born because it's all up to them. They screwed up their face and made noises about not wanting to see me.

They'll see me because Ye Olde Sister's a force to be reckoned with. But I wish they'd see me because they want to. How does somebody you love so much reject you so completely? What even happened?

Not caring. That's the last thing other people would say about me. But anyway it's over, and they're gone. Maybe they'll come back, or maybe this quiet is forever. A nice but sad quiet. I'm wagging school today, to spend the day drawing inside this quiet. And reading books.

And wondering about how I could've been a better mother to somebody who wouldn't let me be their mother at all.

Thursday, 22nd April, 2010.

You Must
Blood Meridian, Cormac McCarthy. Because he makes bleak so beautiful. Because we need to be reminded of what we are, and who we are. Because we've cleft such a dangerous distance between ourselves and history. The malevolence of our species.

I recently listened to it on audio, but the book has arrived and will sit like a bible next to my bed, so that I can read it bit by bit and find those passages that thrilled me so much. That left me feeling bludgeoned and raw. Possibly in a fug of despair.

Best to read in small doses, I think. Digested carefully. Not to be taken in abject conditions, but very effective if you have happiness that needs curing. Hide the razor blades, just in case.

May 2010

Wednesday, 5th May, 2010.

Just Thinkin'
I don't know why, but I had a random memory about Churchy Friend this morning. From before she was Churchy, back in the more embarrassing days when she was Spiritual-y. She'd been to see a clairvoyant and had the channelling sessions recorded. It was against the rules [rules!] to play the tape for anybody, but she played it to myself and Ex-Wife, who was then just Girlfriend. We did things like raise our eyebrows, and frown. And then get all protective.

I then paid money to satisfy my scepticism. I went to the same clairvoyant, using a fake name. I brought the tape home and played it for Pre-Churchy Friend, emphasising the parts of my reading that were EXACTLY THE SAME as hers. I'd done my good deed for the century by pointing out my friend's gullibility and exposing the cruel practice of playing on people's vulnerability.

Friend was upset, very. But instead of learning to live in the real world (which I've since decided is a cruel and horrible place so if you wanna be gullible and live elsewhere then go for it), she went back to the house and confronted Cheap-Ass Clairvoyant, who then convinced her that she was genuine DESPITE EVIDENCE TO THE CONTRARY.

This is why I have bad karmic energy. Churchy-Friend went on to attend an expensive weekend in the hills with a group of people who believe there are aliens among us and lo and behold, what a coincidence that everybody at that particular weekend seminar happened to be one of them! What are the chances! There were numerical coincidences involved!

These aliens are [allegedly] all around us. They come from a more evolved, peaceful and prosperous place, and will be revealed to us when we're ready to be enlightened by them.

After that it was the church. She was offended during a dinner when she told a group of us about the churchy weekend conference she was going to Sydney to attend with Even More Churchy Friend, and I predicted that she was going to come back converted. Which she did, and my having predicted this has been a bee in her bonnet ever since.

She hates monkeys and refuses to believe that we evolved from apes. She gives me primate birthday cards every year, which makes me laugh. When we're texting I occasionally retort with *'Your great great great great great great grandmother was a monkey!'*. Naysayer and believer thus get along beautifully [most of the time].

I love this friend, and the only reason I knew she'd return converted was that I'd watched Even More Churchy Friend go through the same desperate "spiritual" search when she was younger, and saw how she also found refuge from meaningless reality in religion. She was always vulnerable, hence my protectiveness. She thought for a long time that I thought of her as stupid, but I never did. I just thought of her as needing security.

So why am I remembering it now? Was I thinking about desperation, community, or need? Is it just my life flashing before my eyes? I don't know why it's bothering me. Do I really have to trace every thought back through its genesis? No pun intended. Maybe I'm just thinking about how grown up we are now. How adult fairytales are just mature forms of the things we believe in when we're children.

I could use a fairytale right now, but *not that one.*

Churchy Friend's doing great things out in the world, working as a youth social worker. She's interested in histories I was trying to tell her about ten years ago, and I can see her mind expanding. I'm not being patronising. On the other hand, my mind's shrinking as it expands and I feel more and more ignorant every day. Mine's all cluttered and useless, hers is clean and ready and able to absorb.

So maybe it doesn't matter where the thought started, but it matters where it takes me. I want to be like her, because it's better to learn from being in the world than from being on the sidelines of life, watching. I'm missing something. I wish I knew what it was. [And *no*, Smartarse; it's not dog-spelt-backwards [!!!!].)

Vagina-Mite Was No More

Friday, 14th May, 2010.

Believe it or Not

The Family did lunch early this week, and sure I was supposed to be in the studio but life needs to be like this, not like that, so I went to lunch because Me Big Sister is gorn to Europe and we had to see her off. So much love around, you know? It didn't used to be like this, but suddenly it is, long story.

Anyways, I was telling Dad about how Son had seen First-Born walking towards the station the day before, and Dad said First-Born's like the new Abominable Snowman, with sightings so rare they're worth announcing.

I know it's all in the delivery but I can't be bothered writing it with a bit of punch. Just, the Abominable Snowman! Hilarious! Dad cracks me up. And it's so true – those reported sightings are rare and might be the most I get of First-Born for a while to come. At least this makes it something to laugh about.

Wednesday, 19th May, 2010.

All Ya Need is Love…

First-Born turns eighteen next week, and I was dreading Mother's Day this year but I'm dreading that day more because I know it's going to swallow me. I've been planning to spend a day shopping in weird places for something special for them, even though I probably won't be able to give it to them personally. I asked Little Sister to come with me, because what a lonely thing to do alone.

Now I'm not sure. First-Born was here last night. They often come back, sometimes for one night and sometimes for a few. It's been a turbulent few weeks. Sadness has been sadness and has then become something else. Sometimes peace, sometimes not. I didn't want to see a counsellor because I can't be bothered. There's nothing anybody can do. But I finally saw one and I was right, she wasn't particularly useful, there's nothing to be done – it just is as it is. But she said one thing I hadn't realised, and that is that I'm going through a grieving process.

It's private and it's isolating because I'm supposed to talk it out but I have nothing to say. Grieving's exactly it.

But maybe grieving's making me grow balls? Two nights ago First-Born brought a friend here and they started partying. Loud. I told them to leave and they did. I was impressed because they didn't seem resentful.

Which explains why last night I fell into a trap. Something about driving them places, something about a rolling pin breaking in half at my feet. I shouldn't write about that here, but I love the broken rolling pin. As an object it becomes a sacred relic, such a beautiful thing.

Point being, they've kept the door to home open, as a safe haven. Ironically. I know I have to cut them off. I'm so ashamed of having let them speak to me like that for so long. For being cowed by the sheer volume of it all. I'm ashamed of not ever knowing what to do, when what has to be done is a mere demanding of decency. Only I could have given them that. So I'm ashamed of being passive because the alternative was to put them through suffering and I didn't want to hurt them. I didn't want them to ever feel as though I don't love them.

All my life I thought of love as being everything. Not in a sappy and sentimental way, but as the motivation for Every Little Thing. I think the most difficult thing to learn as a parent is that love is nothing. I hear First-Born re-write the past (a result of being troubled by something, I'll point out – not malice), I watch them skew the present before my very eyes, everything coloured by an agenda, and that's all that's left to know. That love means nothing, is nothing, and can be obliterated as though it never happened.

Our whole history was love, and now we have no history. Without it there's nothing. I'm nothing. Just nothing.

Saturday, 22nd May, 2010.

That's Class, That Is

It was like a blind date. I refused to pay a five dollar booking fee – per ticket – for a gold class movie, so we had to get tickets on the day. Instead of being next to them, bad luck had me sitting behind Mum and Son, next to a smelly geek. I knew he smelt before he lifted his arms (and he did lift his arms), because Mum told me. She did that little old lady giggle she does and said *'That's the man who smells like he hasn't had a shower'*. She said it pretty loud and laughed and laughed, and it made me happy, because that's why I dropped my standards to go to gold class in the first place. To hear my mother laugh.

I was squeamish all the way in because it's ridiculously expensive, even before the booking fee. But Mum wanted to spoil Son for his birthday and she wanted to spoil me to cheer me up, so I had my little *complain* and then snuck downstairs to buy popcorn, because it's not on their upper-crust menu. Then I came back up and ordered the mousse with masala anyway because I had to go straight to work afterwards and didn't wanna starve. I kept thinking *this is pretentious,* until I got into the cinema and sat on the seat. It was *nice*.

It's funny how when you look around you at the gold class audience you see lots of fathers with sons and you guess that they're doing divorcee weekend access activities. I wonder what kind of people can actually afford these damn things and why they choose to spend so gratuitously. What is class anyway? Aren't we insulting ourselves and everybody else by buying into something that clearly doesn't belong to our *class*? Seeing a gold class venue full of outer suburban bogans must be amusing to the truly rich.

To me it just felt stupid, and I cared about that until I tasted the mousse. *Faaaark* is an understatement. I might have to pretend I'm rich again even though I don't care about wealth, just so that I can keep ordering that mousse. I'll take Mum with me again, because it's good to have somebody smell people for you. Don't wanna lean over to talk to strangers and get a horrible shock.

The cheering up worked.

Ye Olde

I really love that it's only 8:30 on a Saturday night and I'm well and truly tired and wanting to go to bed. The house is so *quiet*. Growing old isn't so hard; by the time I'm geriatric I'm going to be very, very good at it.

Chris Fontana

Saturday, 29th May, 2010.

Hip Hip Hooray

Recognising good bling when I see it, I bought these jewels, and they were lovely. I played with their sweet weight, let them splay themselves across my fingertips and smiled with wonder as they reflected light. I'm not even a bling/jewel person. And sure they're not valuable stones, just very pretend-valuable fake ones. That's me, middle of the range all the way. But I couldn't wait to give them to First-Born even though it'd mean not being able to play with them anymore.

So on this sad day that's been eighteen years in the making, First-Born actually came home. None of us were expecting it – I was going to leave their present on the bench so that they could sneak in and get it without having to see me. But they came here openly. We all had to rush around like crazy to throw a dinner together for them, so that they'd feel loved.

They opened the present over the table after dinner, and grudgingly admitted that it's very nice. *Very* nice? Try EXTREMELY NICE. They looked at their reflection in the window and yes; a good cross between lovely and gangsta.

It took them a while to find a negative spin to put on the gift, but eventually said *'She only gave me these so that every time I wear them I'm reminded of her existence'*. Clever, half. Wrong, but clever. I also heard them on the phone to Ex-Wife (who had to be reminded by yours truly that it's First-Born's birthday, no wonder First-Born's a mess) saying that they're probably going to give it back (as in not accept it). Ex-Wife said *'She probably still has the receipt'*.

I wonder how I'll feel when they do that. I wonder if jewels are as pretty when they represent rejected love.

Hopefully I'll feel nothing. I'll be too comatose and spun out on amazing thoughts, because one of the many who came over tonight – drove forever to get here – was Churchy Friend, and she gave me "special" cookies. I hope, soon, to try them for the second time in my life. And then I'm going to become a full-time druggy, spend the rest of my days completely mind-fucked, until I die in a gutter somewhere.

I very discretely didn't mention that plan to the new counsellor today. She was a good one, though I feel like shit after talking about myself for so long. She kept me there for 45 minutes longer than she was supposed to. Result is, I feel like I've been on a long date and keep remembering things I told her and cringing. Not because I said anything bad, but because I said anything at all. And now, from things she asked me about, I've realised other things and have gotten very emotional. Like I needed that.

She was *too* good.

Eighteen years. Will I ever get over this? Other things happen, why don't I write about those anymore? What if this is all there is left?

Sunday, 30th May, 2010.

For Instance

I'm dead famous now. Possibly only on a scale of legends in lunchboxes, but it made me smile for a day or two a few weeks ago when I was told I'd won another literary award. Because somebody loved my story. That's always the nicest thing.

I needed to feel like I belong somewhere. Not sure where, but somewhere.

And in one particular class I was famous because a teacher liked my small poem (a haiku, about First-Born). He didn't say whose it was, but he pointed it out on the page of poems and called it *beautiful* and *domestic* and *loving* and *affectionate*. Three weeks later he told the class that he chose to print three poems submitted by a particular student (as opposed to only one from everyone else) because they were so lovely, and I looked and they were mine [!!]. As he read them aloud I kept my face all poker so that nobody'd know, but felt so nice and privately lovely, because there was somebody responding to my words. It didn't matter that anybody else knew about it, only that I exist quietly and somebody notice I'm alive and thinking.

Naturally, I buggered that up by writing the shittest essay of my life for him. Last week was not the best for writing essays. But anyway, it doesn't matter. For that brief moment I connected with another human being in the tiniest way just by loving the same things he does. He said nice things in his emails, as I did. Nothing creepy, I should add. Just, you know how some people come along and you just want to think with them? Like that. Not the sort of thing that withstands a crazy messed up essay. (It even has typos, oh the shame.)

If only I didn't fuck things up like that. Fame just isn't what it's cracked up to be.

Note from the future; it wasn't the shittest essay of my life. I cared about it a lot and turns out it was one of my best. I just didn't like the product of my head.

Monday, 31st of May, 2010.

I'm Wondering…

...why, after spending most of my childhood passionately in love with the times tables, I tried to remember eight eights off the top of my head in the supermarket today and couldn't. I had to calculate[!];

...why Old Battleaxe Cat sometimes bites me when I pat her, even though I've let her inside and she's the one who jumped up on the computer table begging to please sit on my lap;

...why I'm sitting here, trapped, with her on my lap and me not wanting to disturb her, when she just bit me.

If cats wanted to take over the world, they really could.

I'm also wondering why it's not June yet, when I finished with May a day ago.

June 2010

Tuesday, 1st June, 2010.

At Your Service...?

I remember when customer service was a given. When department stores always had staff "on the floor" to help you find the right sized knickers and a jacket that would match your jeans.

When I was a teenager I worked at Venture (poor man's Kmart) and we'd pride ourselves on how well we looked after the customers. We could spot a damsel in distress from a mile away and a little kindness made everybody's day. Not the managers – the managers were [allegedly] arseholes who got off on the power trip of being at the top of the littlest shit heap. But we were lovely, and even the arsehole managers knew that being lovely made us an asset to the store.

So the new Kmart advertisement shits me up the wall. Making a big song and dance about how they're changing their stores so that the customer will find the staff oh-so-much-more helpful from now on. They're using images of cute children to flog their interpersonal wares. As though we're so stupid we won't remember that customer service and having people on the floor in each department was something THEY TOOK AWAY IN THE FIRST PLACE. And that's why shopping there is [allegedly] almost always A SHIT THING TO HAVE TO DO.

Wednesday, 2nd June, 2010.

Stiff Upper Lip

I'm allowed to say whatever I like about Fergie because she's the bane of Rangadom and redheads have been silent about the damage she's done to our hair colour for too long.

For instance, those days when I was unaware of her existence and wore a black ribbon in my hair, only to be told *'You look like Fergie!'*, which was thankfully always followed by *but you're much better looking*. It's a bit like the theory that all Asians look the same, which says more about the stupidity of Australians than it does about Asian characteristics. All Asians do not look the same, Rangas do not all look the same, and I don't look like F...F...F... Her. The black ribbon came out (I only wore it because I had to tie my hair back for work) but the scars, they never healed.

How many years? And now she's back in the media spotlight, so people are going to start saying it again. This time I'm gonna wallop them. Because bits n' pieces of the Oprah/Fergie interview were on the *7 pm Project* and I couldn't help but notice that not one person commented on her face. I know I also shouldn't comment on her face, because women are under enormous pressure to conform to aesthetic standards, so technically the Botox and filler thing's not her fault. Also, it's against all sisterhood codes to criticise a woman's appearance.

I'll solve the problem of my impending cnutiness by speaking about a Generic Botoxed and Dermally Filler-ed Person instead. It's not this person's facial treatments that distress me, but that they've overdone it. Which perpetuates a standard that's becoming too prevalent in aging women, namely the one where their faces are so fully immobilised they stop looking like themselves first, and then stop looking human altogether. They usually have old-person's neck and a smooth face, and if you look not-even-very-closely you can tell that their faces aren't moving when they speak. Or laugh. Or cry. Or *anything*. Especially the lips – upper lips so dead still that when they talk they look like ventriloquist's dolls, their words coming out skewed. The distortion's as ugly as feck. Or is it their personalities? Maybe they immobilise those, as well.

I feel sorry for these women, but also disturbed by what it means for womanhood generally. I'm distressed that they don't know when to stop, and nobody *tells* them when they need to stop. Aesthetic interventions seem to be good stuff (what the hey, stay young for as long as you can), up until that point of distortion.

A lesson for anybody who wants to allegedly-lie on camera: don't immobilise the bejeezus out of your facial expressions because they're much more important than your less-than-regal words.

Anyway I have my karate chop ready to go for when the comments start, and am practising for the sage nod I'll have to give when they follow with *but you're much better looking,* because yes, I am. That's because MY LIPS MOVE WHEN I SPEAK.

Fortunately for me, being better looking than people who've turned into mannequins isn't very difficult. Kudos to them, though. Being better looking than people who've turned into mannequins also isn't going to last, so as I grow old and withered they'll be having the last laugh.

Sunday, 20th June, 2010.

Les We Forget

Memory of an elephant, steer clear of the poison berries. I haven't re-subscribed to *The Monthly* since reading that awful comeback essay by Robert Manne. Re female editor.

But a friend came for dinner and left a recent edition on my table, so I opened it to an essay about one male poet written by another male poet and almost had to spew up my hastily masticated crumpets.

Could the appraisal of the poet be any more sycophantic? If the essay-writing male poet were to lick the other male poet's butt any harder he'd rupture a pile.

Can't take that essay seriously – such a shame – because we read these things to learn something about the man and his work, not to watch you drool. Get a grip on yourself. Geez.

Thursday, 24th June, 2010.

Julia Gillard is in Da House!!!!

I don't know what to be more excited about; the fact that she's a woman, or the fact that she's a redhead. Rangas will rule the world!!

This'll be interesting. And I know I've been disillusioned by KRudd PM's salesperson demeanour, but he did stop the recession, and he did say the ultimate SORRY, and the mining tax is a good thing, and et cetera and et cetera. Also he stepped aside graciously and has to be respected for that. I guess I feel disappointed that he was being attacked so voraciously despite the fact that his political decisions have been successful.

If only he'd saved the planet, as promised. But that's okay, because Julia will do it. Or not. Let's be optimistic about it. For now.

Friday, 25th June, 2010.

Cerebral Hangover

I'm over the whole woman thing now. Today was a little like the morning-after, when you wake up and turn to the person next to you in your bed and wonder how they got there, and what was their name...?* Today I realise I was swept up in the moment of history being made. Because change *can* be exciting. *She's* exciting. *Seeing Tony Abbott not win the next election* is exciting.

But today I paid closer attention to the way things happened and I'm shocked by how power shifts on hearsay in this country. Was it always like that? Has nobody got anybody's back? Everything's such a circus.

I do feel sorry for KRudd PM. Even though as I watched his speech, as my cake rose in the oven, while I was getting ready for a killer picnic, I couldn't help but regret that he wasn't able to add saving the whales to his list of achievements.

There needs to be integrity, is all, even though that's expecting too much of this species. This is why dogs walk around saying *'It's human-eat-human out there'*. I don't know how to feel good about that. I'd like to enjoy her political majesty, but you know? Don't you? There's an ugliness to the whole thing. Maybe I should dye my hair black.

*That never happens to me, by the way.

Wednesday, 30th June, 2010.

Rats, Foiled Again

Son tried to trick me yesterday, but fell for his own trick. When I was going out to get a couple of groceries and address the chocolate situation, I asked him if there was anything he needed. He called out '*Duct Tape*', because he has that male hankering for the stuff and it's been a long time between reels of it in this house.

So I brought home some duct tape, and left it on the bench when I went out to tend to my Other Offspring. While I was out he taped the kitchen light switch so that I wouldn't be able to turn it on, but because I'm a neglectful mother and went to a late movie rather than come home to my child, he's the one who had to turn the light on, and when he went to do so he couldn't understand for a minute why it wouldn't work. Then he remembered and it was *Score One to Mother !!*

So now I can't wait for him to wake up (he sleeps in) because I've duct-taped the fridge shut, and I've duct-taped the cherry ripe bars on the bench, and I've duct-taped the kitchen tap, and I hope he's not busting because I've duct-taped the upstairs toilet shut.

But inside I fear this'll become one of those escalating things that gets out of control. Because if he ups the ante? Are we gonna have a duct tape war? Will he start attaching it to painted surfaces, where the walls will get ripped up? What if we both turn into practical jokers and one of us walks in through the front door, steps on a strategically placed roller skate and skids all the way out to the balcony and plummets to our death? Won't be funny then, will it?

Oh lawdy, responsible parenting's a tough gig.

———

July 2010

Thursday, 1st July, 2010.

Strike One, Gillard

We're watching closely to see her do great things, so when she said an emphatic NO to gay marriage, I shook my head and folded my arms all disapproving-like. Because gay marriage is the next big personal-political frontier. Much the same as once, say, being a woman wanting to shack up with a man in a flat in Canberra *outside of wedlock* might have been. Much the same, also, as a political leader being openly atheist [and shacked up in a flat in Canberra, with a man, out of wedlock].

I'm assuming that when it comes to gay marriage the political can of worms has everything to do with reproductive rights. Family values n' all that. Wouldn't want to rock that boat, because look at the stable lives hetero couples are providing for their children. How could you not hold them up to the light as the "Australian Families" ideal?

Spare me. Next thing you know we'll be allowing white Australians to couple with non-white Australians and have interracial pandemonium on our hands. Women and Indigenous Australians will start demanding the right to vote! Somebody forgot to tell Julia that dramatic changes like these can be a necessary thing?

No, we can't risk giving up those solid, old fashioned values. The fabric of this [effing] xtian society can't survive such gaping holes.

Afterthought: coincidentally, I went to see *A Single Man* this week (movie). I think Julia needs to see the scene where Whatsisname is not only told over the phone (two days after the fact) that his partner has been killed, but also that he's not allowed to go to his partner's funeral, because it's only for "family".

Vagina-Mite Was No More

Friday, 9th July, 2010.

Reanimated [!!!!!!]

A matinee performance at the Crown Casino complex, with Mum and Ye Olde Sister, which we do sometimes. This one's like sticking wire into an electrical socket, a good shock that has me sitting forward on my seat the second it starts. Drum Tao, Japanese drumming. I found it while researching Japan in general, for my novel. This energetic thing. Already excited by its physicality but not expecting the calibre of performance managed by this group. A sensorial explosion, right into my core. Suddenly life back inside my body. Not exaggerating.

During intermission an older woman tells me there's a teacher in Melbourne, gives me his name. It's not enough to watch, I have to eat it. I don't know how anybody can see this and take it in passively.

I have to bring my kids, knowing this will save us. As soon as I'm home I book tickets, talk them into going with me the next night. *Life!* I explain to them. *Happiness!* They're reluctant but I can't stand the idea of them saying no to this; it's like our whole future depends on me feeding them pure joy. Reminding them how to enjoy life. I beg, and they cave in. '*You'll see.*' This'll bring it all back.

It costs me [a lot] more money than I can afford but I know it's necessary. We'll manage.

And then there we are in the audience, First-Born drooling also because the performers are, how you say, hot. Mother, you did good.

———

Tuesday, 27th July, 2010.

Grrrrr

Am so grumpy right now. Have been all night; this is the most sustained amount of grump I've felt in a long time. Because I worked my arse off this morning – instead of writing, as I'd wanted to – moving drawers n' such into Son's room, the final resting place of said pieces of furniture. *Hours. Of hard, sweaty work.* And then when I got home from the studios, I discovered that Son had moved them all back.

He undid my work! I know that motherhood's supposed to be full of thankless tasks, but that's ridiculous. He's funny because he thinks his grumpiness at my having moved his computer is supposed to cancel out my grumpiness, so we're technically even, end of story.

Not end of story. Fuck grumpiness, it's an inadequate word for shitty emotions. I was in such a shit I didn't feel like cooking the nice lamb dinner I'd planned for him. So I didn't. I watched tv instead. Eventually he emerged from his room, announcing that he'd finished the essay he'd been working on (an evil plan to make me feel guilty for not cooking the lamb) and asked *'What's for dinner?'*. I said *nothing because I'm too shitty* and then he reminded me that technically I wasn't allowed to be shitty because of it all being even, and then I sat there feeling even more shitty because he wasn't going to eat the healthy meal that I didn't cook for him. (HIS FAULT.)

There's no end in sight for Dear Old Mother, who's spent a long time trying to make the place peaceful. When I get up in the morning the mess is still going to be there. How will I write the way I'd planned when my head's in organise-the-house mode? A little bit at a time, was my plan. Thwarted.

Have to write have to write have to write. Fucken fucken fuck.

―――

Thursday, 29th July, 2010.

Rejoice!!

I need to embrace my sadnesses for the sake of writing a sad story today, but can't see it happening because I'm way too Happy Hallelujah.

This because of the bird. All last year I wanted to write about the love affair I was having with corellas, who came to the local town for autumn (as usual) but stayed well into summer (unusual). For serious, I love them. I watched them, almost crashed my car because of them (they swing from the traffic lights!), filmed them, photographed them, got close up with my powerful zoom lens and eventually painted them.

So when I dropped Son at the bus stop this morning and saw them swinging on the Australian flag (also as usual) I had a little laugh, and Son did too, and off he went. I took out my camera and started filming, because ya never know when you're going to need a film of a corella swinging from a flag. But after seven minutes I realised something was wrong. It was *stuck*. Some flag thread had twisted around its claw and it couldn't peck itself loose.

I rushed home and rang Safeway (who said they'd do something but then did nothing), rang the station (who said they'd ring Safeway because the flag seemed to belong to them), rang Safeway again (grrr) and then tried the local council. Wildlife emergency, animal rescue, a million phone calls later, we worked out that Parks Victoria would have to help, but they were in a meeting, and then hours passed and the meeting ended and I'd since been up to check on the bird and it was okay, so when the guy finally rang me I *said 'I'll meet you there'*, but when I got there the bird was dead.

I got out of my car, stood under the flag pole and cried and cried and cried, thinking I should have called the fire station instead, because they have a ladder. I was devastated, and by the time Parks Man arrived my face was sopping. I could hardly talk and Little Sister was trying to console me over the phone, but she couldn't. The bird had died because I'd failed to get somebody cleverer than myself there in time. It was wrapped up in the flag, dangling, with only a bit of dead wing hanging out and visible.

Worst moment ever. As I stood and felt usefully bad for a while, Parks Man went to see if he could find a way to open the flag pole, and as he was walking back the bird started flapping. It was Jesus! It was Harry Potter! Take that, evil forces – The Bird Who Lived was still alive and in no time lots of people were paying attention.

A friend I haven't seen for years noticed me and came over to talk. She was telling me about her new boyfriend and the fact that she kissed a woman for the first time yesterday, and is planning to have a threesome soon, and all I could think was *'too-much-information'* and *'corella rescue'* and *'I'm happy for you but please not now'* and for some of it *'please not ever because I don't really need to know'*, although kudos for the kissing of women. Still, corella alive!

Parks Man called another man and together they got the pole lock open and lowered the flag and saved the bird, who was all feisty and tangled and then freed and placed in a cage to recover for a bit and is, as we speak, with a bird-rescuing woman who'll take care of it until tonight. Then they'll bring it back and set it free.

It must feel like it's just spent four hours in a tumble dryer. And the really nice thing is that as it was being tossed about up there, a lot of its corella friends were riding the flag with it, crawling over to where it was trapped, just like humans stopping to see if they can help at an accident scene.

Happy ending! And no misery in sight – how will I manage the day's work without it????

August 2010

Thursday, 5th August, 2010.

Beautiful Thing

Old Uncle died. In his nursing home. Mum can't understand why I feel so happy, but I do. Because for those two and a half years since Aunty died, we've been so sad for him, and it turns out we didn't need to be quite as sad as we were. His Daughters-in-Law (who never contacted us or kept us informed, therefore we assumed didn't care about him or us) had been visiting him all along, just like we had. To me that undoes all of the anxiety I felt about his apparent loneliness, or at least changes it into the acceptable kind of anxiety that comes with the territory of watching somebody develop dementia.

He was still estranged from his daughter and son, but still. The nursing home staff loved him.

Biggest relief: we were with him. A couple of the staff had met me and kept my phone number. We'd been in to see him last Wednesday, and he was so lucid and lovely but we knew it was coming.

I thought the *died peacefully in his sleep* business you hear about was all lies, but it was gentle. He had the dying breathing patterns without the death rattle. He wasn't responsive, was topped up with morphine, but his brow would sometimes knit when we spoke to him. I kept one hand on him at all times but he probably didn't really know we were there. And late that night when we were about to tuck in next to him for a sleep, Mum noticed his breathing change. A longer pause between breaths, longer and longer until finally he just stopped, just like that. Am glad we were there, worried for a long time he'd die alone.

I wrote a eulogy that made people cry. Made me cry, too, and I had to pause a lot. But I was honest, and because it was a Catholic-ish funeral and Catholic funerals can be devoid of humanity I know the warmth it generated made his goodbye special. Dad had warned me the night before to *'keep it nice'*. I told him *'I have to be honest – just trust me, I'm not stupid'*. But he knows me and I know me and I had to work very hard to make sure I addressed the bad things carefully, so that the family who're estranged could be acknowledged and we could love him warts-and-all, instead of the usual dead-people-are-suddenly-perfect crap.

In the car afterwards I said *'You were worried about what I'd write about Uncle; wait 'til you see what I'm gonna write about you when the time comes'*. Because we have cruel senses of humour we spent a few minutes joking about Dad's one-day death, and he was okay about it after that. The plan is to give him a censored eulogy to stamp his approval on in advance, and then read the uncut version at the service. (He said that when he dies he doesn't want one of those funerals that celebrate his life – he wants us all to mourn his loss and be miserable about it.)

I met an estranged cousin, who I haven't seen since I was little, and she's older than me but so much fun, even at a funeral. Also First-Wife Aunty, who was always scary to me and has one leg shorter than the other, wears a platform shoe to compensate, walks with a limp (Polio). She's still scary-as-feck by nature, although the shoe doesn't look half as monstrous as it used to. Still, Cousin later said to me *'Okay we have to go, I'd better get Mum outa here before she gets nasty'*.

First-Born was there. They were affectionate, told me I'd done a good job, looked at me with long lost respect. I love that lost little pup.

The cliché's of death bringing people together. The daughter's in-law; lovely. And the son-in-law, who wrote the other eulogy. I've never hugged so many strangers. Now, how to cheer Mum up... ??

Monday, 9th August, 2010.

Half Mast x Two

The Australian flag has gone altogether now. According to my speculative reasoning, there can only be two possible reasons for this.

One is that it was tried and convicted of attempted bird-murder and is being held in detention until it's no longer a threat to the corellas. Or, the owners of the flag are no longer proud of being Australian.

Having seen the boat ads being run by the Liberal Party, and their transparent attempt to appeal to the [unfortunately zealous] racist instincts of common [i.e. uninformed] Australian people, I myself feel ashamed of my country for the first time since Howard was Prime Minister, so I understand this.

Whatever the reason, good riddance bird-hurting, bigot-loving piece of linen. And don't come back until yer ready to behave yerself.

―――

Saturday, 14th August, 2010.

Let's Get Physical

Yesterday was a veritable cerebral marathon. A good thing happened, so I worked hard at prepping a manuscript, which didn't require much work but kept me on my bum all day, no up-getting until well into the evening, and then time for a walk and a relax. That was a good day.

Today was also a good day. I went to taiko/drumming class [love!], pruned branches from around electrical wires, cut them up into piles ready for tying, and cleaned out the garage. Me and my piece of earth are entering our spring romance early this year. It's not really a relationship you can put into words, the one between you and your garden. I love it more every year, even though it's buggered my elbow and I need my arm.

The garage is a huge burden lifted. I've hated it being used for storage and not for using, and thought today about how your garage really needs to be respected the way your studio is respected. It's a studio for the garden, really, and for toolish stuff that I seem to do a lot of, in a girl way.

I have nothing to say, particularly, just getting used to writing again. I'm content, and want to remember, later, how content I am. Waking up the bits that have been dormant, one by one.

―――

Wednesday, 18th August, 2010.

I Don't Get It

I wonder if, hypothetically speaking, a not-very-published writer would be digging her own grave if compelled to comment about her disappointment with Daughter of Prominent Literary Agent's first novel.

It doesn't help that reviews open with an enthusiastic declaration about the author's literary [family] connections, followed by gushing praise. Does this mean that open criticism's a no-go-zone?

It's just, I really looked forward to reading it. To reading anything, really, but specifically *it*. Because of those reviews, which had me prepared for something exciting. I hate to write not-nice things, but even moreso hate the fear of power that seems to settle over me as I write this. As though that kind of power exists in a malicious form and is out to get you if you don't like the right things.

She writes a good sentence. A strong sentence, a good strong boot of a thing. And for the first third of the novel I admired the writing despite being bored by the content. I don't understand this in itself; the writing's not beautiful, or original, or clever, or exciting. It's just well done, not something you can pick holes in. Accomplished? A product of good education and a love of reading? All of that.

This you can get away with. But not the content, and that's why I don't understand the fuss. I like the intensity of the relationships in the beginning, but as the novel progresses those relationships fail to become substantial. I felt so much emptiness. I could have put it down without returning to it quite easily; the curiosity that kept me reading was curiosity about her as a writer, not about the story.

One of the features I consider weak = her reliance on the narrator's interpretation of a look one somebody gave another somebody. Many meaningful looks being relied upon to carry the interpersonal plot. Combine this with too many descriptions of upper class clothing and decor = she lost me well before we got to the middle.

I kept wondering what was sustaining the writing of this novel, how did she love it? How did she think any of it mattered? Intensity within relationships needs to be fed. Not only that. I understand that young adults can be self-involved, but the dynamics of the world didn't enter the sphere of the story. The BIG world, I mean.

That was the most dissatisfying thing, especially when she started writing about 9/11. It was too much like a narrative tool and not enough like a real thing. The viewpoint was so incestuously fixed in the small realm of their few minds that it lacked the emotional impact it required. And resonance. It came across, to me, as wooden.

I feel deflated after reading it because there was nothing to connect with emotionally as a reader. I started to hate it, hated it fully, and then lapsed into apathy. Mystery did NOT drive this novel forward. Had I read the back-cover blurb before I started I might have given up on it sooner. It basically covers the whole thing. Leaves no surprises. Is dull, everything a blurb shouldn't be.

So now, the resonating emptiness. And the concern, that we laud the safe novels, the ones that can be explained in a couple of paragraphs. The ones that say nothing significant about the world, or that keep their focus fixed exclusively upon a small number of class-and-intellectual-status representative characters who fail to enlighten us about the condition of being human. I guess that's why my reaction's so strong; I've walked away with no insight that I hadn't already had from some other, common source.

Maybe it's me. Maybe there's a subtle profundity that's gone right over my head. Maybe I'm getting blunt and cranky in my old age.

Saturday, 21st August, 2010.

Quiet Other Thought

On to girly bits, I think I'm prematurely attracted to somebody. I shouldn't be because I don't know him well enough. Plus he's a him. But anyway, I saw him yesterday, called out *hello* from a distance, was on my way to somewhere, he ran to catch up, and walked with me to where I was going. I looked at him and realised I think he's beautiful. Potentially.

What a pity I've forgotten how to do this liking people business. Maybe I don't really like him, maybe I just have wind. I hope so; I'm way too old to go back to being a silly teenager. Let that be the end of it.

The Void

I love voting. All of that possibility. It's a bit lonely doing it on your own, though. Such as when you're looking at the order of preferences on the Greens how-to-vote card and you have nobody to turn to to have a good laugh about how they rate the Sex Party in front of Family First.

Also, it's First-Born's first election and it's gut-wrenching not to be able to go to the polling booth with them, what with them having run away from home. But I know First-Born's politically feisty and socially concerned and is voting for a good party, so I can sit back and be proud of them. I even got to ring and give them advice about filling out the forms. Just like a real mother.

All that aside, today's a non-day, and won't become a day until it's over. I'm glad I'm filling in for somebody at work, so that I don't have to think about it. Am dreading the outcome. Todd Sampson was on the ball, on *The Gruen Transfer,* when he commented upon the way Liberal Party [and other] advertising has been aimed at inciting emotional responses that don't involve logic. Bad emotion from hot-headed, under-informed voters. Manipulative.

They played the jingles from past elections, and it reminded me that however poxy they might've been, the past was a place where politicians tried to woo us with a vision of a positive future, gave us uplifting hopes and some sort of aspiration. Now they're just dirty mud-slingers. Way off track.

Please be tomorrow already, with a good outcome to show for yourself. Please don't let my country be stupid.

September 2010

Friday, 3rd September, 2010.

Bad Chemistry

I'm not shallow. And I did say the attraction was premature, which is pretty much a *get out of jail free* card.

The problem is he wore this bright jumper. Really, really bright. Last week. I nodded and smiled my *hello* because I was already talking to somebody else, which is just as well because otherwise I might've been seen with him. Not that anybody would have been able to see me, with that distracting glare, but I work so hard to maintain a comfortable shade of ordinary that I could never take a risk on somebody who threatens to draw attention like that.

I mean, it's really good that he won't ever get hit by a car in that thing, but I'll have to reassess my appraisal of him as "beautiful". Just as soon as my retinas recover.

Saves me the trouble of having to get to know him better, which is just plain hard work. And doesn't it take a year to really know somebody? Unless they wear a hideous jumper, which makes them unfortunately known from the outset.

Today was easy. I left early. I'm on a story, so I had to leave early anyway, but how nice to avoid somebody and not have to care. I'm so on my way to heartless I think I might just make it there in one piece.

Saturday, 4th September, 2010.

The Red Stuff

It occurred to me that meat juice is actually part-blood. So when I make the gravy out of the meat juice from the bottom of the baking tray, I'm making a blood sauce. And feeding it to my children.

I don't know why this makes me squeamish all of a sudden, but I had to force myself to eat it so that I wouldn't succumb to stupidity and not be able to eat meat ever again. Which would be a consequence of a sanitised sensibility that I don't approve of. Even though I was once or twice a vegetarian.

Look where that got me. I already have trouble handling the stuff. If I eat even less meat than I already do, will I lose all of my hard-earned assertiveness? Be afraid to say *oi!* when people push into a queue in front of me? Turn into a hippy? Hell forbid.

Wednesday, 8th September, 2010.

Failure Becomes Me

My bed looks like a site of trauma. Covered in books and papers and my open laptop, a couple of notebooks, an out of control pile of pillows and very tossy-turny sheets.

Hell is a short story and this is the most constipated thing I've ever written. I'm just about ready to chew my own arm off to get away from its clutches. Or I was. Now that I'm a failure I'm quite in love with it again. Well. Not with it, but with writing it.

I'm a shining example of what not to do. And I have to laugh at how stupid I am. Because this was my dream come true moment. The kind of thing any writer of short stories would kill for. An editor who also happens to be a writer I admire very, very much wants me to submit something for an anthology I look forward to reading every single year. Publishing gold. I'd submitted to her already – two stories, in fact, which she apparently liked. But I'd mentioned not being able to finish this one by the time the deadline rolled around and over, because I was struggling with it. UNDERSTATEMENT.

Unfortunately she's really really nice, and invited me to submit it anyway, deadlines be damned. She said she'd wait for it and that's *so* nice. I belatedly threw aside some responsibilities and worked and worked, but it was too late because I was making her late for her own deadline and the pressure was on and the story was too close to home and I could not, for the life of me, SEE it anymore. I changed my mind about it a hundred times. I don't think I've ever slaved so much over one thing.

I sent the bugger-it email and declared myself a failure, sorri sorri, but instead of feeling really bad about failing to submit it, I feel really good. Because now I can see the story again, and I can enjoy it, and I am enjoying it, even though it's a bit of a bitch. I did the right thing. I always do the right thing, and that's why I don't get anywhere.

So tomorrow I'm going to tell my students not to maintain their integrity. To scrape, grovel and churn shit out if they have to to meet deadlines, because integrity makes you happy but it gets you nowhere.

The funniest thing? For over a year I've believed that nothing matters anymore. I know I've been through the wringer and that belief is a result of that, but it's also because I'm realistic about the world of writing and art. I keep asking *why bother?* Nobody's waiting for me. I could write for a lifetime and never-ever be read, so I started to feel like writing was an embarrassing secret I shouldn't tell people about. That changed a bit when I won another award [hence the story requests], but it's only just hit me now [when it's about five minutes too late], that I might've been wrong to feel that way. Because somebody *was* waiting for me this time. And I *fucked it up*.

What a lucky person that makes me. A little on the stupid side, but so lucky. To be able to do this. So I can't get to the story for a couple of days and that's going to kill me, but I can't wait to keep going with it now. I've been gradually returning to the land of the living, and now here I am. With that same lovely writer still wanting to read the story, therefore with the incentive of a friendly exchange that's purely about sharing something. Success would be a good thing, but if this is failure then I'll settle for second best.

Note from The Future: the story ended up winning an award, but I never submitted it for publication. Once an idiot, always an idiot.

Saturday, 11th September, 2010.

A Kind of Infidelity

I'm not sure about this, but I think it's cheating on somebody if you ask them to see a movie with you and they can't because they have to write an essay, but they promise to go the following weekend and you can't wait because you have to see it NOW, so you go without them but don't tell them about it because you figure you'll just go again with them when they're ready.

But how good am I for keeping my big fat opinions about this movie secret for a whole week between viewings?! We're going to see it tonight, and because we're having dinner afterwards I figure I've only half-cheated on her, because I didn't do the dinner part last week.

The movie was *The Kids Are Alright*, and for me it's research because it covers the same territory as my gawdawful manuscript. In case my opinions change during the second viewing, here's what I thought: I thought, *fuck I hate Hollywood sometimes.* Overall I liked the movie. Liked being in its space. I think because it was sunny and had a lot of fresh fruit and vegetables in it. I liked Paul and I liked the kids. And I found the themes moving. Very.

But the other adult characterisations were fugly. The dialogue was often painful, that Hollywood awkwardness exhibited by people who don't know how to hold a conversation.

My biggest, most fattest opinion is about the sex. The lesbian sex was... what *was* that? I found it amusing that the hetero sex was detailed and acted with abandon, but the lesbian interaction was choreographed. I get that they were portraying marital staleness, but really. A woman with her bits being pleasured by a vibrator under a doona doesn't lie so still. Surely? And couldn't somebody in the world PLEASE make lesbian kissing look as sensual as it is in real life? Let's stop smacking heads together like that. I know that not every movie about a lesbian couple needs to be instructional, but could you please show people what the appeal is?

My final opinion is about the resolution. Now I can't talk because my manuscript is about as man-hatey as you can get, but the donor dad got a rough deal. My empathy was with him, and I'm not sure if that was the idea or not. Because in real life, is the ideal really to be able to ask somebody into your life and then to throw them away like that? Isn't there a lot more to be worked through? Again, I know there was more complexity to it than I'm allowing for here, but I think that's an unfinished point that needed to be tidied up.

So much more to think, so I guess it did its job. I wonder what I'll think Take Two.

Monday, 13th September, 2010.

Take Two

What a stupid audience. The audience were so stupid I was more aware of them than of the movie. Lots of lesbians, yah, but also lots of men who laughed aloud at even the subtle witty things. Made the movie even more Hollywood and tacky. Little Friend didn't like it, and I'm pretty sure that's why. Perhaps if they'd let the amusing bits be really amusing and have a bit of a chuckle here and there, instead of beer-bellied guffawing, the rest of us would have enjoyed it more.

It'll be really good when the whole lezzo-poofter-bastard thing isn't treated like such a novelty act. I thought that day was already here, but apparently not. (Let's blame Julia?)

Plus, the female couple in front of me were pashing as the credits rolled as though it had been a romantic experience, and I can only assume it was because they were in an audience of peers watching their people be their people. A bit performative. Surely that movie was enough to make a person not want to kiss. Yes? Yes.

Monday, 20th September, 2010.

It Wzn't Me, Officer – I Wz Out Partying

If you're sitting at home on a Saturday night reading Nietzsche (and really, doesn't everyone?), and you get an e-mail telling you that somebody has sent you a Friend Request from Facebook, it's perfectly normal to wait until Sunday to confirm the friendship so that they don't suspect you were sitting at home reading Nietzsche on a Saturday night. Even though the fact that they sent you the request on a Saturday night means that they themselves weren't out partying, that they were sitting on the computer doing Facebook, which is only slightly more pathetic than reading.

No life, but I do have the illusion of a life. The upkeep of being cool is so taxing.

Tuesday, 21st September, 2010.

Surrender, Napoleon

There's probably a sub-category under the heading of Child Abuse that condemns the behaviour of parents who play ABBA full blast outside their teenager's bedroom, weaponising ABBA in the war against nocturnal lifestyle and all-day sleepery. I swear, I was just trying to wake First-Born up. I figure if I get only four hours of sleep because they wake me by bumping around in the middle of the night, then my giving them five hours is pretty generous.

Anyway, I was stretching canvas and the ABBA made me feel so happy. I don't know how First-Born can hate them so much. At the ripe old age of four or five it was ABBA who taught me about the profound sadness of war (*Fernando*), about the inequality between rich and poor in a capitalist society (*Money x3*), about the tragic dependency of women on a good match [or gambling] to ensure their life-long comfort, about the subsequent need for feminism (*Money x3*), and about love and life and more love et cetera.

I was stapling away, hammering and cutting and getting all nostalgic. First-Born finally got up, screaming. I made them laugh by grinning stupidly and telling them it was the most gentle way I could think of waking them up.

Success! I couldn't turn ABBA off after that. First-Born particularly hates *Chiquitita* but that's one of my favourites, so what's a girl to do? I kindly turned the volume down. And then felt even happier. I'm not sure if ABBA was making me happy, or if I was getting some perverse form of pleasure from torturing my child. ABBA are the best form of evil ever.

Sunday, 26th September, 2010.

Wadaiko

I found the teacher, who runs a school. Have enrolled in the beginner's class, have started, have made a strong group of friends. Taiko requires that you play with your whole body, am every week hungry for it, the deeper the drum sound the better. Can never get enough. How funny, to suddenly have a thing in your life that wasn't there before. To be allowed.

October 2010

Saturday, 2nd October, 2010.

Bullseye !!
There's this cat that's been hanging around for a while now (weeks? months?) and I've almost written about it a few times but then somehow haven't, seeing as I haven't been writing about much at all, really.

This cat's been on my hit list because it's been stealing my cats' food. Because I feed them outside, easier that way, except for the food being-stolen factor. And the fact that they don't defend their territory.

So I, as well as being their provider, have had to do the territorial defending. I don't quite spit or hiss, but I do hide beside my door and wait for the creature to slink down the driveway and edge my cats away. Which happens a little too easily.

The thing about this cat is I can scare it away by saying *psssst* and sometimes swearing at it, and making loud slamming noises with the door, but it seems to understand human psychology because it just hides under the potato vines, waits for the sound of my disappearing footsteps, and then comes back almost straight away. While I admire its tenacity, I can't let the challenge go.

My new method is to stand dead still by the door and wait, sometimes for a few seconds and sometimes for twenty minutes or more; dead dead still, with a bucket of water ready. I've almost gotten it a few times but it's *really* quick. Once I accidentally drenched one of our cats with the water. Once I let it go, because I started to wonder if it was stray and starving. Which my cats will be if it eats us out of house and home. I felt sorry for it! My own enemy! That's just pissy.

But tonight I was cleverer than usual and my empathy has been spent. I kept accidentally scaring it, but had placed the food right in front of the door (no great plan, I was just lazy tonight), so when I saw it I grabbed a jug of water and waited and waited, and eventually it came back, and the main door was open, and I was there, with my arm already sprung back ready for the throw. I threw the water THROUGH the screen instead of opening the screen door first (always my downfall) and I got that cat with the WHOLE JUG. (The whole jug contents, not the actual jug.)

If my cats don't declare me a hero I'll be very surprised. Don't ever let it be said that I can't outsmart a feline. These aren't the actions of a person who has a life, but at least I'm spending my non-life productively.

p.s. No Nietzsche this Saturday night. I'm supposed to be at a party, but instead I'm reading Vattimo. And defending cats. One day I'll say yes to the parties [?].

Wednesday, 13th October, 2010.

The Sullying of Pure Thomas

One thing you shouldn't do in the middle of writing Philosophy essays is book a ticket to Japan. (Japan!! Me!!) Had I not booked my ticket those little parentheses would contain something more along the lines of '*Agamben!! Ranciere!!*', and I wouldn't be quite so distracted from the things I have to do between now and then.

But speaking of trains, I just opened a notepad with my essay notes and found quotes I'd written down when I was at Ex-Wife's house a few weekends ago. For a while I couldn't remember where they'd come from, but then I had the sickening realisation, accompanied by the sickening memory, that they were taken from children's television. She had *Thomas the Tank Engine* episodes running for her younger son, and I was appalled to discover that Thomas has gone musical. I feel really sorry for the author, who's by now turning in his grave, if he is in fact dead, which I don't even know but let's just assume because if he was alive I'm sure he would have protested about this development.

I love the original Thomas tune, but this music was new and it was pure cheese. The lyrics were about *caring* for each other and *helping* each other and all things working out okay in the end, fa la fucken la.

Worst possible melody you can imagine. The whole thing reminded me of *Brave New World* and pre-natal inculcation recordings, so transparently a tool for socialisation that I looked around me for evil-social-experiment cameras.

It was filthy. It transformed the whole Thomas experience in the worst possible way. There's joy to be had in trains squabbling, that was the point. Let them be human, for fuck's sake, because they're much more entertaining that way. If adults want to pretend life and relationships are that easy they might as well tattoo smiles and rosy cheeks on all of the children's faces and be done with it.

So who let patronising children's music wannabes into the recording studio? My opinion of Ex-Wife dropped a little because she didn't seem to see anything wrong with what her son was watching, and failed to vomit when he started SINGING ALONG to that guff. I wanted to whisk him outa there and play the evils of screamo music at him to cleanse his impressionable little mind, see if I could undo some of the damage.

I used to always sing along with the kids' music when my offspring were little, but there's no way I could have joined in with this antiquated sentimentality. Now to cleanse my mind of the memory. Thank goodness that when I forced myself to sit here and dump at least one thought, this is the one I chose to let go. Go free, little thought, and don't bother me again.

Sunday, 17th October, 2010.

A Must See

Well that's me well and truly spent. Over two days I've watched *Earthlings*, which is available to watch for free and not for profit, which impresses me no end. And that's good, because the money you'd normally spend on seeing a film will be required for the mountain of tissues you're going to need when you do watch it. Which you will, because you must.

I wish I could force it upon people, but have yet to think of a way of doing that without traumatising them. I guess it's the kind of thing a person has to come to of their own volition, having prepared themselves. So the next best thing I can do is tell people to prepare themselves. And THEN make them watch it.

Joaquin Phoenix is perfectly pitched as the narrator; it's not overly sentimental, but he does contextualise the content in a heartfelt way. It's not directed towards hippies, but will appeal directly to your emotional sensibilities. It's brutal, but compelling in a way that incites your sense of responsibility.

I use a lot of these political documentaries for my research (and because they're so relevant, and necessary, and it'd be irresponsible not to watch them and be confronted and then use what you've learned to do something), and I want people to watch all of them. This one's different in that it affects everybody's daily life and is therefore inescapably essential. They all are, I know. Just, this one especially?

Fuck. Humans are awful. You can't work within culture without knowing these things.

Tuesday, 19th October, 2010.

Say Cheese

There comes a time in everybody's life when they must confront the full extent of their own fugliness, and that is [apparently] when they see their passport photo for the first time.

I know I'm not drop-dead gorgeous, but for serious? Am I THAT bad? People keep reassuring me that it doesn't matter, but I tell you it does matter. What if I go missing overseas? Let's just say I'm on the Japan Rail underground and there's an earthquake and a whole train-full of people are trapped and we're on the news for months (see Chile), and being a tourist they decide to use MY PASSPORT PHOTO on the evening news every night until they dig out my dehydrated and/or suffocated body? Or what if they never manage to dig us out and instead treat the site as a ready-made grave, but archaeologists unearth me in a hundred years' time and then dig inside the records to identify my skeleton and MY PASSPORT PHOTO ends up in a history book called *Great Train Burials of the 21st Century*?

And THEN what if they look at my photo and say *'I had no idea people were so ugly back then'*?

Of course it matters. Ace Friend was running her fingers through my hair for ages at Art Skool today, saying '*I can't believe how soft your hair is*', and that was I guess a consolation, except that today I'd rather be pretty and coarse than soft and fugly. What's the point of being soft if you're so ugly no one wants to touch you?

Sunday, 31st October, 2010.

Oh That Old Thing

I think I was supposed to have been excited when an anthology containing one of my stories arrived in the post during the week, all shiny and important looking, but I kinda wasn't. And now I kinda still amn't. The only thing I'm excited about is reading the other stories, and when I opened it briefly I went straight to the contents page to see what they were. When I saw my name I flinched, and I remembered how horrible it is to have that first look to see if they printed your work properly.

I didn't have that first look, I just closed the damn thing and left it on my bed. I haven't even told anybody about it, that's how unexcited I am. Not even my parents. How are they going to magnet it to the fridge if they don't know it exists?

I wondered at first if I'm just being snobbish, but I don't think so. It's not the anthology I wanted to be in, and I found the interaction with the editor to be sub-grown-up. In an okay way, but still. That's not it. It's that I'm outrageously excited about everything else, and publication anywhere seems premature right now. As in, I'm not taking anything seriously until something serious happens. I'm on the brink of everything. (Except proper success; I'm not on the brink of that.) I'm not ready for anything until I do these things that I'm on the brink of.

I did my tax return last night, and I only have one more art obligation to fulfill. When I woke this morning and looked at the post-essay state of the house (enhanced by smears of Son's-Friend's blood and the waxed strands of First-Born's Woofter-Friend's legs), I thought about what essential project I had to work on, and was shocked to realise I don't have to work on anything particular. I can do what I damn well want.

I've been persevering to get to this point. All of my burdens gone. While the waxing and the LAN partying were happening here yesterday, I went off for a long swim and a long sauna and then I came home and dug back into my novel research.

The essays, instead of knocking the stuffing out of me, have left me more energised. It'll be a tragedy [for me at least] if I die in a plane crash or an any-crash or by any means whatsoever before my novel manuscript is finished, and my new art series has been well and truly commenced. All the prep done, just lemme at it.

Still Sunday.

Hard to be Humble

I did finally take a look at the anthology. I haven't looked at my story, but when I realised other people's stories had bios attached I thought *oh no*, because I don't remember sending in a bio. So I found mine and discovered the editor had combined a really carefully written humble one I'd sent to elsewhere, but had added a detailed list of awards I've received. It doesn't even make sense; the humble one cancels out the need to list the awards (I was so clever getting away with that). How embarrassing to follow that bio with the stuff it tries to avoid. Ed should have been able to tell that I'm the *cockroach scuttling along the skirting-boards* type. And *this* is why I'm scared of editors.

November 2010

Monday, 1st November, 2010.

Collateral Damage

I killed a chair. And then I dismembered it. Violently. The problem with me is that I don't think this is a big deal. First-Born's tried to kill six chairs; they succeeded with one and left five of them seriously maimed. You can see "us" whenever you walk into our house because maimed chairs are quite unsightly.

But anyway, I killed it. I broke the rule of *'Do Not Engage'*, a rule especially important with First-Born because the cycle's so endless and the words get misdirected. Mostly I keep my mouth shut, or say the necessary minimum and just wait for it to get better, but I was so angry that I grabbed it and smashed it against the ground, and then every time I made a point I picked up its bones and smashed them again, one by one, until smithereens had happened and there was nothing left to smash. (I repeat that I hardly ever get this angry; I'd say *never* but obviously that's not true.)

Screaming out my words and smashing chairs = I was breathing like I'd run a marathon. All of my pent-up frustration came out, because they won't let me get to bed on time no matter how much I beg or [pathetically] command. It seems like so little a point to fight over, but for me it's a point of life or death. Mine, I mean. If I don't' fight to get it back, you know? I don't care if you know or not, it just is that way.

It's stupid that mothers are supposed to be perfectly behaved. We're not robots.

Ironically, First-Born's behaviour is mildly better this time around. We have more moments of *nice*. They're right that I do nag them now, I *am* on their back the way they used to accuse me of being, and their physical presence does stress me in a way that makes me feel torn. I AM IN SOME WAYS THE BAD GUY.

Son said later that we'd both regret it in the morning and I didn't believe him because I couldn't feel a thing, except the feeling of being spent. But I woke up feeling sad, and I stupidly wasn't expecting that. I didn't look after First-Born's feelings after that scene. I'm now the heartless mother they accuse me of being. I love them so much, but every day, without fail, First-Born tells me they hate me in one way or another. It seems so gentle when I write about it here, but they grind the glass-shardy fact of it into my skull. You just have to watch my tic to know what it does to me, and why I think I'm on the verge of death. Literally now. Chest pains when I go to bed at night, and I can't tell if they're heart or muscular because the motor tic's so bad I've torn my insides. (Hence, the chair.)

The horrible thing is that the chair homicide gave them fuel to feel unloved, even though I don't un-love them. But I *am* cold now. I love them sceptically.

I feel sad for both of the kids because I can't fix this. First-Born's the one who rejected me, and Son gets caught in the middle. He handled last night beautifully, and we're a bit mean to him in the thick of things because he tells us to stop and neither of us will. When I won't stop it's because First-Born's saying they're unloved – I can't leave it hanging at that point, I have to know that if they leave the house in the middle of the night it's with words of mine that tell them they're loved no matter what, even if they come out as anger.

Poor Son, who says wise and beautiful things to his angry sibling.

I don't know if it's good that I'm fighting back now. It's too late for us. But First-Born's a confused child, so how do I help them, is the question. How?

Peas/Pod

One more seriously personal thought to think out loud: we're exactly the same, First-Born and I. Except that I'm not hostile. And they're much more attractive and socially more confident and generally cooler than I'll ever be. So not exactly, not even close, but definitely the same.

In a few years none of this will even matter, we'll both just be relieved to have survived and will be enjoying each other's company.

My art themes are centred around this relationship. Very serious, non-sentimental stuff that has me completely driven, with the kids still at the centre of my universe. Just saying.

―――

Tuesday, 2nd November, 2010.

The joy's been sucked out of the house. The proof of this is in the tv. The kids are watching *Ronnie Johns* over and over, and I love *Ronnie Johns* but to me it's not funny anymore. I don't laugh. Because it used to be something we shared, and now I only get glimpses if I walk through the kitchen, not allowed to join them.

Reminds me of the Xmas I bought the *Summer Heights High* dvd for us to share. Because we all like to laugh and it's one of the last things we can do together. But neither of them would watch it with me, so I waited for weeks and then watched it by myself. Laughing alone. Later they watched it together, without asking me to join them.

Feels like the end of togetherness, no opportunities for positive reinforcement. I'm tentative, afraid of not being good enough. Not welcome in my own family. It's like I've died and they've moved on without me. And I could die; who'd notice?

I still have to finish watching it, but it seems too lonely. Is laughter you've forced yourself to release real enough?

―――

p.s.
My passport arrived, which means I can now run away from home. And the good news is that the passport people made my photo look slightly less ugly – they must have felt sorry for me. Just in time.

―――

Monday, 8th November, 2010.

In the meantime...
...a trip to the High Plains in East Gippsland, with family. I was characteristically late, so I missed out on being at the murderer's hut by the river, where Mum lived as a small child.

Couldn't get the kids to come with us. They don't know what they're missing, this extraordinary thing.

Life at home difficult and am struggling to be happy, but I made it there. Didn't think I would. Or even could. Was a quiet weekend for me. But nice. It's always nice.

Was special for Mum, that's the main thing.

Wednesday, 24th November, 2010.

Japan

My first time overseas. With me is Flower, one of my taiko/drumming friends. I'm on a mission to get physical research for my novel, to be there and touch the place where my characters will move about. Flower's on a mission to find a Japanese boyfriend.

Off to a flying start (pun intended), I get a migraine on the plane. A steward, young and classically attractive, classically extroverted, brought me paracetamol and cheese n' crackers. Talked, asked questions. Taiko and writing and whatnot, none of which I'd have thought would interest him. But he gave me his email and said let's meet up in Melbourne. To what end? Kept returning for more. Flower nudging me with her elbow, me fighting off the migraine. I wondered what the steward's mission was, and how many people a person like him collects on his travels. One per flight maybe, a social currency.

Tokyo

We land at night in Osaka but head straight to Tokyo on the bullet train. Flower's so excited, and then disappointed by the men. Says they all have bad skin. Not true, although sometimes true. No worse than anywhere else. Long office hours, men on the train so pale and wan. Not enough sunlight perhaps, low vitamin D, too much airconditioning. At night as we travel around, people heading home so late.

Our other mission – shared – is to buy drums for ourselves and for other friends in our taiko group, so we can practise together and at home, on something other than a phone book. So many drums. Our Japanese friend back in Melbourne gives us instructions on how to get there, using a rickety suburban train line, so different from the bullet trains, and one of my favourite trips. A non-touristic side of Tokyo.

At the taiko store we bring with us great business and they show us great Japanese hospitality. The manager takes us to (and buys us lunch at) a small restaurant over the road. Teaches us what and how-to. Is lovely. I want to keep him, but settle for keeping the drums and his many other gifts, which'll be delivered to the airport before we depart.

———

Tempura vegetables with ramen and miso. A thing to remember. Flower wants to try everything, but I loved it so much I know that whenever I go to a Japanese restaurant I'll be looking for that and only that on the menu. (Why mess with perfection?)

———

I started learning Japanese from a tv program back when I was 18, but didn't progress very far before losing confidence. I can say a few words and about three sentences "fluently", which amounts to not very useful. But Flower's learning Japanese bravely and enthusiastically, maybe so that she can speak to her Japanese husband in his own tongue, when she finds him. Whereas I find things like language much easier to play with inside my head, she fearlessly speaks unfamiliar Japanese sentences into the real world, using a travel phrase book.

I'm in awe of Flower. If I was here on my own I'd be floundering, even though most things that are announced over loudspeakers (on trains n' such) are followed by an English translation.

———

We get up insanely early to catch a train to the fish market in Tokyo. What can I tell you about a fish market? It's full of fish. I'm not a foodie or a fish person, and try not to be distressed by the scale of death, but I love finding and being in these places. I'd love to paint them. The fish. Not practical, not useful.

Flower finds a tiny café buried in the middle of the vast shed network, does her foodie thing while I wander around looking at what gets lifted from the ocean. She's safe, whereas I'm followed by a threatening looking man who appears not to trust gaijin (foreigners). Red hair and pale skin, I stand out like a sore thumb. Smiling stupidly but mostly transfixed. Also overwhelmed. Only so much ocean you can take in with your eyes in one hit.

I feel sorry for Flower, who has an engineering background and a professional job. I travel like a poor person, using a card to spend money from Ex-Husband's bank account, which I'll repay gradually as I earn money when I get back.

Where she wants to visit restaurants and do normal things, I'm disciplined and aware of my limitations. I'm not as into fish as she is, so when she wants to eat at obscure seafood restaurants I take her there but wander around the streets close by until she's done.

I buy most of my food at grocery stores, where it's challenging to find what I want. I don't know what I want. Something chocolate. I settle on chocolate wafer biscuits and become instantly enamoured. And Mandarins are in season, so they become my staple. I've never loved them before, but I love them now. Good to know that no way will I get scurvy in Japan.

The Imperial Palace for me, a famous night time shopping district for her. An electronics shop because she's that kind of girl. Some shrines, some markets. A museum, and a contemporary art gallery that I desperately want to visit but isn't open. Blossoms everywhere. Presents to take home to friends and parents and children and ex-husbands. The book research thing, the tourism thing. A novelty.

At first we wear bathers when we visit onsen, until we're brave enough to go in naked.

Kii Peninsula

And then the real business. Another bullet train, this time away from the noise. Spellbound by green scenery and steep orchards, where the mandarins grow. Weaving through mountains on our way to Kii-Katsuura, where we'll stay while we visit Taiji. A small town on the Kii peninsula, another fish market, a hostel/ryokan with futons and tatami mats instead of bunk beds we have to share with snoring men. A sweet and simple room, an open upstairs window, the constant sound of water. The sound of fisherman alarm clocks going off at 3 am, travelling over the town. Smiling in my sleep.

———

Another rickety local train, with heated seats [!!], we make our way to Taiji to visit the whaling museum. Self-conscious about being a Western person in a Japanese whaling museum. But it's fascinating. Not so much the dolphin stadium, where these beautiful beasts are penned up in small pools. I'm horrified watching them thrash their way from one end of a small run to another, so contained.

Flower thinks she's doing the communication thing by making eye contact with them, because dolphins are "dolphins". That unfortunate smile and the romanticism that goes with it. We go up to the roof of the whaling museum to watch the dolphin show without supporting it financially (therefore encouraging its continuation as a tourist attraction). As if they'll even notice this tokenistic refusal.

I point out the cruelty of their captivity to Flower, lamenting the awfulness of human beings and nudging her away from the dolphin-rainbow connection. Gently. Wondering if or when she'll get sick of hearing me talk about the plight of cetaceans. Knowing what a killjoy I must be, but knowing also that it's necessary.

———

Back in Kii-Katsuura we meet up with Sea Shepherd people, self-appointed "cove guardians". They've taken over a local hotel in town, run their PR operations out of the foyer.

I have thoughts. Am not impressed by the Sea Shepherd people's attitudes. They're adversarial and self-important. Not willing to consider the Japanese viewpoint. Not willing to analyse faults in their own.

This imperious attitude is one of the reasons I'm writing my novel, but still. I didn't think they'd be like this.

The next day they drive us up to a bluff where they do their "guarding', the landscape stunning. Technically we're there to help them, looking out with binoculars to spot the boats and banger poles the fishermen use to herd dolphins towards the famous cove. Big Man is preoccupied with a female film-maker who seems suitably suspicious of him. Which leaves me free to go rock hopping with the son of one of the protesters, over an amazing rockscape beyond the trees, all of it so beautiful. We lose track of time and get called back. Adults spoil things. My muscles want leaping and climbing. Away from Big Man's posturing.

———

They've told us stories about how much of *Whale Wars* was hammed up for the cameras, same with *The Cove*. Am left wondering where the truth is. Realise the Sea Shepherd people are serial pests.

Flower and I wander the town, even more self-conscious, aware that the locals will associate us with the protesters. Smiling pointedly in the local grocery store, our faces saying '*We come in peace*'.

We find the famous cove, which is empty of people, no blood in the water. Unguarded. So pretty. We step over the heavy fortifications (flimsy plastic barriers) so we can climb up through the scrub. Flower uses a stick to write a message into the sand.

———

Flower's nervous about walking at night but it's quiet and beautiful and I can't resist. We head to an onsen in a posh hotel, perched above rocks along the shore, waves washing over as the tide comes in. Mechanical foot massager in the change room, heaven for my feet. I must *have*.

———

Early morning at the tuna market, again photographing fish I'd like to paint but know I probably never will. Wondering about the nature of passive research. What it means to be somewhere. It doesn't mean anything, is just fascinating, even if I'm just observing.

———

Also heaven is catching a bus outside of town, being dropped in a nowhere place and finding our way through small farming properties to the hiking trail that'll lead us up to a shrine.

Something about hiking up steep forested hills that always brings me to life. Not even frustrated by Flower, who isn't a hiker, not even much of a walker. I rush up ahead and then back, rush up ahead and then back to her, over and over, getting my fix of clean air deep into my lungs. Clean air and muscle.

I love this place, the shrine in a forest and so peaceful. Pulling mandarins from my pack and calling them lunch. Still feasting on chocolate wafer biscuits, which I have to ration.

We stay as late as we can, 'til evening, and then have to catch the bus back. That Japanese musicality again, the sing song voice of the woman announcing our arrival at each stop, and then '*Katsuuuuuuura*', her voice high and sweet. A human who speaks like a bird.

We get off the bus. I want to come back here before I even leave; how could anybody not be happy in a place this full of song.

Kyoto

In Kyoto, bad hair. I just want to be normal and not so scruffy, but there's no hairdryer in the hotel. Without a hair dryer, no hair straightening. We're meeting up with an ex-student of one of my favourite teachers from Art Skool. Maybe my only favourite teacher? Anyway. A Canadian student who now lives in Japan.

I feel unsettled, and know it's the hair. Too much of life out of my control. I realise how prepared I need to feel to meet somebody who matters. He's so relaxed and friendly. A real restaurant, with real food. He and Flower both foodies, she practically salivating over the experience, which I enjoy also but in that off way of the person who has no control over the drying of her hair. I discover I'm ashamed of my face. The chaos of inside is plastered all over my exterior.

He walks us through the pleasure district after dinner, a long walk. The conversation is wonderful. It's better in the dark. This is life, I know I'm in it. But still. The deep, deep shame of not being able to be the way they're being. Watching from some distance, unable to feel like I'm actually there. I've failed at something and I don't know why.

Still no reply to an email I sent to Son when we were back in Tokyo. He's being looked after by Ex-H, who's feeding him this time. My insignificance at home is a shock. I realise I'm depressed. Depressed in Japan, living the life but not feeling like I'm living the life. Never quite getting it right.

———

But aren't the autumn leaves pretty. So pretty.

———

Hiroshima

The museums, of course. Shock and reverence. No visible heritage in the architecture, could be any city in the world. Such wide streets. Seems so unnatural, and depressing.

We're here because when planning our itinerary we discovered we could see Drum Tao perform. Was worth going out of our way, and the extra expense. The euphoria. Drum Tao performers have the glowing skin Flower has come looking for.

After the concert we eat in a small café and I get sick afterwards, relieved to be in a hotel with my own room this time, so I can be unwell with privacy. It's not until later that I think of radiation and wonder for a moment. We'd visited ground-zero, I'd put my body there without it even occurring to me that only sixty years have passed. Is it possible that...? Nah. If radiation was still around everybody would be sick, all the time. But still. Stricken.

———

At home my absence was a non-event, but I have drums. And friends to play with, who also have drums. As soon as the skins return from Customs. Waiting, waiting...

———

December 2010

Friday, 10th December, 2010.

Snow White

He's poisoned my apples!! I've waited three years for my first apple tree to grow a full head of fruit, and there it was all cute and budding, so I called out to Ex-H over the balcony *'Please don't spray that stuff underneath my apple tree'*. He was weed killer-ing on the top garden bed. I explained that the killer substance would sink into the roots and be sucked up into my lovely apples, who deserved a good shot at life *please oh please don't you dare*.

I watched through the windows and sure enough, he sprayed under the tree, so I ran out and begged and we argued and I called him a *fucking prick* and now I'll never speak to him again.

He still does that garden-martyr thing, where he comes here and works on the garden and gets angry that I haven't stopped what I'm doing to spend every day in the garden with him, even though I'm working bastard shifts in the kitchen every day and have a lot of things on at the moment. (Note: I don't call him to demand that he come home from he's FIFO destinations when I need help with the garden.)

He accuses me of never doing anything to help. I spend a LOT of energy on that garden, but unlike him I love it and I'm not launching into a longwinded defence here because that's not the point. The point is, when he starts getting mean I avoid him.

He calls my writing and my art work "hobbies" if I explain that I'm busy working on them (which I am), and I've had quite enough of that thankyouverymuch. Who let that non-believer into my church?

The apples won't die, but they won't be pure anymore. This cannot be undone. So. *Enough.* I want to enjoy his friendship and I'm very patient and tolerant of his insulting moods, but he poisons everything. Be gone, poisoner of all things good. I'm very pissed off.

Sunday, 12th December, 2010.

what a happy, happy day

Two good things. One = we performed in our first Wadaiko concert, and the whole weekend was full of rehearsals. That means non-stop euphoria, both playing and watching the big kids play. I'm so, so lucky to be a part of that. My friends and I are the kindergarteny pre-beginners, but we did okay. How can anybody not be happy when Wadaiko's in the world?

Two = Ex-Husband backed down. He didn't apologise, but he expressed regret about the apples and has begun to understand that his attitude is both unkind and unfair. He said he respects what I do and conceded that I'm '*not lazy or indolent*', and I'm quite thrilled that he used the word *indolent* because I'd forgotten about it. It's a fine word. For the first time in years I feel like I can be his real friend and not have to walk on eggshells for fear of upsetting him.

He's never done this before. I wonder if he realised I would have walked away from him this time. Full severance. Anyway it doesn't matter; I got home between rehearsals on Saturday and he opened the discussion and now I have a great deal of respect for him, because he overcame an entrenched behaviour and not many grown people would be able to do that.

My halo's getting very shiny with this endorsement of my good character. As is his. And I'm relieved, because his mother died while I was in Japan. This is an intrinsically sad thing, but is also other-level sad because she and I and the woman he has a crush on in Peru are the only three people in the world he's close to. Son as well, but that's not an adult friendship yet. So if he'd walked away he'd have nobody, and I'd be worried about him. Saved by the bell.

Wednesday, 15th December, 2010.

Pollyanna is BACK!!

The sunny outlook! The irrepressible happiness! The sheer optimism! The joy! I can feel how happy I'm getting. I used to always be this happy, so if getting it back after all this time means I'll appreciate it even more because I won't take it for granted, then I could end up being some kind of Super-Happy. I'll be so happy, people are gonna want to smack the glad off my face.

Why I'm happy today = I got free mulch. Or at least I think it was free. I'm 80% sure it was free. Which means that if it wasn't free, I was only 20% stealing. And frankly stolen mulch is as good as free mulch, so it's a win-win situation.

Also: my taiko skins arrived (Customs treated them), and I assembled my okedo taiko myself. (HAPPY!)

Saturday, 19th December, 2010.

Once More, With Feeling
The non-depressed version of Japan, written into a letter. This is the one I want to remember when I'm old:

Japan! Lucky for you, [Favourite Teacher], that it took me a hundred years to sit down here to think, because the initial rapture would have been excruciating to read.

What an exciting and beautiful country. I enjoyed the shrines and et-ceteras because they were good excuses to be in nice places, but their tidiness wasn't something I could touch. What I really loved was seeing how the Japanese inhabit their land, how they've filled all of its inches and how the paraphernalia of their daily lives is cluttered around the houses, which are unpretentious and practical and colourful and so on and so on. All of the small details. And the farmlets embedded in every type of landscape. And the musicality of the language as it's sung at you from machines and overhead speakers. And water – I love that the sound of water is everywhere, little canals beside the roads and drains coursing underneath you at every turn. I'm glad I don't know the language (yet) because it allowed me to experience things in a sensory way without understanding. Plus holding whole conversations with nothing but words I picked up along the way and wild gestures was so much fun.

Poor [Ex-Student of Yours] was assailed by a million observations and expressions of dumb wonderment. By the time we got to Kyoto we'd found our way through Osaka and a few choice bits of Tokyo, gone to Ina (outer suburb of Tokyo) to buy taiko, seen a small piece of Nagoya (overnight on the way to elsewhere), and my favourite favourite place = Kii-Katsuura. The landscape of the Kii Peninsula is spectacular and I wish I could drag all of the people I know who've been to Tokyo and Kyoto and Osaka through the countryside to see it. I practically got whiplash from spinning around and leaping from one side of the train to the other to see every possible thing. The town itself is quiet and the people are so friendly. The streets smell of onsen (rising up from the drains – a slightly unpleasant but addictive smell) (and the onsen themselves – OMG!), and I lived on mandarins and enormous apples and woke every morning at 3 am to the sound of fisherman alarm clocks going off across the town. We visited Taiji (I needed the whale museum) and cavorted with the American conservationists/Sea Shepherd people for just long enough to be repulsed by them and their arrogant refusal to understand what it is they're fighting.

So, [Ex-Student of Yours] : I felt sorry for him having to be seen with us – one tidy Colombian-Australian (her) and one shamelessly scruffy Regular-Australian who hadn't even brushed her hair (me) and was probably still dripping and flushed from the hastiest shower in the tiniest and steamiest shower cubicle in Japan. By then I was lonely and was so happy to be meeting him I was singing out loud all the way through the long, long subway passageways so that my friend couldn't be painfully silent at me (Plan A, very successful).

That was a strange kind of lonely, actually. The new-ish friend I was travelling with = I couldn't connect with her, or couldn't feel affection for her. We shared small raptures but no thought, or at least sharing thought involved struggle. No joy in her, that was the problem. No humour. Although she's really nice. Just, she's warmest when she's discussing men, which she did a little too often. (We were in Japan! What was she doing looking at men!!)

No, something wasn't right with her and she was uncommunicative whereas I spill out all over the place, so I sang to myself and then there was [Ex-Student of Yours], and he's a lovely creature, isn't he? So comfortable inside his own skin. I want to be just like him when I grow up, though I know I can't be. I would have loved to have talked to him a lot more, but there was sake involved and the conversation went all over the place. He chose a perfect restaurant and the food was amazing and what a generous person, to have given us that experience. A very happy night.

Then I made the mistake of answering questions about my child with more than 'Yes, I have an 18 year old child', and I heard myself using indifferent words to describe something emotionally devastating and reality hit me hard. Being in Kyoto felt not-real then, and a very profound sadness kicked in. I sat back quietly and didn't cry, bully for me, but did keep my distance as my friend told [Ex-Student of Yours] at great length about the sensuality of Colombian women (something I'd heard a lot about by then). Possibly she was flirting with him, and therein lies entertainment.

Actually I was glad she was like that – she had a nice glow about her, all warm and beautiful. We saw Drum Tao perform in Hiroshima the next night, and she spent the entire thing clutching at my thigh because the drummer she has a crush on was playing – if I was the slightest bit attracted to her that could have been pleasant, but let's just settle for "it was funny". Now that we're back I enjoy that about her, even the crazy man-obsession. As happiness is my favourite thing I was disappointed to have let it slip away, but I mustn't have been too far gone that night with [Ex-Student of Yours], because I still laughed out loud when Flower interrupted her own conversation about finding a husband for herself to tell me 'It's okay for you, Chris, you already have your children'. *PEOPLE ARE FUNNY!*

[Ex-Student of Yours] took us for a walk around Gion, which is so beautiful. Overall I found Kyoto the craziest of all the cities we visited. Busier, more overwhelmingly crowded, with a younger-ish population. We found our way around, but it's geography had me stumped (the "creative" tourist map didn't help). Although we intended originally to spend more time there than anywhere else, we ended up giving it only one day, and I'd surrendered my will by then and followed Flower without feeling much, so I'm now curious about the place, and will go back there soon. Ish. I'm working a million extra shifts (day job: nursing home kitchen) to save up for the next trip. Hence, busy and exhausted.

It's sad, I think, that Australian history isn't overly embraced, culturally. There's something so invigorating about grabbing on to the threads of history and using them now. Wadaiko, for example – that's just happiness on a stick, and you can't separate it from the past even though it's such an immediate pleasure. During our concert weekend, last week = the wadaiko community is a wonderful thing to be a part of. I feel very lucky to have access to those threads.

When I was researching for your subject I left a trail for myself that I'm about to pick up and follow, knowing that it leads to an obscure mode of storytelling that I relate to, similar to medieval exemplar in style. I love writing exemplar because there's no limit to how playful and imaginative you can be, and you can shock people as you entertain them because of the rich quality of the form. It connects the childhood love of story to adult experience. And when I start incorporating Japanese styles into my narrative it's going to connect me to the history through a narrative conduit that also connects to European history. I'm going to be thoroughly tied up in knots and it's going to be bliss. It already is bliss.

Now I'm rambling but when I think of you I think of what I found through you and of how I'm using it and again, I feel lucky.

You realise how light you are on your feet when the person you're travelling with isn't, and I practically flew through Japan. Riding on all of this. Now I've got everything that was in the way of my project out of the way, I've prepared my research for both art and writing, and this morning has been the first quiet one of many. My next Japan is one I've invented. (Fun!)

Thanks for adding that nice element to my trip/Chris[.]

Sunday, 20th December, 2010.

Prometheus' Liver

I keep forgetting that I first met Prodigal Friend at an award ceremony, years before we taught together at the university, which is where

I thought we'd first met. I won the award and she was shortlisted; introduced herself to me when I was too overwhelmed to commit her to memory. Even when she reminds me, I have no recollection of our conversation.

I do remember I was recovering from a bad cold and my lips were so dry they were shredded that night, immune system struggling to kick in. I was so self-conscious about it I kept ducking off to the venue toilets to apply Chapstick. Lips are right there on your face, and my face was being looked at by *everybody*. I felt like a leper.

Prodigal always introduces me to new people with this, using our meeting as a song of praise and it surprises me every time. In her memory I'm on a pedestal; in mine I'm diseased and ashamed. And apparently dismissive of well-wishers. A typical example of how I'm never ready for anything outside of the labour, and always wishing I could arrive at a time where I feel somehow presentable, so that even when things go well I'm not skulking and undeserving. I think of Dorian Gray, and know that my memory's the more astute.

Apologies for the obscure mixing of my Greek mythologies with my Oscar Wildes. But the minute I finish writing this, the place where my brain cells have parted to let this memory in will close again, before it's properly embedded. I can't seem to hold onto it. It's not being ripped out, exactly, because it never really sinks in. Which is unfortunate. I wish the eagles would peck out the big chunks of shame that take up most of that space.

Wednesday, 23rd December, 2010.

She's Not Our Sister, and *Yes He Is Sleeping With Her*

When First-Born returned from having dinner with The Biological last night (who they now call their *father*), these were the words they said to Son, who was sitting on the other side of the bench. He and I were discussing how much responsibility people should take for global issues and getting heaps political (he was arguing *do nothing*) [!!!], but with that fat whiff of Pure Gossip we naturally both dropped all interest in global issues (sorry world) and said *what the fuck?*.

Vagina-Mite Was No More

I love First-Born when they're like that – they're hilarious. By like-that I mean drunk, and while it's true that they're just as hilarious when they're not drunk, it's mostly when they are that they stoop to being hilarious with me, at me, as opposed to hating my sweet gutses.

So they threw their two Taco Bill sombreros onto the table and announced that they'd had two fish-bowl margaritas because they couldn't take that situation sober. The situation being, when The Biological turned up for the first time this year to take her for dinner (not Son, just First-Born – OMG men shit me), he had a young bit of fluff with him. I'd forgotten this fluff, although I did meet her this time last year; she's the daughter of his best friend, and at the time I thought he had a man-crush on his best friend because I'd heard them on the phone together and he was all over him. I've never seen him so all-over somebody else. But anyway, there was his best friend's daughter, and I remember thinking well, that man's stupid for letting his daughter spend time alone with this particular man, who hasn't met a vagina that he hasn't wanted to plug.

This young woman's twenty years young, and a redhead. He brings all of his significant people to meet us, so when I met her I knew he must be sleeping with her. I raised my eyebrows and thought it funny for all of a minute before deciding that I really didn't want to know (way too young) and forgetting that she existed.

So I had to think for a minute about what First-Born had said:

'She's not our sister...'

First-Born had been thinking The Biological and I had had another child together and not told them about it? I'd had another little redheaded baby and given it away? The mere thought of this is so funny I wished I was drinking soft drink so it would spurt out of my nose. When I worked out who they were talking about and asked if I was right, they said yes, *'...and she's your fault!'*. They went on to explain that he's with a young redhead because I made him love redheads, seeing as he's always had a thing for me.

How anybody can look at a twenty-year young woman and feel attracted to her I don't know. Young people are stupid. Plus, First-Born's eighteen, so you can see why it might freak them out. Both of them ginger, even though First-Born's hair's never ginger anymore, more like a cross between black and burgundy. They could easily have suspected they were fraternal twins.

But anyway, he's forty-two now and during the dinner First-Born was making the best smartarse remarks at them all night. Such as, 'A*re you old enough to be drinking that red cordial?*', and '*Here, would you like that in a sippy cup?*'. And then they went up the road to get their best friend – a rampant woofter who they're going to share-house with, if they ever actually leave here. He's just as hilarious as First-Born is and apparently they both went back to the restaurant and gave the strange couple smartarse hell.

The way First-Born tells it had us in stitches. I wish I'd been there. Problem is, First-Born gave The Biological a parallel to consider, saying that him sleeping with his friend's daughter is the equivalent of First-Born sleeping with one of his closest friends (who's even older). Instead of considering this parallel seriously, The Biological rang this close friend and the friend said that they were okay with that. Then The Biological said they should all go on a weekend away together. (Meaning, he wanted to arrange for First-Born to sleep with his close friend. *Pimping them out.*) At this point I'm about ready to vomit and will end this little story here.

Gossip, I love it. But *ewww*. Sleeping with a mini-me my child's age. *Our* child's age. I don't know how they both withstood First-Born's humour, which should have knee-capped them. I'm amazed and yet not surprised that The Biological doesn't see how the situation seems so unsavoury. Because he really does think through his penis, and his penis isn't very smart.

This is the sort of thing I wanted to protect my kids from. I made many decisions [and wrote a novel] because of this. I hope it's not really bothering First-Born, but I suspect it is. Now that the alcohol's worn off.

They really thought I'd secretly had another child and given it away. Wow.

Sunday, 26th December, 2010.

Token

Son was telling me about the present First-Born gave him for Xmas yesterday, and I realised that they hadn't given me a present. Even though they're living here, eating the food I provide, having me drive them here and there, waking me up when they walk in and out at all hours, and accepted the bag of gifts I spent my last money on buying for them.

Sigh. Don't have kids, anybody. I don't mean this, obviously, but you may as well know the risks. They'll break your heart and it might just never be fixed.

———

Tuesday, 28th December, 2010.

Alphabet

After weeks of sleeping on a mattress on the lounge room floor, nothing but nothing's going to keep me from my bedroom for one more night. Except maybe paint fumes, if they're still hanging around.

Both figuratively and literally, I'm waiting for the dust to settle. The plaster dust that's floating in the air of my bedroom, to be specific. I started stripping First-Born's graffiti from my wall a few weeks ago. I tried sanding first, but oil paint doesn't really sand off very well, so I took a chisel to the wall and started to strip the plaster all the way back to cardboard, bit by bit. And that's when I started to hate the alphabet.

Every letter I stripped triggered my memory of the whole sentence. I had to start stripping them back to front, and in random sequences, to trick myself into thinking of other words. A is for Apple, and so on.

For a couple of months now I've been acutely aware of how emotionally toxic it's been sleeping under a wall full of red hatred. And how much those words were affecting me. So stripping the wall, empowering as it was, was also traumatic.

When it was finally blank, good. When I'd patched the plaster, even better. It looked like old ruins. I didn't want to paint over it, because old ruins are attractive, but I did, and now I have a white wall.

Chris Fontana

It's a little bit pockmarked, hence the filling and sanding, but still; white. Very boring, is white. But what a symbolic way to usher in a new era. The era of the Clean Mind. The era of our Clean Domestic Slate.

Acknowledgements

Most of the preparation for these volumes has taken place quietly in the shadows – somewhere between Purgatory and Solitary Confinement – where I skulk around as I work. I couldn't survive this lonely business without the feedback of good friends, so thank you to everyone who listened when I leaned out of my turret to scream into the abyss.

Thank you to my mother, for anchoring me in the real world daily, with warm companionship, support,... and an endless supply of chocolate.

A special thank-you to Chris Gabriel for being such an enthusiastic sounding board when I needed to ~~rant~~ think-out-loud, and for your support when I came across inevitable technical problems. Your bystander company was a balm during ad-hoc troubleshooting attempts.

Thank you Tracey Lamb, for friendship and for invaluable practical support.

Thanks also to Sarah Rudledge for being on the technology cheer squad, for generous layout/design advice, and for your practical and moral support. Most of all, though, for teaching me that sharing is the thing that makes "Art" worth it.

Thank you to Diane "Grabby" Glenane, for the sound of your reassuring voice as it echoes across the valley when you call from your own turret. Screaming into the abyss isn't so bad when you know somebody is working away on their own projects at the other end.

Last but not least, thank you to Dr [Empress!] Josephine Browne, for your thoughtful feedback, invaluable conversations, and for *knowing*. Because through all of these endeavours, we are kin xx